PATRICK KINSELLA

CAVING, CANYONING, COASTEERING...

30 EXHILARATING ADVENTURES AROUND BRITAIN

Bradt GUIDES

Bradt Guides Ltd, UK
Globe Pequot Press Inc, USA

First edition published July 2023
Bradt Guides Ltd
31a High Street, Chesham, Buckinghamshire, HP5 1BW, England
www.bradtguides.com
Print edition published in the USA by The Globe Pequot Press Inc,
PO Box 480, Guilford, Connecticut 06437-0480

Text copyright © 2023 Patrick Kinsella
Maps copyright © 2023 Bradt Guides Ltd; includes map data
© OpenStreetMap contributors
Photographs copyright © 2023 Individual photographers (see below)
Project Manager: Anna Moores
Cover research: Ian Spick

ISBN: 9781784778927

British Library Cataloguing in Publication Data
A catalogue record for this book is available from the British Library

Photographs © individual photographers credited beside images and also those from picture libraries credited as follows: Alamy (A); Shutterstock.com (S); Superstock (SS)

Front cover Top: Coasteering in Cornwall (Danielle Devaux/4Corners); Bottom: A rock scrambler on Gillercombe Crag in the Lake District (Izel Photography/Alamy)
Back cover Tree climbing on the Isle of Wight (Goodleaf Tree Climbing)
Title page Patrick during an early bikepacking escapade (page 214), before he'd learned how to pack properly… (Patrick Kinsella)

Maps David McCutcheon FBCart.S

Typeset and designed by Ian Spick, Bradt Guides
Production managed by Page Bros; printed in the UK
Digital conversion by www.dataworks.co.in

AUTHOR

Patrick Kinsella is a writer, editor, photographer and journalist who has spent over three decades travelling around the world and scribbling about outdoor activities. In pursuit of stories he has canoed the Yukon River in Canada, skied across the roof of Norway, climbed Mont Blanc and Kilimanjaro, run ultra-distance races in Mauritius and the Indian Himalaya, mountain biked through the red centre of Australia, hiked to the very bottom of South America, scuba dived on volcanoes in the middle of the Indian Ocean and set speed records for trail running New Zealand's Great Walks. However, it is here in Britain that Pat has experienced some of the most enjoyable, challenging and revelatory adventures of his career, and the realisation that many of the best outdoor escapades lay hiding in plain sight, right on your doorstep, was the seed for this book.

Pat now lives in Devon with his long-suffering wife, two indomitable daughters and an indefatigable dog – most of whom you will meet in these pages. Besides writing for various outdoor-focused magazines and websites, and contributing to scores of guidebooks, he has authored two walking books that explore myriad coastal and countryside paths around Devon and Dorset, plus a book about pub walks around the UK. He has also worked as the curator and director of two outdoor-adventure events for the National Trust: the South West Outdoor Festival (SWOF) and the Top of the Gorge festival.

FEEDBACK REQUEST

At Bradt Guides we're aware that guidebooks start to go out of date on the day they're published – and that you, our readers, are out there in the field doing research of your own. So why not tell us about your experiences? Contact us on ✆ 01753 893444 or e info@bradtguides.com. We will forward emails to the author who may post updates on the Bradt website at ⌀ bradtguides.com/updates. Alternatively, you can add a review of the book to Amazon, or share your adventures with us on Facebook, Twitter or Instagram (@BradtGuides).

ACKNOWLEDGEMENTS

Firstly I'd like to express my enormous gratitude to my wife, without whose support in holding the family fort I could never have gone gallivanting around Britain getting wet, muddy and annoyingly excited in the name of research – thanks Steph, I'll get a proper job one day (maybe…). Big thanks also to my girls, Ivy and Alice, who have accompanied me on many an exploratory adventure over the years, (usually) with boundless enthusiasm and good humour – the memories, mistakes and mayhem we made along the way will keep me grinning for the rest of my days. And I need to say cheers, and perhaps fork out some apologetic beers, to several mates who have been variously dragged on escapades under borderline false pretences, or had days and weekends away hijacked by my irritating habit of combining recreational jaunts with covert research missions.

Huge thanks, also, to my amazing Mum and Dad, who always encouraged a deep appreciation of the outdoors and the opportunities that lie within it, and took me on multiple hiking and camping trips around Britain as a child, not only distilling in me a sense of adventure and wonder, but also opening my eyes to the extraordinary natural environment we enjoy.

I am also immensely grateful to all the outdoor guides, experts and activity providers who hosted and helped me during the research period of this book. Thank you so much for lending me your time, knowledge and skill – you are a truly inspirational group of wonderful people.

Lastly, but most importantly, I want to extend a massive thanks to the excellent Editorial and Production team at Bradt Guides, and especially to Anna and Claire, who have been endlessly patient, understanding and helpful as I navigated my way through a few years of research, hitting pandemic-related potholes and various other obstacles along the way. It's been a suitably adventurous journey, with more than a few bumps and bruises experienced en route, but I would never have reached the finish line without your superb support – it's greatly appreciated, and I owe you a rich mixture of cake, gratitude and apologies.

CONTENTS

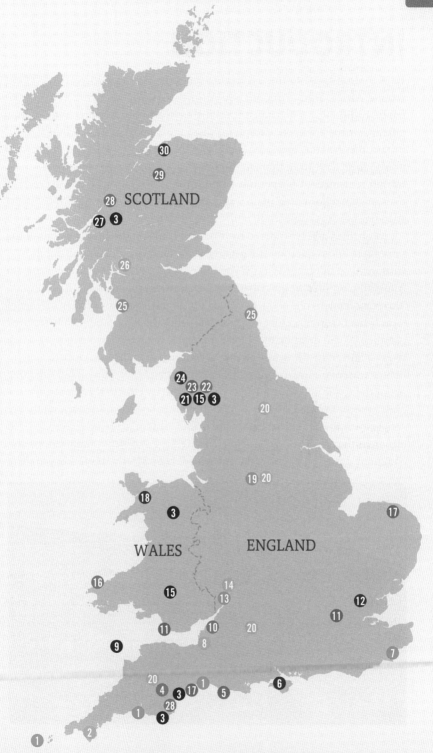

INTRODUCTION

In 2013, I returned to the UK having spent the previous 15 years travelling around Africa, South America and Australasia, and then living in Australia, where I worked as a journalist specialising in adventure sports and outdoor pursuits. Almost without exception, when I told people I was coming back to Britain, they had the same, seemingly heartfelt and visceral reaction: *why on earth would you do that?* Even then, in the afterglow of the London Olympics – now warmly remembered as a period of optimism and hope compared to the years of division that followed – Britain was clearly regarded by many of its inhabitants as somewhere to escape from, rather than explore.

I was baffled and bewildered by this. And I still am (because versions of the same incredulous question still get fired at me now, when I mention our move – what *were* you thinking? Why *did* you come back?). I realise it is human nature to constantly consider the grass to be greener elsewhere, but trust me, it's really not. This place remains one of the most ludicrously and lusciously verdant patches of terra firma I've ever set foot on. Britain also has the most fantastically featured coastline. Not to mention mountains, moors, tors, caves, canyons, gorges, lakes, river valleys and wild vistas aplenty, all of which are relatively close to you, no matter where you live, because this is a little island that – for all our moaning about the roads and the railways – is really pretty easy to travel around. The cities can feel crowded, of course (as metropolises do the world over), yet they're simple to escape, and it's still very easy to find areas of true wilderness scattered all across the UK if you go looking, and we have excellent organisations and community groups that maintain and defend them. Mostly, the people you share

↑ Discovering a letterbox on Dartmoor, page 36 (Patrick Kinsella)

the trails and peaks with – either intentionally, or through serendipity – are a lovely and increasingly diverse bunch of fellow explorers, which is fantastic. And, yeah, it rains quite often – but the topography of this eccentric island has been hydraulically sculpted over millennia by the movement of water, almost to perfection for people into outdoor pursuits, so there's no point whinging when you experience the odd downpour. Put a coat on and embrace it.

You don't uproot a young family and transplant them to a new hemisphere lightly, and there were personal reasons underpinning the decision to return, but I was also very ready to come home, and genuinely excited about getting reacquainted with a place that I had experienced with completely different eyes many years before. As a youngster, I spent a lot of time exploring the coastline and countryside of the British Isles. Dad was a train driver, and while holidays abroad were out of the question for most of my childhood, we did enjoy free rail travel around the entirety of the UK, and used this extensively to go hiking, biking and camping in various corners of England, Scotland, Wales and Ireland. Some of my earliest memories are of epic cycling trips around Scottish islands, ambling and scrambling to the summit of peaks in the Highlands and Lakes, falling asleep to the sound of surf while camping behind wild wave-stroked beaches in Wales, backpacking along the Northumberland coast and taking our two-person kayak on escapades along the River Wey, where I grew up in Guildford. Lots of kids never get to do any of these things, and I'm well aware how lucky I was.

After a hiatus of several years, when more of my adventures started happening in pubs, clubs and bars rather than under the open sky, I returned to the outdoors with renewed enthusiasm as an adult. I now love nothing more than embarking on silly solo missions into the wilds, or convincing my mates and children to

↑ Tree climbing on the Isle of Wight; page 58 (Goodleaf Tree Climbing/Anna Fulford)

come out camping or go exploring in boats or boots, or aboard bikes. Not every adventure goes to plan, of course, and often people get a little tired and grumpy for a bit during a trip, but almost invariably you come away from shared escapades in the outdoors with amusing memories and anecdotes that are retold umpteen times, the details swelling with each telling, that add cement to friendships and strength to family ties. To reflect this, and to illustrate how accessible most outdoor pursuits are, I have deliberately involved family and friends in many of the activities included in this book.

I've often half wished that I'd settled on one outdoor pursuit in particular – perhaps mountain biking, or trail running, or sea kayaking – and invested the time to become properly good at it. Instead I fell in love with all of the above, and plenty of other activities to boot, and have ended up as a Jack of all adventures and master of none. Mostly, though, I have no real regrets about this – life is too short to devote to just one sport, and the experiences and encounters I've enjoyed by trying my hand at myriad activities have been literally life affirming, with many of the most surprising and brilliant outings having taken place right here, within an hour or so of where I live. Which is one of the reasons I wanted to write this book.

ABOUT THIS BOOK

Despite its diminutive size, Britain is the birthplace of an extraordinary number of adventure sports and outdoor pursuits – from sport climbing and fell running to pilot gig rowing, coasteering, ghyll scrambling and cave diving – many of which have subsequently become popular around the planet in various forms,

↑ Coasteering in Pembrokeshire, Wales; page 170 (TYF)

but were initially inspired and shaped by the unique terrain found in the craggy and curious corners of the UK. The idea behind this book is both to explore the origin stories of these activities and their continued appeal, and to seek out other outdoor pastimes and pursuits, such as shinrin-yoku and via ferrata, which have arrived here from elsewhere, put down roots and now offer us even more fascinating ways to experience our natural surroundings.

Each chapter begins with a first-person account of the focus activity, intertwined with some history about the pursuit and why we have chosen to explore it in the area selected. Having, hopefully, piqued your interest, I then provide practical information on how you can go about trying the activity yourself, and where else in the country the conditions and landscape lend themselves to getting the most enjoyment from it.

SCOPE As the title indicates, you will find chapters about caving, canyoning and coasteering experiences in this book, but the activities and ideas explored within these pages are far from limited to these three sports. Also included are adventures involving scrambling, ambling, running, climbing, pedalling, paddling, diving, swimming, skating, surfing and sailing. The common denominator is that all the pursuits are either entirely human-powered, or involve people harnessing the natural elements. Beyond a brief guest appearance by an e-bike in the chapter about bikepacking, no motorised vehicles have been used.

↑ Making a brew before bed while sleeping in a snowhole in Scotland; page 322 (Patrick Kinsella)

Happily, there are already thousands of titles dedicated to hiking, biking, climbing and running in various places around Britain, so I have avoided talking in the broadest terms about these massively popular pursuits and instead approached them from a perspective you may not have considered previously. As a result, many of the outdoor pursuits covered are activities that could be considered somewhat niche. Of course, many readers will have heard of most of them, and you might have tried a few already, but the core concept is to provide people with a few fresh ideas and a splash of inspiration to try something new, or approach an old hobby from a different angle.

GEOGRAPHICAL SPREAD

As you can see from the map on page vii, I have focused on activities that can be enjoyed in various places around the island of Britain (and a few of the smaller islands offshore), rather than the broader British Isles, or the United Kingdom. This means you will find adventures across England, Wales and Scotland, but not Northern Ireland.

For various reasons – ranging from an increasing awareness of the damage that flying does to our environment, to the long-term impact of the pandemic and rising travel costs – more people are now exploring closer to home, and I think that's something to be celebrated and embraced.

ACCESSIBILITY, DIFFICULTY & RISK

While researching this book, I made a conscious effort to feature a wide range of outdoor sports, pursuits and activities, including plenty that are far from fast-paced or adrenaline-based, such as Dartmoor letterboxing, canoe camping and tree bathing. There are some slightly more daunting jaunts too, including whitewater paddling on boisterous rivers and scrambling on the edge of precipitous drops, but not every minute spent outdoors ought to be nerve wracking. It's nice to challenge yourself sometimes, but getting home safe and savouring your time out is far more important.

In each chapter I have included a comprehensive breakdown of the potential risks involved in the focus pursuit. This is not to discourage anyone from trying any of the activities, but simply to make readers as informed as possible. The best way to approach many of the pursuits included here is to seek professional guidance in the first instance. Trying an adventure sport alongside a good guide or as part of a club, with all the correct gear supplied and the risk analysis having been done, will allow you to enjoy the experience fully – if you then decide to progress with it, you can advance your skills and learning to the point where you can do it independently. But everyone has to start somewhere, and most outdoor pursuits are surrounded with their own subcultures, clubs and communities, where newcomers can find guidance, advice, support and comradeship.

↑ A couple diving into some forest bathing/shinrin-yoku in Essex; page 124 (Patrick Kinsella)

And neither do you need to be in exceptional shape to participate and enjoy any of the activities described in this book. Some, such as fell running, do require a decent degree of fitness, but for the vast majority of the ventures covered, a willingness to have a go and rise to the challenge is much more important than any physical attributes.

KIT & CABOODLE

As the old (but nonetheless true) adage states: there's no such thing as bad weather, just bad kit. In the process of researching this book I have undertaken activities in all seasons and conditions. Indeed, some – most obviously snowholing – are only possible in the depths of winter, but other pursuits, such as whitewater rafting, are also best experienced when the elements are at their most feisty. Wearing good gear is the difference between having a great adventure and enduring an absolute sufferfest. It might be amusing to retell stories of epic fails once they're well behind you but, in the moment, being wet and cold is downright miserable and potentially dangerous.

Outdoor apparel can be horrendously pricey, but concentrate on the fabrics and materials used, and their quoted performance levels, rather than the attractiveness of the brand. Read some reviews on trusted websites (not in mainstream magazines and papers where so-called gear testers try the kit out for five minutes before banging out a paragraph about it). Another old adage that isn't always true is that you get what you pay for. In the past I have been let

↑ Fell running in the Lake District; page 238 (Patrick Kinsella)

down by very expensive kit, and impressed by some bargain buys. There are a few golden rules I recommend following: when it comes to clothing, always go with multiple layers, avoid cotton at all costs (go with poly, merino or a mix of both materials for your base, and fleece or down for midlayers), and make sure you have a good wind- and waterproof shell layer. Thoroughly test out your kit before taking it on a multiday, midwinter or high-altitude adventure. Protect your sleeping bag and spare clothes with dry bags. Don't trust digital navigation devices entirely (use them, but bring a sheet map too).

MAPS Another big benefit of exploring in Britain is that we have access to the best publicly available cartography in the world. Ordnance Survey maps (both the paper and the digital versions) are extraordinarily detailed, and besides all the topographical information they provide, the leisure versions are increasingly being updated to show infrastructure details such as canoe and kayak access points on canal- and riverbanks, campsites and even bike centres. If you enjoy the outdoors, it's really worth subscribing to the OS app and getting access to all the maps.

GOOD CONDUCT IN THE OUTDOORS

SHARE THE TRAILS No matter what you are doing while you're out and about, it's massively important to be respectful and considerate both to other people enjoying the trails, peaks, rivers and coastlines, and the wildlife that lives amid these oft-fragile landscapes. This extends from the blindingly obvious (don't shout and scream all the time, or blare loud music; when mountain biking or running on shared trails, be aware that hikers and horseriders might be just around the next blind bend) to the more subtle: when you're exploring very remote terrain, think about what you're wearing, because bright, unnatural colours can impact on the scene as seen by others, even from afar.

It's particularly crucial to heed signage about things such as ground-nesting birds and seal nurseries while you're exploring, and if an area has been cordoned off by a conservation agency for regeneration, please respect that. When you pass people on paths, give them a friendly smile and say hello – the characters you encounter out there are going to be into different things, but enjoyment of the outdoors is a common denominator between us all, and with a bit of mutual respect, potential disputes between, say, walkers and mountain bikers, or climbers and birdwatchers, or wild swimmers and anglers, can be avoided or kept to a minimum.

Access to many wild parts of Britain is far from ideal (more about this in the epilogue, page 344), but the outdoors should be a shared resource for everyone to enjoy, and it's important that we all play our part in making it a welcoming and pleasant place.

LEAVE NO TRACE I'm sure most people are already on board with this, but please ensure that wherever you are and whatever you're up to, you leave the natural environment just as it was when you arrived (or, if you encounter litter and have room to collect it, even better than how you found it). As well as the more obvious things, such as avoiding dropping rubbish, this includes not starting fires in fragile environments or bashing new paths when established trails exist. If you're wild camping, be extra discreet, pitch late and leave early, and don't disturb local wildlife or residents.

It's essential that you pack out whatever you pack in, including vegetable waste such as banana skins, which might be biodegradable, but take around two years to decompose (and much longer in alpine environments). Take a dedicated, strong plastic or material bag for use as a trash sack, otherwise things can get messy. We all get caught short once in a while when out adventuring, but if you need to make like a bear in the woods, ensure you do so 50m or more from the nearest water source, and bury the results in a hole at least 15cm deep – burning any tissue used if it's safe to do so, or packing it out if not.

If you're adventuring with your dog, please clear up after them and always keep them under strict control around wildlife and farm animals. After enjoying an adventure in one area, be sure to clean your boots, boats, tents or tyres off, so you don't spread potentially damaging invasive flora, infective material or bacteria from one place to the next location you go exploring.

↑ A trailhead sign in the Peak District (Patrick Kinsella)

1 CORNISH PILOT GIG ROWING

WHERE	Saltash & the Isles of Scilly, Cornwall; Lyme Regis, Dorset
SKILL LEVEL	Pilot gig rowing is a team sport that requires each person in the boat to put in plenty of effort and, ideally, apply good rowing technique. At an intermediate and advanced level, there's lots of skill and synchrony on display, but clubs are typically very friendly and welcoming to beginners, and will put new rowers with non-competitive crews where good technique can be taught over time. There's much more to being a good sea rower than you might think, but everyone is capable of learning.
RISK FACTOR	Although gigs can capsize and accidents do happen, pilot gig rowing typically takes place in and around estuaries and harbours, and is generally very safe. Highly knowledgeable club officials monitor weather forecasts and will cancel rowing sessions in conditions deemed dangerous. Some teams of rowers do attempt ocean crossings, which is a much more risky undertaking.

↑ Launching a pilot gig in Lyme Regis, Dorset (Patrick Kinsella)

The pull of water is a strong force, and once you've lived by the sea it's hard to move inland, especially if you're into any sort of paddlesport. This visceral attraction to aquascapes has influenced every move I've made for decades, and it's what led to me living in a salt-encrusted corner of southwest England, where I have suddenly (and very unexpectedly) discovered a whole new calling: rowing.

Although I've paddled kayaks and canoes for years, and started stand-up paddleboarding more recently, I'd never even contemplated having a bash at going backwards and taking up rowing. In all honesty, I'd always seen it through the prism of the Oxford vs Cambridge Boat Race, and as an outsider to that world it seemed a posh person's pursuit, surrounded by an air of exclusivity. But that was before I stumbled across sea rowing, specifically Cornish pilot gig rowing, which has turned my view of the activity completely inside out.

Gig rowing is a sport with a deep history, which is woven into the culture of the coastal communities of the southwest and steeped in the universal lifesaving lore of the sea. The boats now used for recreational rowing and competitive racing have a heritage that ripples back across centuries, and the clubs that organise the activity are central to local life. Ever since moving here, I've watched crews take these boats out early on Saturday and Sunday mornings, or spotted them returning just before sunset on hazy weekday evenings. And I've always envied the rowers and the good-humoured camaraderie they share while cutting across the water, with the coxswain in the back, yelling instructions. By contrast, kayaking suddenly seemed quite lonely.

Clearly this was a very different activity to what goes on at places like Henley, but I still assumed rowing was the kind of thing you either grew up doing or just didn't do at all. Until one day a school dad – another blow-in from elsewhere, who'd washed up on the southwest coast – told me the local gig club in Lyme Regis was looking for new blood, and virtually press-ganged me into going to one of their regular open-to-all 'Learn to Row' taster sessions. He insisted the fact I'd never rowed before in my life wouldn't be a problem, but before rocking up I thought it best to at least research the sport.

GETTING THE GIG

Seafaring traditions go deep in the villages, towns and cities that cling to the cliffs and coves around the southwest of England. The culture of the sea defines most of the small coastal settlements of Somerset, Dorset, Devon and Cornwall, where fishing is often the only reason various villages existed at all before the advent of tourism (well, that and smuggling). Meanwhile, the bigger places on the peninsula were all built around their harbours, historically becoming prosperous from maritime trade and naval activity. The sea sustained life, but it also took it away, and tales of shipwrecks, tragedy and heroism are everywhere, from the lyrics of sea shanties sung in local pubs to explainers on memorial plaques in streets and on remote headlands all along the storied shore.

All around Britain, before the invention of dedicated lifeboats in the late 18th and early 19th century, small rowing boats were taken out by men (and sometimes women, famously in the case of Grace Darling) into the most ferocious storms and terrible conditions in brave attempts to rescue sailors and passengers from stricken ships, wrecked on the rocks of the country's gnarled coastline. In the southwest, the vessels used were clinker-built wooden gigs, powered by crews of six rowers, with a coxswain at the helm controlling the rudder. These boats were also employed for another purpose, though, especially in harbour towns in Cornwall and on the Isles of Scilly.

Here, whenever a merchant sailing ship was spotted approaching land, gigs were used to transport a pilot out to meet it. The captain of the larger vessel would commission the pilot – who had intimate knowledge of the local seascape, tides and obstacles – to bring the ship safely into dock. This was lucrative work and more than one pilot would usually be jostling for the job. The first to reach the ship would typically be chosen, so each pilot would recruit a team of the best, fastest rowers they could find, and the activity became competitive, eventually evolving into a sport that helped keep rowers fit and sharp.

As the shipping industry modernised, and motorised craft eclipsed and eventually completely replaced rowing boats, gig rowing declined. After World War I, however, a group of returning soldiers in the Cornish town of Newquay revived the activity and began rowing and racing the remaining gigs again. The popularity of the pursuit ebbed and flowed, and World War II caused another hiatus, but gig rowing resumed in 1947 with renewed energy, and participation grew and spread. In 1986, the Cornish Pilot Gig Association (CPGA) was founded, and now there are over 80 clubs, with more than 8,000 members, rowing some 160 gigs, all made to the exact same design and specifications.

The spiritual heartland of the sport is still Cornwall, where every seaside (and a few riverside) town and village has a gig-rowing team or two they're fiercely proud of, with pictures in pubs taking pride of place even over local football and rugby squads. But the pursuit is popular right across the southwest of England, and a long way beyond. There are now clubs all over Britain and Ireland, and even some scattered across continental Europe, North America and Australia, and most meet up every May, at the annual World Championships in the Isles of Scilly.

My mate, who'd only joined the rowing club the year before, as a complete beginner, told me he was in one of the squads going to the Scillies to compete in the Worlds – something utterly unimaginable in almost any other sport. As soon as I heard that, I was hooked. I'm never going to get to the mountain biking or kayaking world champs, but just maybe I could be a contender in a rowing boat… All you have to do is pull an oar through the water – how hard could it be?

↑ Gig rowing oars are large, but hollow (Teenasparkler/S)   → Correct hand positioning is crucial (Zichrini/S)

LESSONS IN OARSOMENESS

So, early one chilly April morning, I show up at the Cob in Lyme Regis, wearing a hodgepodge outfit comprised mostly of kayaking gear. Beside me are two other newbies, there for the taster session. The gig is already in the water from an earlier session. We're assigned seats, given an enormous oar each, and the more-experienced rowers in the boat take us out of the harbour and on to the open sea, with the cox, Marcus, sitting in the stern (back) shouting directions.

Marcus leads the session, and he patiently takes us through the basic terminology and techniques used. The person sat in the number six seat, closest to the cox, is called the 'stroke' rower. Following the cox's instructions, they set the pace, which is followed by the other five rowers. Rowers are positioned on alternate sides of the gig. The stroke rower sits to the left (port) side of the boat and their oar protrudes over the right (starboard) side, as viewed from the perspective of the cox, the only person facing forwards, looking in the direction of travel. Those in seats four and two are positioned in line with the stroke rower, and this side of the boat is called 'stroke', so if the cox yells 'stroke side pull us round!', rowers six, four and two need to row. The person positioned at the pointier, front end of the boat, in the number one seat, is the 'bow' rower, and they sit on the right (bow) side of the gig, in line with those in seats three and five. If the cox shouts 'bow side pull!', then rowers one, three and five need to get their oars working.

For a gig to move fast and efficiently, all six rowers need to be pulling on their oars in synchrony. Good technique starts with the rower leaning forward with arms stretched out straight, both hands on the oar – the one nearest the end with palm facing upwards, the other with palm facing down. The blade is dipped into the water – not too deep, not too shallow, just covered – and then the rower pulls back until they're almost horizontal, with the end of the oar drawn right into their chest. The blade is then taken out of the water and pushed back to the start position. Us newbies are distributed around the boat, and we're told to keep pace with the oar in front of us – so sat in seat two, I have to keep in rhythm with the guy paddling at four, who is in turn following the lead of the stroke paddler, in seat six.

CATCHING ON It is, all at once, extremely simple and very complicated. The principle is clear enough, but doing it right takes years of practice. Dozens of little factors add up to make the perfect stroke, from holding the oar correctly to how far you bring it back before starting each stroke (which begins with a 'catch'), and where you take it out at the end. Gig seats are wooden, so they don't slide back and forth like on a fancy rowing machine or a river-rowing set-up, and your body – mostly bum and legs – has to absorb all the movement involved. You need to brace your feet against the 'stretcher' (footstop) below the

↑ On the pull – rowing hard in Lyme Bay (Patrick Kinsella) ← Pilot gigs are all made to the same strict dimensions (Patrick Kinsella)

WORLDS IN MOTION

Since 1990, the Pilot Gig Rowing World Championships has taken place annually in the Isles of Scilly, an eccentric handful of five inhabited islands 45km (24½ nautical miles) off Land's End, Cornwall. And it is a big deal. Some 2,000 rowers flock to the islands in late April–early May, doubling the population, and for a weekend the archipelago is consumed by raucous rowing and competitive drinking. During the biggest race, which goes across the lagoon between St Agnes and St Mary's Harbour, over 160 crews might be competing against one another. The UK National Championships are held in Newquay, Cornwall, each September. ⌀wpgc.uk.

seat in front, and really engage your core in order to put in a good strong stroke. If your abs ache after a row, you've been doing something right.

The oars seem enormous. They actually vary in length slightly, depending on where you're positioned in the boat, with each seat number having a corresponding oar made to compensate for the shape of the gig, so all the blades

↑ During the Worlds, rowers take over the Scilly Isles (Glenmore/S)

align in the water. The shafts are hollow, so they're lighter and more manageable than they appear. They also float, which is good for two reasons: they won't sink if they go overboard, and in the event of a capsize (rare now, but not when gigs were used as lifeboats), rowers separated from the boat can cling to them. A leather-covered section of the shaft goes between a pair of pegs, 'thole pins', inserted into holes on the gunwale (the top edge of the hull), which keep the oars in place. In each pair there is a hardwood pin – which goes in the hole closest to the bow and gives you a point to pull against while rowing – and a softwood pin, which fits in the hole closest to the cox, and is designed to break if the rower 'catches a crab'.

And, in a pilot gig, you don't want to catch a crab. This expression describes what happens when the blade digs too deep into the water and you lose control of the oar – something that can throw you right off your seat. If this happens, it's best to lob the shaft of the oar straight up in the air, so it goes in the sea – instead of clouting you (or a team mate), although the pin snapping should avert the worst of the consequences. When this occurs – and it happens relatively regularly with inexperienced rowers – everyone has to stop, the oar needs to be retrieved and a new pin popped in. It interrupts the rhythm of the rowing session and the culprit traditionally keeps the broken pin, as a badge of dishonour.

Inevitably, during our Learn to Row session a couple of crabs are caught, but thankfully I manage to avoid snagging one. I'm exhausted and aching by the end of the hour-long session, though, mainly through exertion but partly because I've been concentrating intensely on not messing things up. I'm used to being on the water alone – sitting in kayaks, kneeling in canoes and standing on SUPs – where my mistakes only affect me, and I feel the pressure of being part of a team. But I love it, too. There's a real feeling of togetherness, and when we all manage to row in sync we seem to skim across the water. I can only imagine how exhilarating it must be during a race, rowing neck-and-neck with a rival boat.

I also realise I've been focusing so hard on keeping time with the other rowers, I've barely looked up during the whole session, and don't have a clue where we've been. The data from my smartwatch later reveals we simply did loops around the end of the Cob, as Marcus gently introduced us to the rudimentary requirements of rowing as a team. Afterwards he makes a point of telling me I've done well, and urges me to come back. He probably says that to everyone, but I'm stoked, and immediately sign up for some Saturday and Sunday sessions.

With each subsequent row I feel things clicking into place with my technique, although I also discover there are myriad more things to learn, as various coxes in command of the boats bellow out orders, instructions and constructive criticism. I keep alternating seat position, but it's all good experience, and as I get to know more of my fellow rowers – who range in age from sixth-formers to septuagenarians – I relax a little and enjoy the experience more. I even start looking around and taking in the views, and on occasions when I join a crew with more advanced rowers, we go right along the coast from Lyme Regis, past Black Ven and West Bay to Charmouth, passing beneath the great blonde head of Golden Cap, the highest point on the south coast.

CORNWALL CALLING

Within months I consider myself a 'rower', which would absolutely astonish my younger self. I'm not a very good or experienced one, but nevertheless, the Lyme Regis Gig Club has welcomed me with warmth, and I'm proud to be a member. And I'm still harbouring dreams of getting to the World Championships. I'm way off the pace for that at the moment, but there's something I feel compelled to do in the meantime, en route to the Scillies (sort of). Rowing with a club based on the Devon-Dorset border is brilliant, yet the sport's spiritual heart and deepest history lies further west, over the River Tamar in Kernow, and I'm keen to join a Cornish crew at least once while submerging myself in gig culture.

Luckily, part of that culture is a welcoming approach to fellow rowers, and after I put out some feelers I'm contacted by several clubs in Cornwall, who say they'd happily host me – even if I am from Devon, where people make a mess of putting cream and jam on their scones. For various reasons – mainly around feisty weather conditions, which regularly force the cancellation of winter rowing sessions for clubs based along the more rugged and exposed parts of the coast – I end up joining a crew from Caradon Pilot Gig Club in Saltash, which is literally just across the Tamar. But it's still Cornwall, and it has an extraordinary record, with the men's squad having won 12 World Championships and the women taking three titles out of the last five. It also boasts one of the more enviable positions of any gig club in the country. With options to go up or down the scenic rivers Tamar and Lynher, or along the Hamoaze estuarine area, there's almost always somewhere to row in the shadow of the wind. 'Unless there's a 50mph southwesterly, we never need to cancel,' I'm told by Steve, who has kindly made room for me on the club's rowing roster.

I listen to the radio as I drive west in the pre-dawn gloom of a soggy Sunday morning, and the shipping forecast reveals the coast is being battered by strong winds, including a lively southwesterly tearing across Plymouth Sound and up the Tamar. Uh-oh. It's still stubbornly dark when I arrive at the gig shed, but there's plenty of activity, and I help get the gig down to the water's edge. Clearly we're still going out, which is great, but sunrise seems to have been cancelled, and looking up at the bruised black-and-blue sky, I put on an extra shell layer and try to stop shivering. I've been allocated the bow seat (one), and climb into the boat last before we push away from the wall and start rowing.

↑ A crew from the Caradon Pilot Gig Club on the Tamar (Patrick Kinsella) → View from the bow seat on the Hamoaze Estuary (Patrick Kinsella)

I'd told Steve I'm a relatively new rower, but either the message hasn't filtered through to the cox, John, or he doesn't care, because we get straight into it, with a fast-paced 15-minute warm-up row up past the confluence point of the Tamar and the Lynher. My fellow oarsmen – Alistair, Crispin, Nick, Mark and Steve – clearly row regularly together, and the standard is good. I just hang on for dear life, following Crispin's oar, grunting with effort and desperately trying to avoid making any embarrassing errors. The sky does eventually lighten, and as we pause for breath and to remove layers, a friendly conversation breaks out. The lads laugh when I explain why I have joined them, before revealing that only one of their number is actually properly Cornish – born and bred – while the others live one side of the bridge or the other. The club and the culture around it, however, is as Cornish as Poldark's pants, so I'm not worried.

After the warm up we put in three seven-minute, high-intensity sessions, with a couple of minutes between each to wheeze and recover. It's a proper workout – seven minutes is a long time when you're rowing hard, with a gut full of fear

ESSENTIALS

GETTING STARTED Many clubs, including Lyme Bay (lymeregisgigclub.com) and Caradon (caradongigclub.com) hold 'Learn to Row' introduction sessions and open days to encourage newcomers. Check the directory of clubs on the Cornish Pilot Gigs Association website (cpga.co.uk) and contact your nearest one.

SPECIAL CONSIDERATIONS Tradition is important in a sport like pilot gig rowing, from the terminology used to the specifications of the boat. All pilot gigs rowed today are based on a vessel called the *Treffry*, built in 1838 by William Peters in St Mawes, on the Roseland Peninsula in southern Cornwall. These clinker-built (overlapping panels) boats strictly measure 32ft (9.8m) in length, with a beam width of 4ft 10in (1.47m).

KIT BAG Rowers wear all kinds of kit, depending on conditions and personal preference. It's important to wear shoes with some grip that you don't mind getting wet. Besides footwear, you require fairly lightweight clothing that allows a full range of movement and protects you from the wind and sun. It's wise to take water and a shell layer with you in the boat, to keep hydrated and warm in the event of a long pause in rowing. Some clubs/harbour masters stipulate the use of a PFD (personal flotation device); most rowers use a compact, waistbelt version, inflated by a gas canister.

GETTING THERE Lyme Regis is reached via the A35 from Bournemouth or Axminster. The closest train station is Axminster – buses run to Lyme Regis from the station.

about failing. We glide nicely across the water, though, shooting past tree-covered banks and beautiful bridges. I manage to keep pace and, most importantly, avoid catching any crabs, which would be a bit mortifying in the circumstances. After the row, while shaking hands, a couple of the guys say they're looking forward to seeing me on the circuit, and out on the Scillies for the Worlds, and I can't tell whether they're joking or not. Anything seems possible with this pursuit.

'Actually, now I think about it, everyone who was in the boat with you this morning is a World Champion,' Crispin casually remarks as we walk together up the pontoon. 'Even John, the cox, who's 80 next week. He rowed with the supervets last year, and they won their category.'

I'm glad I didn't know this fact before I got into the boat. I was already nervous enough, and had I realised I was rowing with bona fide world champs, I probably would have caught a bucket-load of crabs. But as it happened I didn't, and I think I kept pace with them. Maybe the idea of going to the Worlds is not such a Scilly one after all.

To get to Saltash, take the A38 past Plymouth and across the Royal Albert Bridge over the River Tamar. The town has a train station, which is on the line between London Paddington and Penzance, via Bristol Temple Meads.

The Isles of Scilly are served by the *Scillonian III* passenger ferry, which operates once a day in both directions March–November, running between Penzance and St Mary's, the main island (⌲ islesofscilly-travel.co.uk).

PLACES TO STAY There's a wide range of accommodation in Lyme Regis, including the very on-theme **Pilot Boat** (⌲ thepilotboat.co.uk) boutique hotel and restaurant.

Places to stay in Saltash include the **Who'd Have Thought It Inn** (⌲ whodcornwall. co.uk), which has great views over the River Tamar.

The Isles of Scilly have accommodation options ranging from **camping to B&Bs, hotels and self-catering cottages** (⌲ visitislesofscilly.com/accommodation) – but everything gets busy during the gig rowing World Championships.

ELSEWHERE There are gig-rowing clubs all over the southwest, but you can also find clubs in central London (⌲ londoncornishpilotgigclub.org), Bristol (⌲ clevedonpilotgigclub.co.uk) and many other places.

EXTRA RESOURCES
Cornish Pilot Gigs Association ⌲ cpga.co.uk
⌲ gigrower.co.uk
⌲ visitislesofscilly.com

2 FREEDIVING

WHERE	Porthkerris, Cornwall
SKILL LEVEL	To do a freediving course you need to be a confident swimmer and in good health. Freediving independently requires a range of advanced skills and knowledge, including the ability to plan a safe dive.
RISK FACTOR	Freediving courses with reputable providers take place in a well-supervised and highly controlled environment where risks are strictly managed. Freediving independently necessitates careful risk assessment, factoring in weather, tides, currents, environmental hazards and facilities. Done incorrectly or individually it can be a dangerous activity; even basic breath-holding exercises in pools should never be practised alone.

Exploring the subaquatic environment is like entering an entirely new world; an alien place where the laws of nature are different and your senses have to adjust dramatically. With a mask on, in decent visibility, the experience of gliding over rocks and through great fronds of seaweed can feel more like flying than swimming. The problem is, underwater we are literally out of our element, and sooner or later (always too soon) we must return to the surface to breathe. You can, of course, take compressed air down with you, in scuba tanks, but that involves a whole lot of heavy and expensive equipment, means the experience is effervescently noisy, and you're still time limited. Most people get less than an hour underwater from a twin set of tanks, and between dives you need to stay at surface level to allow pressurised nitrogen to work its way through your system, to avoid suffering from the bends.

But what if you could remain underwater long enough to do some real exploring, or interact with marine wildlife, without all that cumbersome gear and noisy bubble blowing? Well, some people can do exactly that – comfortably staying submerged for several minutes on a single breath. It's known as freediving, or apnea, and you don't need to be superhuman to learn how to do it. (Although, at the pointy end of sport freediving, athletes perform feats of endurance that make it seem as though they belong to another species, reaching depths well beyond 100m and staying underwater for over ten minutes.)

To enjoy recreational freediving, however, you simply need to acquire a few skills and some important safety knowledge. In fact, most people have already been freediving, but without calling it that. Every time you duck dive while snorkelling, descending to look at something on the sea floor or trying to keep up with passing fish – that is freediving. But holding your breath can be extremely dangerous around water, even in the shallows. A few years go a friend of mine – a keen spearfisher and freediver – tragically died while practising apnea techniques alone in a swimming pool, after blacking out and drowning, so I want to learn how to do it safely. Which is why I'm heading to Cornwall to learn from a world-class freediver.

← Freedivers use long fins to make the most of every movement (Daan Verhoeven)

BREATHTAKING

You know that burning sensation you experience after holding your breath for a little while? Well that's not your body demanding more oxygen, but rather a build up of carbon dioxide in your lungs, activating a trigger response to breathe. 'You need to become friends with that feeling,' Georgina Millar tells us. 'It's not pleasant at first, but it reaches a point and then doesn't get any worse. Your body has much more oxygen to work with than your brain will readily admit.'

Well, that's easy for her to say. George, a multiple British champion and freediving record holder who competes internationally, can remain underwater for more than seven minutes while still (static apnea) and reach depths of over 65m on a single breath when diving with fins (constant weight apnea). This seems absolutely incredible to me, as I sit on a pebbly beach, puffing and blowing, having just struggled to hold my breath for a mere minute.

There are six of us in the group, and after an introduction to the pursuit and a quick check of our blood oxygen levels, we have been instructed to lie down, close our eyes and, on George's signal, hold our breath. As each person reaches their limit, they sit up. When I can take it no longer I release the carbon dioxide from my lungs, take a big gulp of air and rise. Angela is already sitting, and Jason and Katinka come up for air just after me. About 30 seconds later, Laura joins us. But Graeme just lays there, for what seems like an age. We can see his eyes flickering beneath closed lids, like someone experiencing REM while asleep, but otherwise he remains entirely motionless. I'm almost concerned, but George is grinning – she is clearly impressed. When he finally exhales and sits up, blinking, he seems startled to see us all staring at him. Full of positive affirmation, George gives us our scores. I managed just over a minute and half, while Laura – a yoga instructor who knows a thing or two about relaxation and slowing her heartbeat – has pushed through the two-minute mark. Graeme, though, is nailing it, with a time well north of three minutes. The bastard. Later he explains he's been practising dry apnea (holding your breath outside of water) for weeks, using an app. I wish I'd thought of that.

People take up freediving for all sorts of very different reasons – the ability to remain comfortable and calm underwater for several minutes can be useful for everyone from actors and synchronised swimmers to spearfishers. George runs a special course for aspiring mermaids, where you can learn to freedive and swim underwater with a large monofin. Graeme is a professional photographer, specialising in marine wildlife, and this is a serious matter for him. If he can stay submerged for longer periods of time without scaring animals by blowing bubbles, it will vastly increase his chances of getting a great shot. Others are interested in the competitive side of the sport. For most people though, myself included, freediving is a way of spending more time exploring underwater without the need for cumbersome scuba gear. But to see some tangible results, there's a lot to learn.

↑ Doing breath tests on the beach (Patrick Kinsella) → Measuring blood oxygen levels (Patrick Kinsella)

SEAL SCHOOL The course we are doing is two days long, and the first morning is spent entirely in the classroom – albeit an outside classroom on a beach tucked away on a Cornish cove, where the siren sound of the sea clawing away at the pebbles is ever present. Porthkerris is on the Lizard Peninsula, close to mainland Britain's most southerly point. There's an excellent PADI (Professional Association of Diving Instructors) scuba diving school here, and George and her partner, Daan Verhoeven (a highly regarded underwater photographer and freediver) share the facilities to teach freediving through their company, Aquacity. Our Level 1 Freediving course is accredited by SSI (Scuba Schools International), but you can also get internationally recognised freediving certificates through PADI and AIDA (the International Association for the Development of Apnea).

I'm a qualified advanced diver, but soon learn I'm going to need to put aside virtually everything I remember from scuba training in order to get anywhere with freediving. For starters, when learning how to dive with tanks you're instructed never to hold your breath, and obviously that won't work when you're attempting to master the techniques of apnea, which literally means the cessation of breathing. Before long, George calls a whiteboard into action and it all gets pretty scientific as she explains some of the physiological reactions the human body experiences

DIVING BACK IN TIME

People have been freediving for thousands of years all across the world, to harvest resources and claim treasure. In Greece, freedivers were collecting sponges from the sea floor during the lifetimes of Plato and Homer. Japan's *ama* ('women of the sea') are legendary, freediving for shellfish and pearls in freezing cold water and often working into their 70s and 80s. Post World War II, freediving developed into an endurance pursuit and then a competitive sport, with pioneers such as Raimondo Bucher, Bob Croft, Jacques Mayol and Enzo Maiorca constantly exceeding the boundaries of what scientists believed was possible. Jacques Mayol was the first person to go beyond 100m, but extraordinary new feats continued to be performed by the likes of Tanya Streeter.

RECORD-BREAKING DIVES There are multiple freediving disciplines, but the current world record for static apnea (where competitors just hold their breath underwater) is 11 minutes and 54 seconds (held by Branko Petrović). The record depth for Constant Weight Freediving with fins is 131m (set by Alexey Molchanov in 2021), while in the dangerous discipline of No Limits Freediving (where divers use a metal sledge to descend and an air bag to come back up), Herbert Nitsch reached 214m in 2007.

when you stop breathing. As carbon dioxide levels rise in the lungs and you feel that burning sensation, your spleen releases more red blood cells, which direct oxygen to your vital organs, and at the same time your heartbeat slows down. This is known as the 'mammalian dive reflex', and it's what enables marine mammals such as seals to stay underwater for so long. Newborn humans are good at utilising this (think of the baby on the cover of Nirvana's *Nevermind* album), but as adults it takes a while to push past other bodily reflexes screaming at you to breathe.

For a successful dive, your intake of oxygen immediately before going underwater is vitally important. George leads us through some diaphragmatic breathing techniques, whereby you take long deep breaths and use your stomach muscles to pull your diaphragm down, efficiently filling your lungs to their real capacity. She stresses this is very different to hyperventilation – taking lots of quick, short, sharp breaths – which is extremely bad for apnea, and needs to be avoided. Calmly breathe in. Then out. We're encouraged to spend two full minutes doing this before getting one last big breath in, forcing the air down into our lungs, and then holding it. The urge to exhale becomes almost unbearable really quite quickly, but I try to push through. On dry land it's easy to release some of the carbon dioxide to relieve the pressure, but when you're underwater it's best to keep it in, otherwise it will affect your buoyancy. And when you surface, it's important to take at least three recovery breaths – again, long intakes of air, pushing oxygen deep into your lungs.

Because you're taking in air (a mix of oxygen, nitrogen and other gasses) at sea level, where the pressure is 1 bar, there's very little risk of getting the bends while freediving recreationally. Depth still does strange things to your body (if you have 6-litre lung capacity at the surface, for example, by the time you descend to 20m, where the pressure is at 3 bar, your lungs will have shrunk to a third of their size) but as you return to the surface the nitrogen in your system (which is what causes the bends) dissipates. Freedivers can experience the bends, but you'd have to do multiple deep dives with very little surface time in between for compressed nitrogen to build up to problematic levels.

Instead, the big danger with freediving is hypoxic blackout, when you lose consciousness underwater through lack of oxygen and drown. For those who really push the limits, visiting the kind of depths George and other competitive athletes reach, hypoxic blackout out happens quite regularly in the last 10m of the dive, or even at the surface. But it can occur at any depth when you're holding your breath, which is why you should never, ever practise apnea in water on your own. Not even in the bath. Safety and rescue skills form a big part of the course, and just like with scuba, the buddy system is crucial for freedivers. During events, well-trained spotters observe competitors all the time, and they're primed and ready to perform a rescue when required. But even when freediving

recreationally in relatively shallow water, it's vitally important to keep a very close eye on your partner.

After lunch, it's time to hit the dive school pool, try on the equipment and learn some rescue techniques with Alex, another elite freediver, and Luca, a trainee instructor. Because the human body is naturally buoyant, and even the tightest wetsuit makes it want to float more, weights are required. It's a delicate balance – obviously you need to be able to propel yourself back to the surface without too much effort, and unlike scuba diving you can't borrow air from a tank to inflate your BCD (buoyancy control device) to help with that. Being neutrally buoyant at 10m is considered perfect. The ballast is distributed differently too, with many freedivers wearing neck weights to help them descend headfirst. It's a little unnerving initially, being weighted down in water without tanks, but I soon get used to it as we practise pre-dive breathing and do lengths underwater, attempting to kick ultra efficiently. Graeme, of course, blows the rest of us out of the water with the number of lengths he can do on single breath, but still, I feel like I'm freediving.

With the help of a mannequin aptly nicknamed Creepy Martin, the rest of the afternoon is spent on safety, repeatedly rehearsing what to do when someone exhibits signs of hypoxia (oxygen starvation). In addition to a full-on blackout, indicators include a loss of motor skills, befuddlement, the shakes, and occasionally sufferers might even go a bit blue. After observing any of these symptoms, you immediately need to get your buddy's face out of the water so they can breathe. Then remove their mask, gently slap their cheeks and blow air across their face – all while talking to them. If none of these things elicit a response, you may need to administer a rescue breath and, keeping their face above water, get them to a boat or ashore to seek additional help. Poor Martin endures multiple slaps, the occasional smooch, and is dragged hither and thither until Alex is happy we've mastered the procedures.

DOWN TIME On the second day we put all our learning into practice in a proper diving environment. Unusually, the wind is blowing in from the east and the typically calm water of Porthkerris Bay is too choppy for us to get in the sea, so instead we meet at a local quarry. Initially we're all a little disappointed by this – Porthkerris is close to Manacles Reef, a Marine Conservation Zone famous for its biodiversity, whereas the chances of meeting marine life are zero in a flooded quarry. However, as the day goes on, I'm increasingly grateful there's nothing to distract me from the set of new skills I'm struggling to master.

While we kit up, Alex rigs a number of lines between surface buoys and the bottom of the quarry. We split into groups, a pair of students with each instructor,

↑ Luca enters the training lagoon (Patrick Kinsella)   ← Georgina Millar can make one breath last over 7 minutes
(Daan Verhoeven)

and take it in turns to dive. Before descending, you must clip a lanyard on to the line, which prevents you from getting disorientated and also means the instructors know exactly where you are. When it's my turn, I go through the pre-dive breathing drill, fill my lungs with air, jettison my snorkel, perform a duck dive and set off down the line, headfirst.

It immediately becomes apparent that the biggest hurdle isn't how long I can hold my breath, but whether I can equalise sufficiently to get to a decent depth before running out of air. (To pass Level 1, you need to reach 20m.) Equalisation is necessary in all forms of diving. If you've ever swum to the bottom of a pool and experienced ear pain, that's because the pressure in your ear and sinus cavities is different to the outside pressure, causing discomfort that can only be relieved by equalising. Venturing deeper without successfully equalising is excruciating and causes permanent damage to your eardrums. The most common equalising method when scuba diving is the Valsalva technique, when you pinch your nostrils and blow air from your lungs against your now blocked nose, forcing it into your ear and sinus cavities. However, this doesn't work for freediving, because it uses up valuable oxygen and becomes impossible to do as you get deeper and your lungs shrink. Instead, you must master the Frenzel technique, whereby you still pinch your nose, but use your tongue to open the soft palate and force air from above your vocal cords into your nasal cavity, equalising your ears and sinuses. It sounds complicated, and it feels it too, when you're submerged upside down, operating on a single breath like some half-baked Houdini wannabe. After time it becomes second nature – but it's well worth practising this technique before doing a course, so you can make the most of your time in the water.

Once we've been through the requirements of the course, there's an opportunity to explore. And, while it's not the Manacles – where harbour porpoises and seals commonly cavort amid a dramatic rockscape, the skeletons of myriad sunken ships lie in water up to 80m deep, and divers can enjoy swimming at shallower depths among pink sea fan, cup coral and gorgeous jewel anemones – the quarry does hold some submerged secrets. We investigate several caves and swim-throughs, and dive into a drowned forge complete with an old kiln. There are mysterious markings along the lower reaches of the sheer walls, and while I'm trying to decipher one of these, during a dive that's nowhere near as deep or as long as I'd like to claim, a shadow passes way below me. It's Graeme, of course. Cruising along like a sodding seal, and showing no signs of needing to surface. Sadly, my jealousy runs deeper than my dive profile. But I'll be back to Porthkerris before long, better prepared with my apnea training and equalising techniques, and I can't wait to get out among the Manacles to meet the locals.

ESSENTIALS

GETTING STARTED Aquacity Freedivers (⌀ aquacityfreediving.com) offers a range of freediving courses.

SPECIAL CONSIDERATIONS Always freedive with an experienced buddy, a group or an instructor.

KIT BAG Freediving equipment is similar but subtly different to scuba gear. It's important to reduce the size of any air pockets, which make descending harder, and to cut down on effort, because exertion eats up oxygen. So freediving masks are very low volume (close to your face), and wetsuits are super tight. Fins are longer, to provide more propulsion when kicking. Some freedivers use monofins (like a mermaid's tail).

GETTING THERE Porthkerris is on the Lizard Peninsula in Cornwall. Drive via Helston.

PLACES TO STAY There are self-catering apartments and a campsite in Porthkerris, with sensational sea views.

ELSEWHERE Cornwall is particularly good for freediving, with multiple sites ideal for shore dives. However, you can freedive around most of the British coast if you know what you're doing. **Go Freediving** (⌀ gofreediving.co.uk) offers courses near Bath, while **Apneists UK** (⌀ freedivers.co.uk) runs freediving courses in the north of England, Wales and Scotland.

EXTRA RESOURCES

⌀ aidainternational.org
⌀ divessi.com/en/get-certified/freediving
⌀ padi.com/education/freediving
Freedive (app)
⌀ youtube.com/c/AdamFreediver

↑ A freediver explores Cornwall's colourful underwater forests (Daan Verhoeven)

3 SURFSKI PADDLING

WHERE	South Hams, Devon; Lake Bala/Llyn Tegid, Wales; Windermere, Cumbria; Loch Awe, Scotland
SKILL LEVEL	Although there are some crossover skills, paddling a surfski is very different to paddling a sea kayak – it's much more like handling a K1, and core balance is one of the first things you have to master (along with the ability to get back in the boat after capsizing). With a rudder to steer with, you're free to focus on perfecting your all-important forward stroke, and then it's mostly about being efficient with your energy expenditure and learning how to harness the helping hand that surf, swell, waves and wind can provide.
RISK FACTOR	All watersports carry with them an element of danger, but risks can be vastly reduced by good decision making and the use of appropriate safety equipment. Beyond big events such as Hawaii's legendary Molokai Challenge, surfski paddling is typically enjoyed in the sea or ocean relatively close to shore, but dangers include getting blown out to sea, becoming separated from your craft, and collisions with larger powered boats or ships. You should always wear a PFD (life jacket), paddle within your limits, use lights if visibility is poor, and pair up with a partner or group when adventuring independently (at the very least, let someone know your plans). Avoid busy shipping lanes.

The first time I ever set my eyes on a surfski I was hooked. This was a completely different style of paddling to anything I'd seen or done before, and watching an experienced surfski racer in action, suddenly sea kayaking and canoeing seemed somewhat pedestrian. These long craft are lean and sleek - in the right hands, and when travelling downwind on a decent swell, they scythe through the water like a shark closing in on its prey, picking

↑ A surfski in its natural environment: the ocean (Chris Ord)

up speed with each precisely placed stroke, until the power of the ocean takes over and the paddler gets to sit back and ride the rolling wave. It's spellbinding to watch, and even more incredible to experience – if you can perfect the paddling skills required.

Surfskis and oceanskis are much more akin to a competitive K1 boat (like the solo craft used to race on flat water in the Olympics) than a sea kayak, except they're intended for use on open water, where you have waves and other wild factors to contend with. There are variations in the design of the hull compared to a kayak, but the most obvious difference is that the cockpit is open to the elements. And this is just as well, because it makes them a whole lot easier to remount when you fall in, which happens with frustrating regularity when you first start out. This is largely due to the narrowness and V shape of the hull, designed as they are to move quickly through the water, and the more advanced and race-orientated the ski is, the more skinny and tippy it will be.

These boats are made for racing and paddling fast over relatively short distances, not for leisurely day adventures, long-distance touring or camping out (see the boatpacking chapter, page 310, if this is more your scene). Some events are endurance length, however, so building up some stamina and fitness is important too (and there's no better way to strengthen your core and earn a six-pack than putting in some serious paddling time). But the most important thing is nailing your technique and finding a surfski that is right for you – otherwise you're likely to spend more time swimming next to your boat than paddling it. And the only way to do that is to get out on the water regularly. So, where in Britain can you do this, getting a taste of the sport and trying out some craft without investing a big chunk of money and buying your own ski? This was a question I was asking myself not so long ago.

THE DOWN LOW

I first came across the pursuit while in Australia, where a massive percentage of the population grow up on the coast and ski paddling is part of the very strong surf lifesaving culture. I'd done plenty of kayaking and canoeing, but when I first plonked my posterior in the cockpit of a surfski (and promptly fell out), I realised I was going to have to forget everything I knew and learn to paddle this craft from scratch, while most people around me already seemed like experts.

During my time Downunder, I spent years attempting to master the art of surfski paddling, with some – albeit limited – successes. I graduated from beginner boats made from heavy plastic and began paddling proper skis, constructed from carbon fibre, which made me feel like I was flying across the tops of the waves. I began to understand how to harness the white horses, ride the runners and use the swell to maintain speed. Over time I fell in less often, and even survived a few ocean races in exotic places like the Coral Sea around the Whitsunday Islands, and amid the big rollers of the Southern Ocean, although I was generally (okay… always) the shark bait at the very back of the pack – you certainly learn how to clamber back into your boat quickly after a capsize in those great whitey waters.

Leaving Australia and returning home to the UK, I thought I was also bidding goodbye to a sport I'd learned to love. But I was wrong. While I'd been gone, the pursuit of surfski paddling had taken hold here too, especially, as luck (and logic) would have it, around the surf-stroked shores of the southwest – the wild coastline of Cornwall and Devon – which is exactly where I was heading.

BRINGING IT HOME

The best thing about paddling a surfski here in the UK is that you're not constantly surrounded by loads of other people who have been brought up on such boats, for whom core balance seems to be second nature. In Britain, a lot of ski paddlers are relative beginners – except for the K1 kayakers, who blow everyone out of the water. The next best thing is that, when you rock up at a British beach with a surfski, you're guaranteed to get a gaggle of people gravitating towards you because they're totally bamboozled by the boat. The sport has taken off here recently, but it's still nowhere near as popular as it is in Australia, New Zealand, South Africa and the United States, and the sight of a 6m-long fibreglass surfski being carried on to the beach over someone's shoulder is usually enough to cause a significant ripple of excitement to spread across the sand.

Of course, the downside to pulling a crowd is that you then feel like a proper plum if you subsequently fall straight off the ski into the sea, mere metres from the beach. With this in mind, and feeling a bit rusty after spending far too much time landlubbing, I started looking for a way of doing some structured sessions and getting to know the boats again.

I contacted one of the brands I used to paddle in Australia, Think Kayak, and they put me in touch with Neil Gilmour, who had been running a fantastic organisation called Head For Adventure, helping to rehabilitate people impacted by serious head injuries through involvement in outdoor pursuits. Neil has a couple of skis, one of which he's happy to lend me, and we meet up for an intro paddle in Salcombe, on the super-scenic south Devon coast. Enveloped in a spooky sea mist, we paddle out past Bolt Head and attempt to hitch a lift back on the swell that accompanies the incoming tide. My attempts at catching runners aren't particularly successful, but at least I don't fall in, which is a result in my eyes. The ski I'm using, a Think Ace, is a relatively new model, which combines comparatively good stability with excellent pace and performance, and it doesn't feel too tippy or twitchy, which is a great relief.

This little corner of the southwest, I soon discover, is a hotbed of surfski activity. Located right on the beach at South Sands, Sea Kayak Salcombe paddle sports centre has single and double surfskis for hire, and I soon get to know the owner, Ben Sherring, a kayaking instructor and expedition leader who is passionate

SURF TURF

Surfski and oceanski paddling should not be confused with surf kayaking, which is a different pursuit altogether, where paddlers use specific craft to catch breaking waves in a similar way to surfboarders. Custom-made surf kayaks are short, flat-bottomed, sit-inside boats, designed and made for maximum speed and manoeuvrability. The best places in Britain to enjoy kayak surfing include beaches and breaks all along the Atlantic coastline of Cornwall, Devon, Wales and Scotland, and put-in points on the North Sea coastline of Scotland and northern England. For more information, including details about lessons, coaching and competition, see the British Canoeing website: ⊘ britishcanoeing.org.uk/competition/surf-kayak.

about paddling in all forms, but especially wants to help grow the surfski scene in Britain.

Through Neil and Ben, I learn about a group of surfski paddlers that go out every Wednesday evening during summer from Exmouth, a bit further up the Devon coast. The informal sessions are organised by Jim Taylor-Ross, who has paddled for Britain on the international stage in disciplines including Ocean Racing, Wild Water Racing and Marathon, and is now the GB Ocean Racing Team manager, a member of the British Canoeing Safety Advisory Board and a National Race Coach Tutor. Suffice to say, he knows one end of a paddle from the other, and now represents Epic Kayaks, another boat brand that makes excellent surfskis.

With another friend, Rich, I start joining Jim for weekly training sessions. And between these outings and regular paddles with Ben and Neil in Salcombe, gradually my form starts to return. I get confident – or cocky – enough to enter the Epic Bay Ocean Race, a 16km (10-mile) event that happens each May off the coast of Exmouth. Without all the elite Aussies to content with, I finally don't come last in a surfski race, although I'm still a long way off the pointy end of the pack. I only take one involuntary swim during the race too, after misjudging an incoming wave and getting caught side-on, but at least there are no sharks to worry about here.

THREE LAKES

Races are good fun, and there's a whole series of them to take part in – spread right across Britain from deep in the southwest to Scotland, via Wales and Brighton – but I'm not an especially competitive person, and what I really want to find is some sort of surfski paddling mission. And then, one evening in the pub after a paddle, we hit upon the perfect plan.

British Canoeing (BC), through their Go Paddling website, has come up with a challenge: to paddle the longest lakes in England, Wales and Scotland, consecutively, in the shortest time possible. Although BC are careful not to spell this out, many people, including us, interpret this as a 24-hour challenge – so the clock starts with your first paddle stroke and keeps ticking, even when you're driving. It's just like doing the Three Peaks hiking challenge, but wetter.

The paddling sections are out-and-back along Llyn Tegid in Wales (11km/7 miles) and then end-to-end across the longest part of Windermere (18km/11 miles) and Loch Awe (40km/25 miles). As far as we can see, no-one has yet attempted this in surfskis. This will be our mission. Ben has a business to run, so the paddling posse will be me, Rich and Neil, and we recruit one of Rich's mates, Dave, as our designated driver – because previous experience on these sorts of escapades has shown me that it's much safer having someone who isn't taking part in the challenge behind the wheel of the vehicle most of the time. We pick a weekend in the middle of summer, giving us plenty daylight hours, and start to prepare in earnest.

When the day arrives, we roll away from Rich's house in Totnes, Devon, in the early hours of a sun-splashed Saturday morning. The far shore of Loch Awe, way up in the Scottish Highlands, feels like a terribly distant place. If we manage to get there at all, let alone within 24 hours of starting the challenge (which will get going properly once we're afloat on Llyn Tegid), it will feel like a minor miracle.

By the end of the driveway, though, we've already set ourselves a new target. Rich lives by a pub, the name of which – the Waterman's Arms – suddenly assumes a whole new significance as we drive past. Okay, so we're aiming to paddle this

↑ About to start the Three Lakes challenge on the shores of Llyn Tegid/Lake Bala (Patrick Kinsella)

trio of lakes in 24 hours or less. But the real, overriding objective, we suddenly decide, is to get back here before last orders on Sunday, to see if our wannabe watermen's arms are still willing and able to pick up a pint.

We had originally intended to start in Scotland, but that plan is ripped up and reversed just hours before we set off. Our hastily reconfigured route is designed around drive times, prevailing winds and daylight hours. If we've worked it out correctly, we will be travelling during the night on quiet roads and paddling in the light. It does, however, mean a midday start, straight after a 5-hour car journey, instead of beginning at dawn after a full night's sleep in the Loch Awe hostel.

WALES: LLYN TEGID (LAKE BALA) Llyn Tegid's family-friendly foreshore is an unlikely place to begin an expedition. When we arrive, the beach is busy with sunbathers and squealing kids in inflatables bob on the water. It's 2.15pm when we start the stopwatch and begin threading carefully through the flotilla of rubber dinghies and blow-up crocodiles. Once clear of the kids, we begin burying blades into the water with intent, and the challenge starts in earnest.

Despite his inexperience on a ski, and the fact he's paddling a relatively heavy plastic boat, Rich sprints ahead. Neil has the best paddling technique in our group, but he knows this is a marathon and keeps the pace steady. I just try and hang on as we power up the lake into a fairly feisty headwind. This leg requires kayakers to do an up-and-back loop of the lake, as there's no take-out point at the far end. Fortunately, Bala (Tegid in Welsh) is only 5.5km long, so this isn't too tough (in fact, as we paddle we pass open-water swimmers doing the same distance as us) and it means we have a tail wind for the return journey.

I'm more concerned with ensuring we cover the right distance – I get a bit OCD about these things, and I'd be gutted to reach the end only to find out that we should have paddled an extra 100m on the smallest puddle of the lot – so I insist on doing a jellybean-shaped circuit of the lake. We still get back quicker than expected, after 1 hour 12 minutes, taking Dave by surprise. After a few minutes back on the beach, we spot him, scouring the water with binoculars. To redeem himself, he's dispatched to get ice creams – the recovery food of champions – while we get the boats back on the wagon.

ENGLAND: WINDERMERE The drive to the Lakes from north Wales is the non-paddling bit that had worried me most, but we breeze it without any delays, despite a threatened road closure just a kilometre or so from the put-in point at Fell Foot Park, which we tactfully ignore. It's gone 8.30pm by the time we begin paddling, though, giving us just over two hours to get to the other end before darkness descends.

Although the pressure is on, the dying day is a thing of beauty, and a gentle following wind helps push us along a lake that looks like a mirror until the reflection is shattered by a ferry, followed by a yacht and then a speedboat pulling a wakeboarder. When other boats pass, we ride the ripples and harness their wash, and keep up an average speed of just under 10km/h. By 10pm the lights of Ambleside loom into view, and a fantastic full moon has climbed above Windermere to watch us paddle into the port after exactly two hours on the water. Dave is ready and waiting this time, and we head north for Scotland.

SCOTLAND: LOCH AWE
If there's a perfect time to drive through Glasgow, 2.30am is it. I still manage to take a couple of wrong turns, navigating via a GPS with the sound off while the others slumber, but they're none the wiser and the streets are deserted, so we make good time. We rotate drivers regularly, and I'm unconscious for the final part of the drive, but wake with a jolt as we pull into the car park just past Torran Bay Hostel in Lochgilphead, at the southern end of Loch Awe.

It's 5.30am when we tumble out of the wagon, which is rapidly resembling a wheeled skip full of the detritus of half-a-dozen motorway service station stops. A new day has broken, and it's full of rain. We're shivering, stiff and sleep deprived, but anxious to get started on the crux move of this challenge: a paddle over twice the distance of anything we've tackled thus far. Dave waves us off, drives to the opposite end of the lake and gets some kip.

The drizzle is persistent, but we have a tail wind, just as forecast, and soon warm to the task at hand, surfing on the back of little running waves that help to propel us northeast, towards our goal. The loch – allegedly home to a Nessie-like beast called Beathach Mòr Loch – is immense. Punctuated by little uninhabited islands, its banks are completely wild and undeveloped. Bar the very occasional hint of a house in the hills, there's no sign of life, man or monster, beyond our own paddling party.

After about 24km, muscle fatigue really starts to kick in, along with the bum-numbness that's unavoidable during any long-distance paddle. We're flagging, but bananas, chocolate bars and energy gels work their magic, and eventually the silhouette of Kilchurn Castle looms out of the mist, signaling the end. As we approach the 15th-century ruin, built by the powerful Campbell clan of Glenorchy, there's some confusion about where the paddle officially stops. We're comfortably within the 24-hour time limit for the challenge, so spend a good 20 minutes taking photos beneath the castle, before paddling around the corner to the take-out by the railway bridge, where a grinning Dave eagerly awaits.

'What kept you?' he quips, as we hit the button on the stopwatch to record a time of 4 hours 51 minutes on the loch, to make a combined paddling time of 8 hours, 3 minutes and 55 seconds, and a total expedition time of almost exactly 20 hours.

↑ Setting off: Neil on Llyn Tegid, Wales (Patrick Kinsella) ← Rich in full flow on Lake Windermere (Patrick Kinsella)

Already stoked with those results, it's not until we get in the car and look at our phones that we realise we may have set a new fastest ever time for individual paddlers. The quickest recorded completion of the paddling legs is 6 hours 16 minutes, set by Craig Duff and Steph Roberts, two competitive kayakers paddling a K2 (two-person racing kayak), but we appear to have shaved over an hour off the fastest time set by people paddling individual boats. We're record breakers. Very tired ones. All that remains now is an 11-hour down-country dash to get to the pub and celebrate before last orders.

Swinging into the Waterman's Arms car park at exactly 10.30pm, we're just in time to see the lounge-room lights going out. Panic overrides fatigue, and we dash for the door, only to find it locked. No! The side door is still open, however, and we bundle into the bar where the startled landlord confirms our worst fears.

'Sorry lads, we're shut.'

After hearing our story, however, he pours four pints. 'How could I say no to that,' he says. 'You idiots.'

ESSENTIALS

GETTING STARTED To try surfski paddling for the first time, look for a provider offering boat hire and, ideally, instruction and training sessions, such as **Sea Kayak Salcombe** (⊘ seakayaksalcombe.co.uk) and **Surfski Dynamics** (⊘ surfskidynamics. co.uk) in south Devon. Contact Jim Taylor-Ross at **Epic** (⊘ epic-kayaks.co.uk) to join a paddling session at Exmouth in the summer, where you can try out various surfskis from the Epic fleet.

SPECIAL CONSIDERATIONS There's no time for sightseeing if you do the Three Lakes as a 24-hour challenge, but this trio of inland seas are each located in the loveliest parts of the UK, so consider paddling them separately and spend time exploring the local areas. Loch Awe is in the Scottish Highlands, between Loch Lomond and the Trossachs National Park and the wonderful west coast (where the sea kayaking is truly awesome); Llyn Tegid is just east of sensational Eryri/Snowdonia National Park; and Windermere is within England's Lake District, which was awarded UNESCO World Heritage Status while we were paddling.

KIT BAG People have completed the Three Lakes challenge in kayaks, canoes and on SUPs, but the ideal craft is a surfski: fast on the water, light to carry and easy to remount in the event of a capsize. It's also handy to have a good set of binoculars for your driver, and two-way radios for communication. For planning, Ordnance Survey maps are perfect – *Explorer* sheets 360, OL7 and OL23 cover the relevant areas. You should also have a lightweight (carbon) wing-style paddle for stroke efficiency, a type-3 PFD (life jacket), a

hydration sack with a hose, paddling apparel (including a cag), and warm clothes stashed in a dry bag.

GETTING THERE To get to Salcombe, take the A38 southwest from Exeter; Totnes is the closest train station, from where there are buses to Salcombe. Exmouth is due south from Exeter, along the A376; there's also a train station, serviced from Exeter St Davids. Figuring out the best route for the Three Lakes is part of the challenge.

PLACES TO STAY There are various hotels and B&Bs in Salcombe, but one particularly lovely and centrally located option is the **Fortescue Inn** (⌖ thefortsalcombe.co.uk). To stay right by Sea Kayak Salcombe, check out the **South Sands Hotel** (⌖ southsands.com) or the **Harbour Beach Club Hotel** (⌖ harbourhotels.co.uk/harbour-beach-club).

ELSEWHERE You can find excellent surfski paddling conditions in Wales, especially around the Pembrokeshire Coast National Park (Parc Cenedlaethol Arfordir Penfro), just off Fishguard and St Davids. The west coast of Scotland is also a stunning place to paddle.

EXTRA RESOURCES
⌖ britishcanoeing.org.uk
⌖ gopaddling.info
⌖ epic-kayaks.co.uk
⌖ thinkkayak.com

↑ Finishing the Three Lakes challenge on Loch Awe (Dave Bassett)

4 DARTMOOR LETTERBOXING

WHERE	Dartmoor, Devon
SKILL LEVEL	Medium. You need to be able to tackle some technical terrain on foot, and the ability to use a compass and read the landscape and a map is hugely helpful.
RISK FACTOR	Low. But be aware that parts of Dartmoor are extremely remote, the terrain is often very rugged and exposed, and conditions can change quickly. Dress accordingly and take sustenance, a map and compass, and a phone.

There are tall, craggy tor tops, rushing rivers, ancient forests, voluptuous valleys, prehistoric standing stones, picturesque villages and wonderful wildlife encounters to be found within the bounds of Dartmoor, but for many people, the moor's magical allure lies in its delightful desolation. You can really lose yourself here – accidentally, or on purpose – but you also never quite know what you might find along the way. An enigmatic expanse, full of mystery and haunted by myths and stories, it's the perfect place to bury secrets, or go searching for treasure – both tangible and ephemeral. If there were ever a Hide-and-Seek World Cup, this would be the ideal natural arena to host it.

A long-running game of hide-and-seek has, in fact, been going on here for over 150 years. Dartmoor letterboxing, an activity endemic to Devon's great moor, is the granddaddy

↑ Alice and Kaye search for letterboxes on Dartmoor (Patrick Kinsella)

of more modern pursuits such as geocaching, and the concept is quite simple: leading participants place a 'letterbox' (a physical container, with a unique rubber stamp inside) somewhere out on the vastness of Dartmoor, and then others, following a few clues, attempt to locate the box, collect an imprint of the stamp and leave a signature of their own (often another stamp), along with the date they visited.

Letterboxing on Dartmoor dates back to the mid 19th century. In 1854, a guide called James Perrott built a cairn at Cranmere Pool in north Dartmoor and, amid the pile of rocks, he placed a bottle, in which passing walkers were encouraged to leave messages for one another. A permanent letterbox now stands on the site, and it even appears on Ordnance Survey maps (♀ SX 60325 85802). The site became a destination in its own right and more letterboxes were subsequently set up at Taw Marsh (1894), Ducks' Pool (1938), Fur Tor (1951) and Crow Tor (1962) – all far out on the moor, sited in remote and challenging locations. The tradition took hold, and now there are tens of thousands of letterboxes buried across Dartmoor.

Exactly how many people are involved at any given time, no-one really knows, but we can say with certainty that quite a few of the players have been engaged in the pursuit for several decades. The traditional element of the activity runs deep, and some devotees dedicate several days a week to letterboxing, venturing out in oft-wild weather all year round, while others approach it as an occasional challenge, a good excuse to explore the more remote corners of the immense moor.

It's an adventure activity that has fascinated me since I first heard rumour of it in the midst of a rambling conversation one evening in a Dartmoor pub, when I scribbled down some details on the back of a beer mat and swore I'd investigate further. That was some years ago, but now, finally, I'm heading back to Dartmoor to meet some real letterboxing champions, true veterans of the activity, to discover more, and try my hand at this historic challenge.

LETTERBOXING – GETTING INTO THE RING

Dartmoor can be a dark and foreboding place. In pursuit of other adventures I've been here in all kinds of conditions, including alone in the middle of the night, bivvying atop Hound Tor in a swirling mist with an inquisitive sheep's eyes demonically bouncing the beam of my headtorch back at me – a memory that still gives me goosebumps. Today, however, the moor is bathed in the glow of a beaming summer's afternoon. Instead of growling, the exposed granite head of Hound Tor seems almost friendly as we drive past, and when I look down while crossing the River Dart at Two Bridges, the water looks positively inviting. I'm glad the moor is in a benign mood – not least because I have my nine-year-old daughter with me, and it's so much nicer introducing a child to a new outdoor endeavour when the landscape isn't snarling at them

Alice thinks we're going on a treasure hunt. Which, I guess, we are. Sort of. I have tried explaining the concept of letterboxing to her en route, to manage her

expectations about the kind of 'treasure' we're likely to unearth, but she still seems suspiciously excited, so we'll have to see how much she has taken in. Perhaps it was a tad disingenuous to compare it to playing Pokémon Go – although both pursuits involve a physical search for elusive eggs/boxes – but one of the covert objectives of this post-lockdown mission is to distract her from gazing at digital screens for a while, and I'm not above using sneaky tactics. Letterboxing is one of a small number of adventure pursuits that is truly multigenerational, appealing to people right across the age spectrum, and we're about to meet Chris and Kaye, who have been involved in the activity since the 1970s and have kindly offered to take us out for our first round.

Despite the generous August sun, a stubborn shadowy darkness still pervades the site of Dartmoor Prison at Princetown, right in the heart of the moor. A place of punishment to this day, the infamous jail was originally built in the early 19th century to confine French and American prisoners from the Napoleonic Wars and Britain's 1812 War with America. It was purposely constructed far from the coast, surrounded by ominously empty moorland, to deter the POWs, mostly sailors, from entertaining any thought of escape – a bit like an inverted Alcatraz – but many of those imprisoned souls never left at all, and their restless remains lie buried in the grounds. Little wonder Dartmoor is so busy with ghosts. Historically, groups of hardened letterboxers would meet in the prison officers' mess, but thankfully we have arranged a rendezvous at a small car park nearby, rather than amid the cells.

When we arrive, Chris, Kaye and their friend and fellow long-standing letterboxer Lynda are already geared up, ready and raring to go. With decades of combined experience, they are absolutely steeped in the activity and all the traditions, tales and anecdotes that revolve around it, and they greet us with the wonderful warmth of true enthusiasts about to introduce new recruits to something they really love. They have brought along several spare trekking poles, which in letterboxing circles are used less for balance and walking efficiency, and more to assist with 'firkling'. Firkle is the verb used to describe the action of searching for letterboxes, which are commonly hidden away in holes beneath rocks and gorse bushes, both to make them more of a challenge to find, and to keep them out of the way of the destructive elements and nosy non-letterboxers. Alice is delighted with her stick and immediately starts firkling around some boulders beside the road to see what she can find.

Our new friends are impressed with her enthusiasm, but of course, there's a bit more to it than this. Letterboxes are typically squirreled away in much more remote locations – although some can be found in places such as pubs, and a few, known as 'Travellers', even move around (there's at least one in an ice cream van). Chris has printed out a sheet of potential targets we will be searching for

↑ Chris has hunted down over 5,000 letterboxes on Dartmoor and has the patch to prove it (Patrick Kinsella)

← Following clues, Alice firkles for a letterbox on the craggy moor (Patrick Kinsella)

MOOR INFORMATION

A diverse, upland landscape balanced on a massive granite base, Dartmoor sprawls across 954km² (386 square miles) of central Devon. Topped by over 160 tors (hilltops) it is home to thousands of species of wildflowers, trees, birds and mammals, including red deer (Britain's largest land mammal) and free-roaming Dartmoor ponies, a distinctive breed. Although the area is wonderfully wild and sparsely inhabited now, humans have lived here for millennia, and Neolithic standing stones and the remains of prehistoric settlements can be found all over the moor. It's one of Britain's best adventure locations, with superb tracks, crags, woodlands and rivers for hiking, biking, trail running, wild swimming, rock climbing, kayaking, canoeing and camping.

↑ A wild and windblown place, Dartmoor has many secrets to discover. (Jason Hobson)

today, and under his arm he has an up-to-date copy of the *Catalogue of Dartmoor Letterboxes*, which lists all existent boxes on the moor, along with a six-digit grid reference and a one- or two-sentence description of how to locate them. This book is a bible for boxers, and traditionally you could only get hold of a copy once you'd earned your place in the 100 Club, membership of which is reserved for people who have located 100 letterboxes and bagged a century of stamps using other clues and their own initiative. The rules are slightly more relaxed these days, and the pursuit has become very inclusive – even dogs are allowed to join the 100 Club now, which is good news for our snuffle hound Rosie, who has joined us for the adventure.

THE SEEKERS Our focus is an arc of targets that will take us on a round walk across the open moorscape between the village of Princetown and Dittisham Woods, exploring Foggintor Quarry and King's Tor. We set off in search of our quarry with Chris energetically bounding off in the lead. On the back of his pack I spy a badge revealing that he has over 5,000 letterbox finds to his name, and he tells me that was awarded several years ago, so he has hundreds more stamps under his belt by now. Clearly we're in good hands here, and it's not long before he announces that we're in the vicinity of our first letterbox. According to the book, the box was set by 'The Owl from Germany' and the clue is quite detailed, informing us that we should be looking for an '80cm ridged lichen-covered rock next to reeds, resting on an approximately 1m embedded rock',

↑ Success! Alice locates a letterbox (Patrick Kinsella)

and giving us compass bearings for surrounding landmarks: 'Swell Tor 241°. Leather Tor 185°. King's Tor 297°'. We zero in on a rock that fits the description, and Chris directs Alice to start firkling around beneath it for hidden bounty. Sure enough, her trekking pole hits something that sounds hollow, and she pulls out a tightly sealed container.

Any concerns I have that the experience isn't going to live up to my hype evaporate when I see how excited Alice is at the unearthing of this simple treasure, and the revelation of the unique stamp, which features a dog (always a crowd pleaser). We take an imprint, and then Chris and Lynda add their own stamps to the visitors' book, which reveals a history of other letterboxers who have been here in recent days, months and years. Unlike geocaching, this is all there is – no little toys or novelty items to swap with tokens of your own – but the simplicity keeps things tidy, and collecting the stamp is surprisingly satisfying. There is a message-in-a-bottle feel to the discovery of something deliberately hidden by human hands, which is intended to be found by like-minded people, and adding your name to a list of other successful searchers and then carefully concealing the box back in its hidey-hole gives you a feeling of connection to a community.

With one box in the bag, Alice is extra enthused and strides ahead to keep pace with Chris. Viewed from behind, they make an odd couple. She bounces over boulders and keeps up a constant stream of questions, which he manages to field while remaining firmly focused on the search. He has a map and compass around his neck, but most of the time keeps his eyes glued to a GPS unit, where

↑ Letterboxers leave a personalised stamp in the box booklet (Patrick Kinsella)

he has uploaded all the relevant grid references and clues. Unlike in orienteering or fell running, it's entirely acceptable to use a mixture of traditional and digital devices when you're navigating to letterboxes, but even this and many years of experience doesn't guarantee success. Over the course of the afternoon we locate lots of letterboxes, but several elude us. Boxes do occasionally fall prey to foul play, of course, and can disappear altogether, but some are just extremely tough to find – and therein lies part of the appeal. Hitting the harder targets is often the most satisfying element of any sport or challenge, and some of the best stories stem from heroic failures to achieve an objective. Chris and Lynda know many of the people who have placed the letterboxes out on the moor, although often only by nickname and reputation, and some are renowned for leaving particularly opaque clues or selecting impenetrable locations.

As we work our way around, the moor reveals all kinds of hidden secrets that have nothing to do with letterboxing. We discover a disused railway and a couple of atmospheric ruins, walk past prehistoric settlement sites, encounter a string of wild ponies and chance upon a series of immense, precisely shaped stones, which Lynda tells me were made as corbels to support London Bridge. In 1903, when

ESSENTIALS

GETTING STARTED You can take up letterboxing whenever you like, without having to do anything special – just head out and try your luck. To apply for a catalogue, write to Colin Richards at **e** letterboxingcatalogue@gmail.com, or attend a Letterbox Meet – these twice-a-year gatherings are traditionally held on clock-change Sundays each March and October at Lee Moor Village Hall, on Dartmoor. There's no official letterboxing committee, but an informal Letterbox 100 Club exists for people (and dogs) who have proof they have visited 100 boxes. Badges are also issued to those who have bagged 200, 500, 1,000, 2,000, 3,000, 4,000 and 5,000 letterboxes. There are regular meet ups at pubs such as the Dolphin in Bovey Tracey and the Plume of Feathers in Princetown. Visit ⊘ letterboxingondartmoor.co.uk for more information.

SPECIAL CONSIDERATIONS After collecting your stamp and signing/stamping the visitors' book, it's essential you reseal and replace the letterbox exactly where you found it. People adding letterboxes shouldn't place them where they might disturb wildlife (for example near a badger sett or close to nesting birds). There's a code of conduct in the catalogue.

KIT BAG Wear sturdy walking boots with ankle support (some veteran letterboxers prefer wellies, because of the marshy terrain often encountered), and pack plenty of layers, including waterproof protection. Take snacks, water, a map and compass, mobile

the old bridge was being expanded to accommodate the capital's growing traffic demands, these huge chunks of Dartmoor granite were carved to specification right here, in the place where the stone was quarried. Too many were made, however, and the surplus stones were just left, lying in the middle of the moor, looking almost as incongruous as the rest of the bridge does now that it resides in Arizona, having been sold and shipped to America in 1967.

By the time we get back to the car park, we have ticked off seven letterboxes, leaving us with a lot of future firkling to do if we want to join the 100 Club, let alone bag one of those illustrious 5,000 badges. By way of encouragement, Chris gifts us a copy of the coveted *Catalogue of Dartmoor Letterboxes*, so we have no excuse not to keep searching. And I'm keen – it really is a great way to explore the moor, and I think I might combine my next letterboxing foray with a spot of wild camping, another great Dartmoor tradition. And, as for Alice, she is beaming, and seems well and truly hooked. The Dartmoor letterboxing community has unearthed itself a couple of new recruits, and I have a feeling that's what Chris was really searching for today. It's mission accomplished for me too, because Alice is full of chat all the way home, and doesn't mention her phone once.

phone (for taking proof-of-find photos, and in case you need to make an emergency call), a book for collecting stamps, and a stamp of your own to leave your mark.

GETTING THERE The A38 skirts the southern part of Dartmoor en route to Plymouth, while the A30 goes across the north of the moor on the way to Cornwall. The moor's main gateway towns are Okehampton (north), Ivybridge (south), Bovey Tracey (east) and Tavistock (west).

PLACES TO STAY Dartmoor has abundant accommodation, ranging from B&Bs and inns to camping and glamping sites. It is also the only place in England where wild camping is legal (at least it was at the time of writing).

ELSEWHERE Although letterboxing was born on Dartmoor and is regarded by most enthusiasts as endemic to the moor, letterboxes can be found elsewhere, including the New Forest in Hampshire and the North York Moors. Dartmoor diehards refer to these as 'out of area' boxes. Geocaching, a direct descendant of letterboxing, takes place all around the world.

EXTRA RESOURCES
⊘ letterboxingondartmoor.co.uk
⊘ visitdartmoor.co.uk

5 SPORT CLIMBING

WHERE	Portland, Dorset
SKILL LEVEL	To do a sport lead-climbing course, it's useful to have some climbing experience, even if it's just indoors, and to know the basics of how to tie-in to a harness and belay. To enjoy sport climbing independently, more advanced skills are required, covering the use of quickdraws with fixed bolts and being able to thread the belay so you can descend safely and clean the route.
RISK FACTOR	All rock climbing has an element of risk, but done carefully and correctly, with good gear and knowledge, sport climbing is a relatively safe pursuit. If you're doing a lead-climbing course with a reputable guide, the dangers will be well managed. When climbing independently, it's up to you and your climbing partner to ensure the conditions are safe, the equipment is in good order and correctly used, your skills are up to scratch and the risks are minimised.

Strangely, most people's first experience of the sport commonly referred to as rock climbing isn't on rock at all – it's at an indoor climbing gym, scaling a manmade wall using deliberately placed plastic hand- and footholds, usually dangling from an auto belay device. It's thrilling and fun, and even highly experienced climbers return to the gym on a regular basis to keep fit and train on rainy days and dark evenings. But it's nowhere near as exciting as getting outside and clinging to a crag with your fingertips and toes, with a wild drop below you and your life clasped in the hands of a climbing buddy who has you on belay.

Unless you're lucky enough to have experienced rock-climbing friends who are willing to take you out and show you the ropes, however, it can be a bit intimidating making what feels like a huge jump from the gym to the crag. Where do you start, and what do you need? The sudden exposure – both to real danger (if you get something wrong) and the perceived judgement of other more-experienced climbers – is terrifying. These sorts of fears are even more pronounced if you're trying trad (traditional) climbing, when you have to place your own protection in nooks and crannies while you ascend, but sport climbing can be an excellent stepping stone for those still finding their feet – especially when done with a guide or on a course.

In sport climbing, you have to locate natural holds to place your feet and hands – so you are genuinely climbing a real rockface, using your own skills and judgement to trace a route to the top – but while ascending you clip pieces of equipment (known as quickdraws) into bolts that have been permanently fixed to the rockface. A quickdraw is comprised of two karabiners with a short length of cord between them – one of the karabiners is clipped on to the bolt, and the other is put around the rope that's attached to the climber's harness, providing protection in the event of a fall. When you lead a sport climb, you are belayed from below by a partner, who needs to stay very alert to your progress, because when falls happen, they can be quite heavy, with the person dropping past the last bolt they have clipped into, potentially lifting the belayer right off their feet.

It's a truly exciting form of proper rock climbing, which doesn't require tons of kit, but you still need to know what you're doing, especially to lead a route. I'm heading to one of the best places in Britain to learn how to do exactly that, while exploring some superb sport-climbing routes on breathtaking coastal cliffs.

GOOD SPORT

Dorset is a beautiful, bucolic county, with rolling hills and winding rivers leading to fossil-rich beaches, passing farmland and market towns en route that form the tapestry against which Thomas Hardy set his rural but radical novels. It also has some of Britain's best coastal climbing, including some sensational sport routes at super-scenic spots such as Dancing Ledge near Swanage, where climbers can often be seen clinging to cliffs above restless waves. Just west of here, further along the World Heritage-listed Jurassic Coast, clinging to the mainland by the skinny arm formed by the spit at the end of Chesil Beach, the Isle of Portland juts out into the English Channel. This place is different to the rest of Dorset; it's harder, somehow, and more ominous. Portland is home to several prisons, a lighthouse and a castle, and there is a severe, fortress feel to the rocky outcrop – as you approach, naturally castellated cliffs loom out of the waves, giving it an almost Alcatraz appearance.

Besides being excellent for climbing on, Portland limestone's legendary strength makes it a highly prized material, and it has been used in illustrious buildings all over the world – from the Cenotaph, St Paul's Cathedral and Buckingham Palace in London to the United Nations headquarters in New York City – and the island is deeply gouged with quarries. Perhaps inevitably – being an almost-island semi cut-off from the rest of the country, heavily and historically populated by prisoners, guards and quarrymen – it's also a pretty eccentric place. For example, you are not allowed to say the word 'rabbit' out loud here. Seriously. It's believed to bring bad luck, and they *really* do not like it. Rabbits, with their tunnel-building tendencies, have been blamed for landslides and quarry collapses in the past, and as a result locals refuse to mention the furry little blighters by name, instead referring to them as 'underground mutton' or 'jack-a-doodles'. The superstition runs so deep that, when the Aardman film *Wallace & Gromit: The Curse of the Were-Rabbit* was released in 2005, promoters had to come up with a totally new strapline for posters appearing in Portland, eventually settling on: 'Something bunny is going on'. True story.

After driving across the isthmus to reach this curious place, I meet up with another animated character with movie links, though thankfully not a cursed rabbit. Tom Hatt is a professional stuntman who also guides punters on various

↑ Tom goes through the gear and shows us the ropes (Patrick Kinsella)

adventures around southern England, and offers instruction in numerous outdoor pursuits to small groups, such as the one I have just joined. After a round of introductions, during which it transpires that I'm the greenest of the five-person posse in terms of climbing experience, we run through the objectives of the exercise. By the end of Tom's one-day course, we should all know how to lead a sport-climbing route, so we could come back here – or visit any other sport-climbing crag with fixed bolts around the world – and independently attempt to climb the routes on offer.

Portland offers multiple crag options, all detailed in a guidebook to Dorset climbing that Tom carries with him, but the first place we head to is the Bowen, part of the Cuttings area on the east coast of the isle, where there are several sport routes suitable for relative beginners. From the car park, where other climbers are busy pulling gear from their vehicles and setting off along the footpath with harnesses on and ropes slung over shoulders, it's a short wander in, and then a fairly dramatic down-scramble to reach a ledge halfway between the crashing waves and the cliff top.

↑ Tom demonstrates how to 'spot' a climber, at the Bowen (Patrick Kinsella)

Tom assumes nothing in terms of our knowledge and starts from the very beginning, scrutinising all our gear (we have all come equipped with harnesses, shoes and helmets, and several people have their own quickdraws) and running through the knots we will need to repeatedly tie today. Tying and untying on is a big part of sport climbing, so by the end of the day you can tie figure-of-eights and stopper knots without even pausing to think about it. He also checks our belaying skills. We've all learned to belay at gyms, using a top rope system, pulling slack in to keep the line tight and our climbing buddies safe and secure. In sport climbing, however, you feed the rope out from below as the climber progresses up the route, giving them enough slack to make progress, but not so much that they will injure themselves in the event of a fall.

We pair up and take it in turns to climb a couple of simple routes with a top rope to warm up, before practising with quickdraws as we go. When he's happy we know what we're doing, Tom removes the top rope and it's time to try our first lead climb. When leading, until you've clipped on to the first bolt, you're entirely unprotected, so on routes where that doesn't happen for a few metres,

CLIMBING BY NUMBERS

Sport climbing was born in France's stunning Verdon Gorge in the late 1970s and early 1980s, when Stephane Troussier and Christian Guyomar controversially began rappelling down from the top and fixing permanent bolts in the beautiful but brutally unforgiving and inaccessible sections of the crag, so they could attempt to climb them safely, unimpeded by loads of gear. It outraged many traditionalists, but soon spread to the United States, Britain and across the world, and one version of it is now an Olympic sport.

The grading system used in the UK is the same as the French one, with a number (one through to nine – the higher the number, the technically harder the climb), often followed by a letter (a, b, c) and occasionally a plus or minus sign too, to highlight additional factors, such as exposure or length. A route graded 4c is more challenging than one rated 4a, and a 4c+ indicates another small increment of difficulty.

↑ Someone seconding (following the lead climber), using bolts in Verdon Gorge, France, birthplace of sport climbing (Erik Tanghe/S)

it's necessary for climbing partners to 'spot' one another. A process used a lot in bouldering, where there are no ropes, this involves standing below a climber with your hands upstretched, ready to break their drop if they lose grip on the lower reaches of a climb. It's a little like being a one-person crowd supporting a reluctant stage diver, except you're not expected to actually catch your buddy, just soften their fall and help them land on their feet.

In my eagerness to get off the ground and avoid the embarrassment of early failure, I sacrifice any semblance of good technique or style, and end up skinning my knees across the rock. 'Relax,' Tom cautions. 'Take your time and read the route.' It's good advice. Reaching the first bolt and snapping a quickdraw into place feels good – partly because I'm now on belay, but also because I'm actually leading a sport climb, which is a new experience. At the top of each of these easier routes are a pair of anchors descriptively known as 'pig tails' or 'ram's horns', which allow you to pass the rope through them without the need to untie from your harness, after which your belayer can lower you down on a top rope, and you can 'clean' away all the quickdraws as you descend.

So far, so good, but then Tom throws in a bit of extra excitement by encouraging us to try a route that starts on the ledge we're based on, but then edges out around a corner of the cliff. At that point you're climbing above a massive drop, all the way down to water level, where waves wallop at the rocks. The procedures are all exactly the same, and the risk level remains consistent too, but the feeling of exposure is massively heightened.

HIGH JINX For the afternoon we decamp to the wild western side of the isle, where the walls are massive and the whole feel of the crag is different. Parking near the main prison we hike a short distance in to an area the climbing guide calls Battleship Back Cliff. A guy with dreadlocks long enough to tie into a harness is halfway up a towering route to our right, carefully contemplating his next move before performing some extraordinary contortion to progress up the sheer wall. Thankfully, Tom is eyeing some much easier routes on 'the Block', a smaller hump of rock opposite the intimidating main edifice. Again we buddy up into pairs, select a route, perform our safety checks, don helmets and take it in turns to begin a battle against gravity, fought with fingertips and toes.

Although the grades are still modest, these routes are a tad trickier than those we tackled earlier, and there are no pig tails at the top. This means that, when (if) you manage to complete the climb, in order to lower off the route it's necessary to use an extra couple of pieces of kit to secure yourself, and then completely untie from your harness before threading the rope through the anchor point (which can take various forms, including welded rings and maillon rapides) and then retying yourself in. This is a crucial skill for sport lead climbing, and one where there is zero margin of error, because it's all done at the top of the route, where a mistake and an unprotected fall could have fatal consequences. Many indoor climbing centres around the UK have simulator stations at ground level, so rookies can master these moves without risking calamity, but Tom has drilled the skills into us, and the reason he has brought us here is to practise the procedure in a real scenario. It's a little nerve jangling, but without nailing this knowhow, we won't be able to explore the vast majority of sport climbing routes around the country and beyond, so this is the crux move of the course.

I belay Sam, my partner, on a challenge of his choice, a slab climb named 'This is This', graded as a 4+. A decent and fairly experienced climber, he completes the route without too much trouble, reaches the final bolt and clips his last quickdraw in. Keeping him tight on belay, I watch him go through the process of securing himself at the top, before he lets me know he is 'in hard' – which means he is connected directly to the anchor point with another piece of equipment – in this case a sling. Clear communication is crucial during this process, especially as the procedure is unique to sport climbing, so even experienced people who might be more familiar with other forms of climbing can make errors if the language used is not precise. I can relax the rope a little now, but I must keep him on belay. He goes through the process we have practised on the ground, threads the rope through the rings, reties on, lets me know before removing the sling, and then I lower him down.

And now it's my turn. I examine the book, study the rockface and select a route. Today is more about mastering the safe use of equipment and technical knowhow required to go sport climbing, rather than pushing the limits of what we can actually climb, so I'm looking for a line that I'm confident of topping out on – especially because I want to make sure I really get my head around how to safely thread the rope for lowering back down. Getting to the top of a climb, as mountaineers often ruefully observe, is only half the achievement.

My choice is graded as a 4, and the initial section looks eminently doable, which is a bonus – there's nothing worse than getting frustrated and tired right at the outset of a climb, trying to locate elusive holds. But then I notice the name: 'Brer Rabbit'. In climbing culture, the person who completes a new route gets to name it, and in this case the first ascender (Steve Taylor according to the book) clearly had a twisted sense of humour and scant regard for local folklore. Tom asks me which one I'm going to attempt, and reluctant to say the name out loud, I just point. This is stupid. I'm ultra cynical about all superstitions, yet, already teetering on the edge of my comfort zone, I find myself unwilling to tempt fate by deliberately poking Portland's peculiar traditions. I could always try a different route, I realise, but most are evidently trickier than this one, so I'll take my chances.

All too soon I'm questioning that decision. After clambering up the first part of the route easily enough, I reach a section where the slab is smooth and offers

little to work with. I rush a move, fumble my hold and peel away from the rock with a yell: 'falling!' Sam is on it and catches my fall, getting lifted off his feet in the process. I end up not too far from the ground, so he lowers me down, I take a few deep breaths, rub chalk on my hands, and start again.

In the gym, on a manmade wall, every feature is a hold, and most are brightly colour coded – they might not be easy to reach, but they are at least obvious. On real rock, however, you need to locate all the little nodules, cracks and crevices that might offer sufficient purchase to pull or push yourself up on. Many are tiny, barely blemishes on seemingly smooth rock, but as you gain experience and climbing confidence, you realise that the smallest toehold is enough to support your weight. And it's so important to trust your feet. Novice climbers – men in particular – tend to try and muscle their way up routes, using their upper body strength, and on all but the shortest, quickest lines, this is doomed to failure. Arm muscles tire quickly and lactic acid builds up, leaving limbs pumped and useless. But legs can keep propelling you upwards for hours if you're confident in the ability of your feet and toes to stay put on little lumps or ledges (which, helped by halfway decent climbing shoes, they will).

I've been taught all this before, but it's one thing knowing it and another altogether putting it into practice. Now, though, extra determined to get to the top, I clear my mind, ignore the fact that others are watching, fight the urge to

ESSENTIALS

GETTING STARTED Hatt Adventures (thehatt.co.uk) offers a range of guided climbing experiences and courses across the country, from intro sessions for complete beginners through to the one-day sport lead-climbing course described here, and two- and five-day trad lead-climbing courses.

SPECIAL CONSIDERATIONS Wherever you are climbing, be aware of local considerations such as nesting birds.

KIT BAG Course providers will typically supply most essential equipment (although it's best to have at least your own harness and climbing shoes). To go sport climbing independently you require a harness, climbing shoes, multiple quickdraws, a sling, several karabiners, a helmet, a belay device and a climbing rope. Wear comfortable loose-fitting clothes and take a warm jacket.

GETTING THERE Dangling off the Dorset coast, to the west of Poole and Bournemouth, the Isle of Portland is accessed via the A354 from Dorchester. The closest train station is Weymouth, from where buses travel to Portland.

hurry and focus clearly on the line I want to take. Putting renewed faith in my feet, taking my time and scanning the route for chalky residue – the telltale sign that someone else has used a barely perceptible feature as a handhold in the past – I climb past the point where I had previously fallen, and scale the rest of the route without incident. Jubilantly I clip the last quickdraw, secure myself with a sling and sing out to Sam, letting him know the situation. Before congratulating myself too much, I realise the scary bit is still to come, and in order to return to terra firma, I need to thread the rope, untying and then tying myself back into my harness in the process.

But it all goes seamlessly, and soon I'm being lowered off, collecting the quickdraws as I descend and returning the route to the same state we found it in. Back on firm ground, Sam high-fives me and we remove the rope, an umbilical cord that's been connecting and protecting us. I'm stoked. I've beaten the bunny – defied the curse of the Brer Rabbit – led a bona fide sport climb and got myself down in one piece to tell the tale. Turning around, I spy the dreadlocked climber way above us, calmly and expertly making his way over the brow of the Battleship, unwittingly putting my meagre achievement into perspective. But it's a start, and the thought that there's a whole world of sport climbing routes out there, and I now have the knowledge to start exploring them, is an exciting one.

PLACES TO STAY There is a range of accommodation on Portland, from campsites to B&Bs and hotels including the **Old Higher Lighthouse Stopes Cottage** (⌖ oldhigherlighthouse.com) by Portland Bill, which offers fantastic views of the famous lighthouse from a tower.

ELSEWHERE Besides Portland and close-by sites on the Dorset coast such as Dancing Ledge near Swanage, there are excellent sport-climbing crags all around Britain. Some that the British Mountaineering Council (BMC) recommend for beginners include Horseshoe Quarry near Stoney Middleton in Derbyshire, Wyndcliff Quarry in the Wye Valley, Castleberg Crag near Settle in North Yorkshire and Trevor Rocks overlooking the Upper Dee Valley above Llangollen in northeast Wales.

EXTRA RESOURCES

Dorset: Portland, Lulworth, Swanage by Mark Glaister and Pete Oxley, published by Rockfax, is a bible for rock climbers tackling trad and sport routes on the county's spectacular sea cliffs.

⌖ thebmc.co.uk/climb-skills-sport-climbing
⌖ ukclimbing.com

6 TREE CLIMBING

WHERE	Appley Park, Ryde, Isle of Wight
SKILL LEVEL	No previous knowledge or skill is required for the course, but a basic level of fitness is an advantage and you are encouraged to do some homework about trees and knots prior to participation. To do it independently, you require good rope-rigging and climbing skills.
RISK FACTOR	Minimal during tuition stage. After that, you're perfectly safe so long as you remember to do your checks and your knots are good.

Isn't it weird, when you think about it, that we grow out of climbing trees? It's almost an instinctive activity for kids – like a nod to our membership of the great ape club – and then, suddenly, we just stop. As adults we take up plenty of other pursuits and sports, including rock climbing, often paying good money to clamber up a wall with manufactured foot- and handholds in a sweaty climbing gym. But when was the last time you climbed a tree? They're still there. Even inner city dwellers are never that far from a tree of some sort, many of them with easily scalable lower limbs. But, past a certain age, we seem to lose the impetus – or, more accurately, bury the urge – to climb them.

↑ Tree climbers get a bird's-eye view from the branches of an Isle of Wight oak (Goodleaf Tree Climbing)

Suggest it to a friend the next time you're wandering through woods or a public park and watch their reaction. In my experience, unless you're on the way home from the pub (when it definitely *is* a bad idea), their response will typically flicker between nervous excitement and self-conscious fear. People wonder whether it's even legal for adults to climb trees and, being so terribly out of practice, they fret about getting stuck. No-one of long-trouser age wants the emergency services to be required to rescue them from a tree.

Admittedly, places like Go Ape have become popular in recent years, but even these experiences are aimed more at children than anyone else, and they are mostly focused on scrambling along top ropes, rather than actually getting your hands and feet on the branches of a real tree and exploring the canopy of a natural wood, or the features of a forest. I for one miss it. In fact I occasionally wonder if the main reason I had children was to give myself an excuse to start doing things like climbing trees again – but why do we feel the need to have an excuse to do something as natural as scaling a tree? I wouldn't be embarrassed to climb a crag or cliff – quite the opposite, actually - so why is tree climbing so different? In search of some answers, and with my inner Tarzan whooping with excitement, I set off to the Isle of Wight to meet Paul McCathie from Goodleaf Tree Climbing.

TAKING A BOUGH

The leaves to my left suddenly explode and I look up to see a red squirrel scampering along the branch I am clinging to. It's been years since I've seen a red squirrel and, regrettably, at least as long again since I've been this far up in the arms of a tree. The encounter is brief – the flame-coated, furry-eared fellow is fast, his aerial expertise is extraordinary, and he leaps into the next tree long before I have time to extract my camera from where it's buried in a pocket below my harness. Never mind. His intervention has shaken me out of my fixation with the practicalities of what I'm doing, and reminded me that I need to pause for a moment and take in my new perspective on the world.

For the past half hour, I have been concentrating so hard on the mechanics of what I'm up to – making sure my knots are right and that my karabiner is closed, and scoping out the next move that will take me further away from the humdrumness of terra firma – that I've forgotten to absorb the joy of the experience. I stop, slow my breathing, and let my surroundings sink in. From my present possie, about 12m up in the leafy canopy of a several-centuries-old oak tree in a suburban park on the Isle of Wight, I feel quite detached from the hubbub below. On the ground, people are rushing around, walking their dogs, talking on phones, pushing prams and returning, panting, from the nearby Saturday morning parkrun. Occasionally, someone will spy the trailing ropes that give us away, and notice the ring of bunting our instructor has placed around the tree in order to keep people out of the 'drop zone'. Then they look up, spot us, journeying through the branches, and usually stop to stare. Some are intrigued enough to holler up, enquiring what we're up to – a note of worry in their voice indicating a degree of fear that we might be about to fire up chainsaws. And that's not surprising – it would probably be my first concern too. Because it's just not normal to see adults up in trees, unless they're chopping them down.

There are four of us in the branches: me, two other rookie climbers and our instructor, Paul. We have spent the last day and a half learning a range of skills employed by tree surgeons, but we are definitely not here to damage or dismantle any of the magnificent oaks that have been standing proud in Appley Park since long before Queen Victoria started coming to the Isle of Wight on her holidays. Thus far, Paul has spent a large part of the three-day tree-climbing course teaching us about the trees themselves, imparting tips and tricks about how to determine species by leaves, berries, bark and profiles. He can identify a poplar tree in the midst of a moonless night by the unique sound wind makes going through its leaves – I'm a long way from that, but I can feel myself evolving into a budding tree-spotter. And this is an important skill, because some species are far better and safer to climb than others. But we're encouraged to view the trees as something far more complex and extraordinary than mere climbing frames. Each one has

a history, an interactive relationship with the other trees and plants around it, and they support a whole host of other living things – as the rendezvous with the red squirrel has just reminded me. Accordingly, we have also been schooled in techniques and the use of equipment that helps avoid damaging trees while you're exploring their upper reaches.

BRANCHING OUT Paul, who originally hails from New Zealand but has put down deep roots on the Isle of Wight, is a tree man through and through. He has an immense appreciation and knowledge of the various species that we are lucky enough to share both this park and the wider planet with, and a passion for climbing them. An arborist by training and profession, he developed a visceral aversion to interfering with healthy trees that was making his day job a bit awkward so, several years ago, he branched out and set up Goodleaf Tree Climbing. He regularly takes groups of big and little kids on two-hour quick-try tree-climbing experiences, and also offers a more immersive three-day course where you can learn how to scale trees with the skill and safety levels of a professional, but purely for fun. I'm doing the latter, and loving every minute of it – helped by the fact that in between bouts of climbing, Paul has been refueling us with the most fantastic flapjack I've ever tasted (it's the stuff of legend I later learn, made to a secret Kiwi recipe, and I half suspect that the squirrel's surprise appearance earlier was an attempt to snaffle some),

These recreational courses are unique in Britain, but there is a vibrant tree-climbing community out there, with its own international body: the Global Organisation of Tree Climbers. There are annual meet-ups and co-ordinated events (such as The Big Canopy Campout, where people all around the world

↑ Paul at the base of an ancient oak (Patrick Kinsella)

ISLE OF GREEN?

The Woodland Trust produced the first ever *State of the UK's Woods and Trees* report in 2021, which revealed that woodland currently covers 13.2% (3.2 million ha) of the UK's land surface, which is low compared to the average forest cover in countries in the EU (38%) and worldwide (31%). Much of the deforestation of Britain happened hundreds – even thousands – of years ago, and the good news is that woodland coverage is now expanding, and has doubled in the last 100 years. Sadly, however, the overall health of woodland species is still in decline. The UK is rich in veteran trees, though, and Little Appley Park is an area where you can engage with a truly ancient woodland. The main section of Appley Park, where the tree-climbing course takes place, was once part of the grounds of Appley Towers. Overlooking the Solent, it was landscaped in the late 18th century by Humphry Repton, a friend of the famous Capability Brown.

IS IT LEGAL TO CLIMB TREES? This is quite an opaque area. Goodleaf works with the local council, but rules and regulations (and the way they are enforced) vary from place to place. Discreet climbing in trees on common land is unlikely to raise too many eyebrows – but remember you are entirely responsible for yourself and your actions (in case of accident or injury to yourself or others). If you are using equipment (ropes, harnesses and so on), then, strictly speaking, you will likely require the permission of the local land management agency and/or landowner.

FURTHER READING Peter Wohlleben's *The Hidden Life of Trees* is a truly mind-opening book about the interconnectivity of trees. *The Tree Climber's Guide* by Jack Cooke is an excellent adventure through the treetops of London, a surprisingly green city when seen from this perspective.

sleep in trees on the same night of the year) and even tree climbing competitions. Most elite tree-climbers are, unsurprisingly, arborists, but Paul gets all kinds of people coming on his courses, including some environmentalists who go on to take up temporary residence in trees and forests that are under threat from destruction and development. The motivations of my fellow course members are more personal. Cary is a social worker in a big city, which can obviously be extremely intense at times, and in her spare time she likes to do challenging activities that completely clear her head. Fred lives in London, works in an office and spends too much of his life staring at the concrete jungle – he just wants to get into the greenery of some real woods.

We are all fully grown adults, but on the morning of the first day there's a frisson of almost childish excitement in the fresh island air. However, it's a serious business, and it soon becomes clear that this won't be the kind of carefree caution-to-the-wind tree-climbing clamberfest we used to enjoy when we were saplings ourselves. Back then, when our boughs were more bendy and quick to heal, a fall was a minor setback, but the older you get, and the higher you climb on the family tree, the more a sense of responsibility and appreciation of your own mortality seems to weigh you down. So it's largely with relief rather than reluctance that we learn how much reliance we will be putting on ropes and harnesses over the following three days. In fact, several weeks prior to the course starting, Paul sent us homework to do, in the form of practising tying a range of knots for use in various tree-climbing scenarios.

For most of the first day, we keep our feet firmly on the ground, learning how to identify good (and bad) trees to climb and perform risk assessments, and repeatedly going through all the equipment and skills required to keep us and others safe when we start to climb (because adults falling out of trees like giant dropbears would also pose a danger to the people innocently going about their business below, and probably cause Paul more than a few legal problems). There is an awful lot to take in, but by late afternoon we have mastered the art of throwing a rope over a branch, learned how to rig up a three-knot system (a figure of eight, a Blake's hitch and a barrel knot – in case you were wondering) and use a lanyard. At Paul's behest, we repeatedly rehearse the safety mantra of checking and rechecking all our gear, stage by stage, using the acronym HAKK (harness, anchor point, karabiner, knots).

Despite all the gear, it is still magically thrilling when we finally get into the treetops. And while there is a fair amount of hoisting yourself up into the branches – especially at the outset, when you need to get off the ground and past the first few metres of sheer trunk – once up in the canopy, where there are many more

↑ A squirrel's eye view of tree climbers in the canopy (Patrick Kinsella)

branches, you can use your hands and feet to climb properly, and experience a far more tactile engagement with the tree. As with mountain climbing, ascending is only half the challenge – you also need to get yourself and your climbing partners down in one piece, and learning the technique for doing this keeps us well occupied for the rest of the day.

We spend most of the following two days in various trees, putting all our new knowledge into operation and learning a whole range of more advanced skills, such as climbing in stages, which is like doing a multi-pitch rock climb, and allows you to ascend much higher in the tree. Even on a three-day course, the morning and afternoon sessions are crammed full, and absolutely fly by, as we get schooled on the benefits of climbing with a two-rope system, and even learn how to perform in-tree rescues. It's a great physical and mental workout, and by the end of each day we're all exhausted.

By the third day, however, I'm starting to feel very at home in the gently swaying top of my carefully chosen oak, securely attached to the tree by my lanyard and rope, happily taking in the view out over the Solent and hoping the red squirrel will come back and say hello. I have my camera ready this time. But he's not getting any of my flapjack – I need all the energy I can get to keep this activity up.

↑ Fledgling tree climbers (Goodleaf Tree Climbing/Anna Fulford)

ESSENTIALS

GETTING STARTED Goodleaf Tree Climbing (⌀ goodleaf.co.uk) offers experiences ranging from 2-hour classic tree-climbing experiences through to the full three-day course described here.

SPECIAL CONSIDERATIONS If you're climbing trees independently, be extremely mindful of wildlife (including nesting birds) and take precautions to prevent people walking beneath the tree you're going to be climbing. Full risk assessment skills are taught during the course.

KIT BAG All climbing equipment is supplied by Goodleaf, but be sure to wear comfortable and reasonably loose-fitting clothes that don't impede your movements, and shoes or boots with good grippy undersoles and ankle support. Also bring warm layers, because the entire course takes place outside. Those who go on to climb trees independently after the course will need to invest in a tree-climbing harness (different to a rock-climbing harness) and tree-climbing rope, which is less dynamic than standard climbing rope (because you shouldn't be falling on it), both of which can be purchased through arborist outlets. Other bits of useful kit include helmets, eye protection, a whistle (in case you do get stuck), a first-aid kit and a folding knife.

GETTING THERE The Isle of Wight is accessed via car and passenger ferries that run daily from Portsmouth and Southampton. To reach Appley Park, where the tree-climbing courses take place, take the Portsmouth–Fishbourne service (⌀ wightlink.co.uk), and head east towards Ryde. The tree Goodleaf most often uses is even marked on Google maps.

PLACES TO STAY There are plenty of places to stay in Ryde to suit all budgets, and further around the coast at St Helens you'll find campsites. For something different, check out the quirky **Windmill Campersite** (⌀ windmillcampersite.com) in Carisbrooke, in the middle of the island, where you can stay in a converted helicopter or a submarine that once appeared in a James Bond film.

ELSEWHERE Other companies such as Big Tree Climbing (⌀ bigtreeclimbing.co.uk) and Climb Trees (⌀ climbtrees.co.uk) offer short tree-climbing experiences – often at festivals and National Trust properties – but Goodleaf's three-day recreational tree-climbing course is unique.

EXTRA RESOURCES

Big Canopy Campout ⌀ bigcanopycampout.com
Global Organisation of Tree Climbers ⌀ gotreeclimbing.org
The Woodland Trust's **British Tree Identification app** is good for budding tree-spotters.

7 SAND YACHTING

WHERE	Romney Sands & Greatstone-on-Sea, Kent
SKILL LEVEL	Like any form of sailing, you need to learn the ropes used on the craft and understand how wind works as a force of propulsion. Lots of the skills required for sand yachting, such as tacking, are the same or similar to those employed in wet sailing, but the steering is very different. To become an expert land sailor obviously takes lots of practice, but going for a spin during an introductory session is very easy and accessible.
RISK FACTOR	Recreational sand yachting under the supervision of an instructor is very safe, but competitive sand sailing can get pretty fast and feisty, and accidents do happen, often at high speed, causing breakages to both sailors and yachts. Remember, there are no brakes.

Kent is quite a curious county, where not everything is always as it seems. Tradition has it that if you are born east of the River Medway, you are a 'Man of Kent' or a 'Maid of Kent', but if you enter the 'Garden of England' to the west of the Medway, you're a 'Kentish Man', or 'Kentish Woman'. There is some debate about the exact nature of the dividing line and, believe it or not, people get into fights about such things, but the vast majority of the Kentish coast lies indisputably within the territory of the Men and Maids of Kent. If you're heading off for a day's sailing here, however, you might not be getting wet. You may not even venture out on the waves at all. Because this stretch of seaside,

↑ Land yachts racing along the beach (SS)

especially between Dover and the eccentric cuspate foreland of Dungeness, is home to possibly Britain's biggest community of land sailors.

The flat, fairly hard-packed and often wind-swept beaches here have square-shaped sand granules. This is a fact that would elude most normal people, but land sailors have a keen eye for such detail, and they know this kind of sand has a firm but sticky quality that makes it absolutely ideal for rolling across. As a result, this corner of Kent has become the heartland of an adventure activity variously known as sand yachting, dirt boating and Blokarting. Just like sailing boats, sand yachts have a sail to capture and harness the power of the wind, but instead of racing across the waves, they feature wheels and travel across land (typically beaches, but sometimes wide-open areas of grass, gravel, dirt or sealed surfaces such as old airports). In good conditions and with the right pilot at the helm, they can be driven over long distances and at high speeds, with zero carbon emissions.

More traditional yachties might snobbily see this as sailing for landlubbers, but there's evidence to suggest that it predates the waterborne version of the sport/method of transport. And it's certainly faster. In fact, the only wind-driven vehicles speedier than a high-end sand yacht travelling at full tilt are the futuristic foiling boats used in the America's Cup, and when it comes to racing, land sailing is a full-on adrenaline pursuit, where no prisoners are taken or quarter given. The land speed record for a wind-powered vehicle was set by a British-built craft called *Greenbird* in 2009, when it was recorded sailing at almost 203km/hr (just over 126mph) on a salt lake in the Mojave Desert.

The reason sand yachts can go so much faster than sailing boats is because of the absence of water resistance. And this degree of speed, combined with the proximity of the pilot to the ground, makes it a highly exhilarating experience. Or so I have been told. To find out more and attempt to go for a spin myself, I got in touch with a land-sailing instructor, Mark Serejko from Kent Land Yacht Club, who not only races sand yachts and Blokarts, but also runs introductory sessions for interested newbies like me, who want to have a go and learn the ropes.

BLAST FROM THE PAST

As I drive along the Kent coast – past the intriguing, post-apocalyptic-looking landscape of Dungeness, watched over by lighthouses, beached boats and a pair of brooding nuclear power stations – not a single tree gives me so much as a shiver. Even across this great open weirdscape, there's barely a breath of breeze. Usually, on a trip to the beach, I would be celebrating such conditions. But this isn't usually. This is the day I want to try my hand at sand yachting, and the signs are not looking good.

True to his word, Mark is waiting for me at the Kent Land Yacht Clubhouse in Greatstone-on-Sea, by Romney Sands. And, despite the decidedly unpromising conditions, he has kindly brought along a yacht or two to show me. The forecast isn't great, but to give the wind a chance to wake up, we grab a coffee in the club and Mark talks me through some of the basics of the sport. 'Land sailing' and 'sand yachting' are umbrella terms that cover all pursuits involving wheeled vehicles propelled by wind, he explains. These craft come in various sizes and are built to different designs, and that's where the subdivisions and categories come in, but they all work on the same basic principles.

There is a very strong tradition of land sailing in France and Belgium, where every coastal village and town has a sand yachting club, typically funded in part by the government, because it's a widely recognised sport. Here in Britain the pursuit is nowhere near as big. In fact, very few people seem to have heard of it at all… except, that is, on the coastline facing France and Belgium. The terrain is pretty similar either side of the English Channel, of course, but there are also historical strands and cultural connections that splice the two places together through the sport of land sailing. Back in 1909, airplane pioneer Louis Blériot performed the first successful fixed-wing flight across the English Channel, setting off from Calais and 36 minutes later landing in Dover, where he was greeted by large crowds. Besides being an adventurous aviator and engineer, Blériot was an inventor, and he is also famous for developing the 'Aeroplage' – a seaside beach-based land yacht. And perhaps this flying Frenchman sowed a few seeds in the imagination of the Men and Maids of Kent while he was here, because now the county is the home and heartland of the sport. Although, when it comes to races and competitions, the cross-Channel rivalry is fierce.

BLOWING ON THE WIND

The history of land-based sailing craft dates back to ancient Egypt. Wind chariots were documented in China 500 years ago and a wheeled, wind-powered vehicle designed by Belgian mathematician and engineer Simon Stevin of Bruges was used as a fast troop carrier during the 1600 Battle of Nieuwpoort. In the 1820s, British inventor George Pocock developed a 'Charvolant buggy', which was pulled along by kites and was capable of covering distances like that from Bristol to London. These vehicles were even built large enough to carry a pony on board, as an alternative engine in case the wind died. During the 1830s in the United States, several railroad companies developed sail cars that ran along railway tracks, propelled by the wind, transporting men and equipment and travelling as fast as the coal-powered trains of the day. And when gold was discovered in California, a few of the fortune seekers going west on a quest for riches travelled in 'wind wagons'. Designs were gradually refined and sand yachting evolved into an adventure pursuit and a racing sport in the early 20th century, especially in continental Europe, where it remains massively popular. By the 1950s, there were several sand yacht clubs at coastal towns dotted around Britain, from Blackpool to Hoylake and Westward Ho! Racing became increasingly popular, and the first official European Championships happened in 1963 in Germany. An epic Trans-Sahara Sand Yacht Race took place in 1967, with several British entrants, and the pursuit has continued to grow in more recent decades, with ever faster craft being developed. In colder countries ice yachting is also popular, with skis where the wheels are on a land yacht, and kite buggying is another variation of the sport.

FURTHER INFORMATION *Sandyachting* by Andrew Parr (published by Gomer Press) is an excellent, very comprehensive book about the sport, from its origins to where it is today.

BECALMED The history of the sport is fascinating, but I'm itching to go for a spin. By the sounds of things, Mark has a veritable fleet of sand yachts of various shapes and sizes at home, but he has brought two along for me to try out during this introductory session, a Blokart and a classic Class 5 sand yacht with a fibreglass hull.

Initially we manoeuvre the higher-spec sand yacht down on to the sand, and Mark shows me how to get into the driving seat, which involves lying virtually flat on your back. The profile of the yacht is a little like a dragster, with the single front wheel way out in front and the two back wheels positioned on either side of the pilot, creating a triangular-shaped base. Looking up from a near-horizontal position to see where they are heading, the pilot steers using their feet (to turn the front wheel left or right) and controls the speed of the craft by pulling down on a rope, which feeds through a pulley system attached to the sail. Once you have wind in your sail, the tighter you pull this rope the faster the yacht will travel. And, of course, when you change direction, the boom (the pole that runs along the bottom of the sail, angled horizontally to the mast) will whip around, just as it does on a water-based yacht, at which point you need to keep your head down and well out of the way. Different sails can be deployed, depending on how strong the wind is blowing and how fast you want to go.

This is one of Mark's fastest yachts. He travels all over Europe taking part in races and events, and is full of stories about the thrills, spills, rivalries and dastardly shenanigans of competitive sand yachting. Sadly, however, no matter how good it is, a sand yacht is dependent on the elements and the wind is definitely not coming out to play today. Even with a large sail rigged, and a few starting pushes to get me moving, the craft only crawls along the sand before coming to a halt. The tide is racing in now, anyway, and the sand is rapidly disappearing, so we load the yacht back on to Mark's trailer and call it a day.

SHOOTING THE BREEZE Fortunately, the forecast for the following day looks a lot feistier, and I do a wind dance in the evening, appealing to the Anemoi for assistance. It works, and dawn delivers a view from my window full of huffing and puffing promise. Mark is teaching another group of beginners in the morning, but we arrange to meet later in the day, as close to low tide as possible. Because, besides a stiff breeze, for a successful land-sailing session you also need the sea to be out, so that enough of the beach is exposed for racing around on.

As I approach the coast in the early afternoon the treetops are dancing an encouraging jig, and before I set eyes on the sand or the sea I spy colourful kites aloft in the sky. Getting closer, I see these are pulling the kitesurfers of Kent (or, perhaps, the Kentish kitesurfers) along behind them. In sharp contrast to yesterday, the conditions are pretty perfect for a learner pilot to have a play. The tide is out, the sun is shining and yet the beach is still fairly quiet (the risk of careering into dog walkers and beachcombers is yet another factor the responsible land sailor needs to take into account).

The tide will turn soon enough, though, and the sand is gradually getting busier as the sky turns ever bluer, so Mark wastes no time getting me sorted with a helmet and harnessed up in the pilot's position in the yacht. I'm trying out a completely different craft today, a much smaller and more manoeuvrable Blokart. Made in New Zealand to a very distinctive design, these nimble little carts still have three wheels mounted on a triangular frame, but you sit much more upright in the seat and steer with handlebars while grasping the rope controlling the sail in your hand. Once again, the tighter you pull the rope, the faster you go.

↑ Sailors on the sands (Mark Serejko/Kent Landyacht Club) ↗ Switching to a smaller Blokart as the wind picks up (Patrick Kinsella) → Sailing a Class 5 sand yacht (Patrick Kinsella)

Mark talks me through the basic techniques required to go with the flow of the wind, then explains that I need to turn with enough speed to get in a position where I can tack back in the other direction. And then he gives me a push and I'm off, racing down the beach at what feels like 100 kilometres an hour, with my bum centimetres from the sand. I'm actually going a much more modest speed, but the proximity of the ground as I rush across it accentuates the feeling of acceleration, and it's instantly exhilarating. A long arc of beach extends invitingly in front of me, but not wanting to get stranded too far down towards Dungeness if I fail to keep the wind in my sails, I pull a tight right turn. The wheel on my left leaves the ground and I hear myself let out an involuntary whoop of excitement as the super-responsive cart whips around.

I know next to nothing about sailing, and sure enough, after pulling off what I'd like to think was a textbook turn, I make a complete mess of the return trip up the beach, where a bit of tacking is required to go against the wind. Hopping out, I have to do the push of shame for a bit, until Mark jogs down to meet me. He gives me a good shove to get the yacht rolling again, and shouts a whole load of instructions about how to keep her moving. Before too long, I get the gist of it – relaxing my grip on the sail and ducking at the right moment, to let the boom swing around without braining me, and then drawing it in to re-capture the wind.

ESSENTIALS

GETTING STARTED Mark offers half-day introduction sessions for people interested in trying their hand at sand yachting. To find out more, contact the **Kent Land Yacht Club** (⚓ landyachting.co.uk). To do a taster session elsewhere in Britain, contact your local club.

SPECIAL CONSIDERATIONS Land sailors need to be able to interpret weather forecasts, looking carefully at the speed and direction of the wind and planning their adventures accordingly. When sailing in coastal areas, tide charts also need to be consulted. Sand yachting is not permitted on all beaches in Britain, and even where it is allowed, great care must always be taken to avoid other people when travelling at speed.

KIT BAG Aside from the sand yacht itself, which can be quite an investment, land sailors should wear a helmet.

GETTING THERE Greatstone-on-Sea is on the A259, which runs along the south coast between Folkestone and Hastings, and can be accessed via the M20. The closest mainline train station is Folkestone, but a small-gauge light railway, the Romney, Hythe

Soon enough I'm able to pull off a whole series of long figure-of-eight laps of the rapidly narrowing shore. The secret, it seems, is to keep up plenty of momentum as you hurtle around the bends, pulling the rope as hard as you can even if it feels as though the cart is about to flip. There are no brakes on these things, and the sensation of zooming along the beach, centimetres above the sand, swooshing through puddles and sending sheets of saltwater flying into the air is properly thrilling. I'd love to get a taste of what a real race feels like in one of these carts. The adrenaline rush as you go wheel-to-wheel with other competitors, vying for position on the turns, must be fantastic. But for the moment I can only pit myself against the kitesurfers who are speeding along the waves just a few metres away from me, getting closer all the while as the area of sand shrinks and the sea comes in.

Sadly, time and tide wait for no man (of Kent, or anywhere else), and the white horses of the English Channel keep racing ever closer to my wheels as I make whooping, looping turns. And eventually, very reluctantly, I have to heed Mark's waved instructions and steer the Blokart back up the sand to the sailing centre. The sea has reclaimed the beach for a few hours, and the land sailors, sand yachters and Blokarters are temporarily forced out of their element and into the bar. But only until the tide next drops and the wind begins to blow – then they'll be straight back out, shooting the breeze. And I've a good mind to join them.

& Dymchurch Railway, operates steam trains along this coast too, from the Cinque Port of Hythe to Dungeness via Romney Sands.

PLACES TO STAY There are multiple accommodation options in and around Folkestone and along the coast, including B&Bs and hotels to suit all budgets. Dungeness is a very unusual and interesting place, with a weird end-of-the-world feel, like a scene from *The Road*, but the Dungeness National Nature Reserve is home to a wide variety of wildlife, and the lighthouses and beached boats create a unique and intriguing atmosphere that has inspired artists and adventurers alike. Various idiosyncratic huts and cottages can be hired, including the 150-year-old Watch Tower (available to book via various websites). For more accommodation options, check out ⊘ dungeness.org.uk.

ELSEWHERE Outside of Kent, land yachting is popular (and permitted) in various places around the British coast including Brean in Somerset, Penzance in Cornwall, Hoylake in the Wirral and St Andrews West Sands Beach in Scotland.

EXTRA RESOURCES
⊘ landyachting.co.uk
⊘ britishlandsailing.org.uk

8 CAVING & POTHOLING

WHERE	The Mendip Hills, Somerset
SKILL LEVEL	Independent caving and potholing demands advanced knowledge and specialist skills, which you can only acquire by joining a club, doing courses, teaming up with experts and getting underground with experienced spelunkers. To enjoy a guided caving adventure, you require average-to-good levels of fitness and flexibility (depending on the route being explored), and you need to be comfortable in confined spaces. Potholing involves more vertical travel, but some caving experiences involve climbing and abseiling. During 'wet' caving adventures you'll encounter water (sometimes flowing, sometimes static), and there might be sumps (flooded sections which, when they're short, advanced cavers can negotiate by ducking through).
RISK FACTOR	The dangers associated with independent caving and potholing vary enormously, depending on the cave being explored, but it is an inherently risky activity, and even experienced spelunkers do sometimes suffer injuries (or worse) from falls, floods and getting stuck in tight squeezes. Cave diving is another level altogether, and the risk to life is high. Never attempt to explore underground extensively unless you're an experienced caver and know what you're doing. However, during guided caving adventures with reputable providers the risks are very well managed and the subterranean route will be extremely familiar to the guide, which significantly reduces the dangers. In areas where potholing is popular, such as the Mendips, dedicated cave rescue organisations provide expert assistance to people experiencing problems while underground.

Caving, it has to be said, is not for everyone. Every time I venture underground there are moments when I seriously wonder whether this is an activity I'm cut out for, mentally or physically. And, in terms of real exploration or anything even remotely extreme, I'm certainly not well suited to the subterranean art of spelunking (as it's known in America), or potholing as it's commonly called in Britain, although potholing traditionally involves more vertical tunnels. I'm quite a large bloke, who simply does not easily fit through many small spaces, and although I'm not seriously claustrophobic, the thought of getting wedged down there in the damp darkness does fill me with horror.

And yet, I can't walk past a cave entrance without at least peering in, and usually take a torch when hiking for this very reason. (Although, tragically, I haven't discovered any long-forgotten pirate treasure, smuggler's swag or secret scrolls yet.) And whenever an opportunity to return to the underworld proper has presented itself, I've always jumped at the chance. There's an almost instinctive and certainly highly addictive appeal to such subterranean adventures – I think they must speak to the residual caveman/woman that

← Exploring the underworld in Swildon's Hole, beneath the Mendip Hills (Steve Sharp/A)

still dwells deep within us. But it's more that that. Once you've experienced the thrill of passing though a tight squeeze to emerge into a large chamber – elaborately decorated with flowstone and resonant with enigmatic echoes – it's a little easier to understand why some people spend their spare time worming around underground in boiler suits, helmets and headtorches.

Britain is blessed with several world-class cave systems so it's possible for punters (like me), with no training in how to behave in a cave, to explore – so long as they're accompanied by a guide. One of the best places for such adventures, a real potholer's paradise, is the Mendip Hills, an Area of Outstanding Natural Beauty located just north of Bristol and Bath, in the bucolic midst of scenic Somerset. Boasting brilliant trails for running, riding and walking, and some of the best climbing crags in the country, the Mendips is a surprisingly underappreciated area. Cleft by great gorges and honeycombed with caverns, these hills offer a plethora of opportunities for outdoor-active types, yet they get a fraction of the attention showered on other hotspots. One reason, maybe, that the Mendips' charms have remained such a secret, is that the area's most magnificent adventure assets of all lie underground.

To delve deeper, I donned a hard hat and a headtorch, swallowed my anxieties and set out to explore two very different caves in the limestone labyrinth that burrows beneath the Mendip Hills, starting with a doorway into the dark realm that opens up right in the middle of Cheddar.

THE UPSIDE DOWN

Cheddar Gorge is a magnet for day-tripping tourists and school groups, but this is also a place that pulls in serious cavers and climbers from the world over. Britain's grand canyon, the gorge is a deep, steep, 2km-long scar in the Mendip Hills, with a series of snaking, high-walled hairpin bends formed by the tallest inland cliffs in the country, which soar over 100m into the Somerset sky. Way up on the near-vertical walls, goats graze and peer nonchalantly down at cyclists and walkers below. Equally lofty, but often not-half-as-nonchalant humans can usually be seen clambering up the crags.

This is one of the UK's most iconic climbing areas, with 579 established routes spidering up the sheer cliffs on either side of the canyon. The north of the gorge is owned by the National Trust and the south by Longleat Estate, which offers adventure pursuits and tourism experiences under the trading name Cheddar Gorge. These include innovative outdoor climbing sessions in a relatively new beginners' area, where artificial holds have been added to the limestone wall. Cheddar's chock-a-block rock offering ranges across a rich mixture of sport and trad routes, mostly single-pitch and ranging in difficulty from easy to the ultra-difficult 'Bristol's Got Talent' line on Sunset Buttress, first ascended by local climber Chris Savage in 2009, when it was hailed as the hardest sport-climbing

↑ Cheddar cheese being cave-aged (Patrick Kinsella) → Cheddar squeeze – Pat going deep into Gough's Cave (Wyl Menmuir)

route in southern England. And then there's the 115m line called Coronation Street (graded E1 5b), which ascends High Rock, the tallest section of the gorge, famously first climbed by mountaineering legend Chris Bonington in 1965.

But hidden behind this craggy face lies a much more mysterious realm, regularly occupied by underground explorers, where sunlight never penetrates and the walls echo with strange stories – some of them as dark as the corners where the events took place. The most famous caverns here are Cox's Cave, discovered in 1837, and the larger Gough's Cave. Both have been attracting tourists for well over a century, and were occupied by our ancient ancestors many millennia ago. When the opening to Gough's Cave was expanded in 1903, some of the oldest human remains ever unearthed in Britain were discovered near the entrance. The near-complete skeleton of the so-called Cheddar Man, who died around 10,000 years ago, was found alone and in good condition, but the bones of other bodies in the cave system have shown clear signs of cannibalism.

The show caves here form the epicentre of the gorge from a visitor experience point of view, with hordes of tourists traipsing around, eyeballing stalactites and stalagmites, and chewing on chunks of Cheddar's famous cheese, mature varietals of which are aged right here in the ambient gloom of the cavern. But Gough's Cave extends well beyond the reach of the casually curious, burrowing almost 3.5km into the belly of the hills. It contains Cheddar Yeo, Britain's biggest underground river system, is home to a huge colony of horseshoe bats, and is also a portal to much more exciting caving opportunities, if you're willing to put on overalls and get filthy.

↑ The incredible subterranean architecture of Gough's Cave behind Cheddar Gorge (Peter Lytle/A)

THE BIRTH OF CAVE DIVING

The extreme pursuit of cave diving, practised by true specialists, takes potholing to a whole new level. The margin for error is very small, but it allows cavers to explore the full extent of long cave systems, where they often find dry chambers beyond flooded passages. The very first cave dive was done in Wookey Hole, where Graham Balcombe and his partner Penelope 'Mossy' Powell dived to a depth of 52m (170ft) in 1935, reaching Chamber 7. Cave divers continue to explore Wookey Hole, where there's a museum dedicated to the sport. In 2018, experts who honed their craft here in the Mendips were flown to Thailand to help rescue 12 young boys and their football coach who had become stuck deep in the Tham Luang Nang Non cave by flooding. There are several films about the dramatic rescue, including *Thirteen Lives* starring Colin Farrell, directed by Ron Howard.

CHEDDAR SQUEEZE Several years ago, while organising an adventure festival for the National Trust, I was lucky enough to explore this special space with Paul Ballantyne, the long-serving Rocksport Manager at Cheddar Gorge and an experienced caver. We were accompanied by the author Wyl Menmuir, the festival's writer in residence that year, who was researching a fictional story set in the mysterious Mendip underworld. Paul took us both far into the cave on an extended subterranean journey, to chambers deep within the limestone lair, and many of the places we saw are explored during the 'Adventure Caving' experience now offered at the site.

On the spelunking spectrum this is introductory-level stuff, but for someone totally new to caving at the time, it felt fairly full-on. The escapade began with an underground abseil and before long we found ourselves edging around a drop called the 'Bottomless Pit' and sliding headfirst through the 'Letterbox' – one of the nerve-wrackingly narrow gaps and holes in the rock that cavers rather cavalierly call 'squeezes'. Some are terrifyingly tight, so much so that helmeted heads have to be turned sideways and shoulders need to be contorted in order to squirm through. I don't mind admitting that I felt panic pulsing through me during some of these squeezes, and I had to focus on fighting it back, but each time Paul gave us the option of taking a more technical route rather than an easy one, Mr Menmuir insisted on the scary option. You have to suffer for your art, and so it seems do your companions – but I thanked him for it at the end.

Wyl wasn't the first writer to draw dark inspiration from this enigmatic terrain. The Mendips is one of many places that can lay claim to having influenced JRR Tolkien in the creation of the epic literary landscape explored in *The Lord of the Rings*. The author visited Cheddar Gorge and the caves on his honeymoon in 1916 and again in 1940, midway through writing his magnum opus. Helm's

Deep in *The Two Towers* is based on parts of the gorge, and Tolkien's fictional Glittering Caves were a direct reflection of what he witnessed while in Cox's and Gough's caves. The latter are real portals to extraordinary worlds with sublime architecture that sparkles with minerals when artificial light ricochets off the rocks.

At the outset, these features have magical monikers like 'Home of the Rainbow', but once you progress beyond the well-trodden tourist terrain into the deeper reaches of the catacomb, the names become more prosaic, such as 'Sandy Cave 1'. There's a good reason for this, and it's not that cavers lack imagination. If their lights fail (bearing in mind the early explorers used candles and flaming torches) and they have to try and feel their way back to the entrance without the benefit of light and sight, cavers need to rely on their other senses to know where they are, and naming sections after how the surface feels to touch really helps. It's a tactile tactic.

And, believe me, you have never experienced true darkness until your light is extinguished several hundred metres into a cave, something Paul encouraged us to do when we reach a chamber called Boulder Cave. Complete sensory deprivation is extremely unsettling, which makes it all the more astonishing that, for four months in 1966 – during the period when England won the World Cup and the rest of the country went nuts – a man called David Lafferty set a new world record by staying right here in this part of the cave, alone and in darkness for 130 days. Emerging back into daylight, even after just a couple of hours in a cave, completely reinvigorates your senses, with colours and smells assuming a new vibrancy, so Lafferty must have been completely discombobulated when he returned to the surface.

THE HOLE HOG But, as thrilling and occasionally chilling as the experience Wyl and I shared was, I know we only scraped the surface of this phreatic network of natural tunnels, created by buried streams and rivers running beneath the Mendips for millions of years. These are regularly explored by more serious cavers – a group of whom discovered Britain's biggest underground chamber, the 60m-long Frozen Deep, in 2012.

Several kilometres south, starting in a place called Priddy, the longest cave of the lot (so far as anyone knows), Swildon's Hole, snakes along a subterranean route for over 9km. Committed cavers occasionally duck dive through small sumps (submerged bends) here, and some specialists even scuba dive in the longer flooded sections. An underground stream connects this to the famous and wonderfully named Wookey Hole (which never fails to put a smile on the faces of *Star Wars* fans), where cave diving was pioneered and continues to be perfected (page 79). Like Gough's Cave, Wookey Hole has a long history of

↑ Cave diving was first done in Wookey Hole (Patrick Kinsella) → A horizontal traverse along via ferrata deep within Wookey Hole (Patrick Kinsella)

human habitation and an accessible section of the cavern has been turned into a touristy show cave. But beyond this family-friendly façade, a fantastic fissure in the limestone flanks of the Mendip Hills continues underground for many kilometres. Exactly how far the hole goes, no-one actually knows, because no cave diver has ever reached the end, but at least two people have perished here while exploring its further reaches.

Despite being a scuba diver and a cautious convert to caving, there's no way I'll be combining the two activities any time soon, but I did jump at the chance to see the spot where the first ever cave dive was done, while on the 'Wild Wookey' experience. Besides visiting the entry pool where Graham Balcombe and Penelope 'Mossy' Powell did that historic dive in 1935, this 2-hour adventure goes well beyond the show cave and involves squirming through several squeezes, exploring dramatic chambers and hidden passages, tackling a horizontal traverse above a section of the green River Axe (via the longest underground via ferrata route in England), taking a row boat across a subterranean lake, rising to various abseiling and climbing challenges, and braving a thrilling descent along a zip line to finish.

Exciting as all this is, I do want to progress my proper potholing experience in a less touristy and more traditional setting, and soon find the ideal place to do exactly that, with Mendip Outdoors, local providers of adventure pursuits, who guide beginner cavers through the intriguingly named Goatchurch Cavern.

↑ The Wild Wookey experience includes an underground boat trip (Patrick Kinsella)

GOING TO GOATCHURCH The entrance to Goatchurch Cavern is an innocuous-looking hole in the ground beneath a tumble of rocks on the flank of Burrington Combe, on the other side of beautiful Black Down, just north of Cheddar. If it wasn't for the sign with the contact details of the Mendips Cave Rescue crew, you would never guess that this small opening leads to a cave that travels three quarters of a kilometre through the hill to an equally inconspicuous exit hole. The first people to explore these natural tunnels – in this case, lead miners in the mid 19th century – must have been nuts, especially when you consider they were doing so with no idea where they would end up, and only candles for illumination. My thoughts on this are only crystallised further as we progress into the cavern, where our guide Matt explains that several of the squeezes are one-way affairs. This means you have to tackle them headfirst and turning around to beat a retreat is tricky, if not impossible. The thought of this sends a shiver of panic right through me.

My daughter, Ivy, has accompanied me on this adventure, and I'd wondered whether I might have to coax her through some of the scarier parts of the cave. How wrong I was. While I'm fretting, she's absolutely buzzing. And as I grunt, shunt and get stuck, she slithers through each of the squeezes with aplomb, and then tries to encourage and school me on how to do the same. I just about manage to keep up through features such as Drunkard's Walk, an off-camber shuffle between two nearly touching slabs of rock. But then we get to a challenge that

↑ Matt emerges from Goatchurch Cavern (Patrick Kinsella)

completely defeats me: the Superman Squeeze, where you have to go headfirst with your arms fully outstretched in front of you, like Clark Kent in action mode, pushing yourself along with fingers and toes. To me this stony squeeze feels more like a Kryptonite cuddle.

Ivy and the rest of the group – all significantly smaller and more slender than me – successfully slide on through, but I can't make much progress. Increasingly convinced I am about to get properly stuck, I pause. Josh, our second guide, who is acting as sweep at the back of our little pack, calmly tells me to slow my breathing down and try to relax. When you become anxious, he explains, your chest expands and that's unhelpful when you're trying to get through a tight squeeze. This makes sense, and I try to do as he suggests, but it's easier said than done to relax when it feels like the hillside is literally biting down on you. Eventually, I conclude it's better to concede defeat than wriggle any further into a place I might not be able to reverse out of. Especially since Josh tells me there is another option over to my left, so we will still be able to carry on through the cave. I swallow my pride, edge back out and take the long way around, through a squeeze comfortingly called the Jaws of Doom, which is wider, but still has a good chew on me.

Despite my inglorious encounter with Superman I do enjoy the rest of the route – even if Ivy relentlessly teases me as we squirm through more squeezes (some with alarming names such as Bloody Tight), scoot down rockslides and emerge into wide open caverns including the Boulder Chamber and the Water Chamber, both bejewelled with most amazing natural architecture and stone sculptures. The most challenging section of the whole experience is the notorious Drainpipe,

ESSENTIALS

GETTING STARTED Throughout the year, climbing and caving sessions can be enjoyed in Cheddar Gorge, Wookey Hole and Burrington Combe, led by expert guides from Cheddar Gorge & Caves (⊘ cheddargorge.co.uk), Wild Wookey (⊘ wookey.co.uk/wild-wookey) and Mendip Outdoor Pursuits (⊘ mendipoutdoorpursuits.co.uk) respectively.

SPECIAL CONSIDERATIONS Caving expeditions can last for several hours and it's not easy to take supplies with you - make sure you've fuelled up on food and water, but also ensure you go to the bathroom before you set off, because there are no toilets in the underworld and it's a sensitive environment that should not be fouled.

KIT BAG Caving can be a filthy activity, but good guiding companies will always provide protective gear, including a helmet, headtorch, overalls and wellies (sometimes you need your own footwear - boots with grip are best). Many caves - including Gough's

a very narrow 12m tunnel that you have to worm through on your belly, with no chance of turning around until you get to the bottom, where there's a little chamber. This is the deepest part of the cave – so it's like reaching the inverted summit of a mountain – but it's also a dead end, so back up the Drainpipe you must go.

Eventually, after a good two hours of underground exploration, we exit from the cave at an entirely different place to where we started, and stand blinking in the sudden sunlight. Even after such a temporary experience of sensory deprivation, the colours and aromas of the woods around us seem extra vibrant and fresh, and now we're back under the sky, everyone babbles at once. During these chat-filled, euphoria-laced, wide-eyed moments when cavers first emerge from a hole in the ground, having just shared and survived an underground adventure – squishing themselves through the dark, damp confines of a cavern – someone inevitably comments about feeling as though they've been born all over again.

After the initial endorphin rush has evaporated, however, talk soon turns to how physically tired everyone is. Because caving, I've discovered, is a full-on all-body workout. There's a reason – beyond the obvious – why you never see a podgy potholer. After the Superman Squeeze shenanigans, I wonder once again whether this really is a pursuit I'm cut out for. Josh and Matt tell me not to overthink it. 'Happens to loads of people,' Josh says. Before revealing that a guy got stuck for several hours in the Superman Squeeze just a week before (albeit not on their watch), and had to be freed by cave rescuers. Wow. I'm glad he didn't let that slip when I was caught in the cave's grip. I would have expanded like a panicking pufferfish, and then they'd never have got me out.

Cave, Wookey Hole and Goatchurch Cavern – have an ambient temperature year round, often around 11°C, so dress accordingly (a fleece is about right).

GETTING THERE Cheddar, gateway to the Mendips, is clearly signposted from the M5. The nearest train station is Weston-Super-Mare; buses run to Cheddar.

PLACES TO STAY There are myriad B&Bs, holiday cottages and hotel options in and around Cheddar. To camp, or stay in a shepherd's hut, bell tent or even an American school bus, I highly recommend **Petruth Paddocks** (⚭ petruthpaddocks.co.uk).

ELSEWHERE There are multiple excellent caving destinations around Britain, from the Brecon Beacons in Wales to the Yorkshire Dales.

EXTRA RESOURCES
⚭ british-caving.org.uk

9 SCUBA DIVING WITH SEALS

WHERE	Lundy Island, north Devon
SKILL LEVEL	To do any level of scuba diving you need to have a PADI or SSI open-water qualification.
RISK FACTOR	Medium. Diving carries some inherent risks, but this is a shallow dive, so they are much reduced. Wildlife encounters are never fully predictable, but seals are usually very friendly.

British diving has something of an image problem, and I think I've got to the bottom of why this is. A lot of people do their initial PADI or SSI open-water scuba diving course in the UK before going on a trip abroad to somewhere like the Red Sea, the Caribbean, Thailand or Australia, where they do a concentrated batch of recreational dives. So this means that, while you're learning all the boring-but-essential stuff you need to know in order to stay alive while breathing compressed air at depths humans aren't designed to visit, you're usually floundering around in a freezing cold quarry in the Midlands.

↑ A diver gives the 'OK' sign (Zoe Masters/Easy Divers)

As thrilling as it is to first put tanks on and start blowing bubbles underwater, no-one can pretend this is a particularly exciting location to explore – and that's exactly why it makes the perfect learning arena. There are few unpredictable distractions, so you can get on with practising how to remove your mask or BCD underwater, provide your buddy with air from the spare regulator, and all the other things you need to get the qualification.

However, once most people have their licence to dive, they head straight off to warmer waters and go exploring reefs and sites where they find themselves in the midst of a kaleidoscope of colourful corals and flashy fish. It's mindblowing. Then they come home again and don't dive at all for ages – until they're planning their next trip overseas and have to do a refresher course, which means going back into the pool or quarry, or perhaps a shallow shore dive off a pebbly beach near a big city. Again, there's nothing much to see, and that's what they subsequently associate with British diving.

In reality, the marine environment around the UK is extraordinarily diverse, and there are some genuinely world-class dive sites to explore and underwater experiences to be had. Sure, the water isn't very warm, and year round you're going to need a full 7mm wetsuit with a hood and gloves (and sometimes a second layer, or even a drysuit), but you can always get the right gear from good dive centres.

Unsurprisingly, given the country's naval history and all the shenanigans that have taken place on the waves around our craggy coastline over the centuries, the ports, channels, seas and ocean-facing shorelines of Britain are absolutely littered with shipwrecks – including numerous submarines and a few aircraft, too. With the right training, or a divemaster with appropriate local knowledge, these are fantastic features to explore.

But the underwater wildlife around the British Isles is also exceptional. There are 13 species of marine mammal, and sometimes leatherback turtles even stray this way. Besides that, there are an estimated 8,500 species of marine plants and animals in UK waters, including two species of seahorse. You can dive amid kelp forests, and see basking sharks, lobster, nudibranchs, octopus and conger eels. Oh, and seals.

SEAL DEAL

Lundy Island, an exposed granite outpost in the gaping gullet of the Bristol Channel, usually only passes the periphery of my consciousness during pre-dawn drives, when the Shipping Forecast is playing on the car radio as a somnolent soundtrack to my journey. This morning, though, while I am en route to north Devon, my ears properly prick up when the forecast comes on, because the conditions will directly affect the experience I'm about to have while diving with Atlantic grey seals off the coast of Lundy.

'Lundy, Fastnet and Irish Sea,' the announcer finally says. Here we go. 'East, 3 to 5 at first, otherwise variable. Moderate or good.'

As I understand it, Lundy usually experiences westerly wind, roaring straight in off the Atlantic. Right now, however, an unusual easterly is blowing – exactly as forecast – and that means we will be diving off the island's west coast, in the wind shadow. I worry that might mean we'll miss out on the best wildlife action, but when I reach the harbour and meet Simon Barker, our divemaster and the owner and operator of Ilfracombe-based Easy Divers, he seems excited.

'The west coast is amazing,' he enthuses, as we chug out to sea beneath the pregnant belly and stern stare of Damien Hirst's controversial *Verity* statue. 'We don't often get to go there, because of the prevailing westerly wind, but it's gorgeous. Really rugged. The puffins have just left for the season, I'm afraid, but the seals will seek out the sheltered side too. They're not daft. Don't fret – they'll be there.'

He's not lying about the craggy beauty of the island's west coast, which has been sculpted by the wind and waves that howl in from across the ocean below the southern tip of Ireland, utterly untamed by any landmass between here and North America. To our left – sorry, port – side, towers an immense 125m sloping slab of rock known as the Devil's Slide, rumoured to be the biggest chunk of granite

TREASURE ISLAND

Lundy Island, which is just under 5km long and 800m wide, is owned by the National Trust and managed in conjunction with the Landmark Trust. For a little place, it has a huge history, and has been used as a base by pirates, smugglers and merchants.

Besides the colony of Atlantic grey seals that live on the island's largely inaccessible beaches, Lundy is famous for its population of puffins – in fact it takes its name from the Norse word for puffin: *lund*. The charismatic birds call the island home between March and August every year, after which time they return to the ocean.

Lundy was one of the first locations in Britain to be designated as a protected marine area. Thanks to the action of the Gulf Stream, it is regarded as one of the richest non-tropical marine environments on the planet. According to the Landmark Trust, '2,500 different creatures can be found in a single square metre of seabed and it is the only place where all five types of British cup coral can be found'.

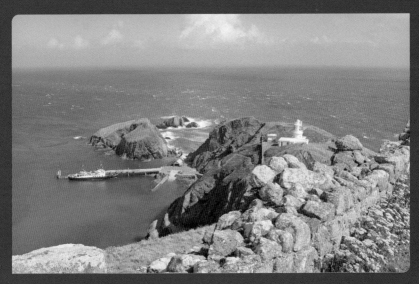

in Europe, and revered as a sea-cliff classic by trad climbers. It's stunning, and it drops almost exactly into our first dive site at St John's Rock.

As we approach the site, Simon addresses the whole party, which numbers 12 – most of us scuba diving, but there's also a small group of freedivers. 'We always advise people against pointing at the seals when we first see them,' he says. Sadly, fishermen used to shoot the animals, and either seals have very long memories, or they pass down cautionary tales from generation to generation – or maybe they are simply self-conscious. But, by all accounts, if you start your interaction

↑ Lovely Lundy Island offers encounters with wildlife ranging from puffins to seals (Diana Mower/S)

↑ A curious grey seal gently nibbles a diver's knee (Simon Barker/Easy Divers)

with them by pointing things like fingers and long lenses right at their heads, they seem to fear the worst and dive. This seems entirely commonsensical on all fronts but, inevitably, as soon as a seal's head pops up on the starboard side, every non-crewmember aboard the *Obsession II* starts vigorously finger stabbing and jabbering loudly in its direction.

For its part, this particular seal seems to be far from shy or scared. If anything, his expression sits somewhere between intrigued and indignant at the sudden arrival of a boatload of noisily excited land mammals. The reason for the latter response soon becomes apparent, as he decides to forget about the rude interruption and get on with his important morning activities. A second, smaller seal head emerges right next to the first, and there's something of a commotion in the water. 'Ah… there's some adult seal activity happening right there,' grins Simon. 'It's the time of year for it,' he explains, before yelling over his shoulder: 'Get a room!'

We turn around and give the amorous animals some privacy, while getting our scuba gear on and listening to the dive brief. And then, before we get in, Andrew, our skipper and onboard wildlife expert, gives us the talk about what to expect from our meeting with this colony of Atlantic grey seals. 'If you see a seal in front of you, there are probably two right behind you,' he begins. 'That's how they hunt.' A salty smile indicates he is joking. Sort of.

'Don't swim towards the seals. Let them come to you. Actually, it's best to pretend they're not there. They can't abide being ignored, and won't allow it.' The encounters are all on the seals' terms, Andrew emphasises, explaining that it all depends on what sort of mood they're in – aloof or playful.

'If you feel something tugging at your fins, that will be a seal. They love doing that. They may also nibble at your wetsuit – like a dog playing with your arm. If it gets a bit too much, blowing some bubbles by purging your spare regulator should give them the message to leave you alone for a bit.'

By the time we're kitted up, fully briefed and ready to go, the courting couple have disappeared – which, frankly, is a relief. I'm all for seeing seals up close in their natural environment, but I'm not a flipping voyeur. Besides, several other heads have since popped up to see what's happening, so it doesn't look like we're going to be short of company.

We have been buddied up into pairs, as is standard practice on any dive, and I am with Steve, who tells me this is his third time coming out to dive with the seals. 'It must be good then?' I suggest. 'You'll see,' he smiles.

MEETING THE LOCALS One by one, we take the big-stride scuba step off the side of the boat. As I'm getting my neutral buoyancy sorted and fiddling with weights and the air in my BCD, I spot a seal about 50m away, comically pushing its head and upper body up out of the water to get a better look at what I'm up to.

Once everyone is in the water and happy, we start to descend on the anchor line, equalising every couple of metres. You need to focus on a few things at the outset of a dive, and by the time I'm ready to go exploring, I look around to see Steve indicating something important in scuba sign language.

'Look', he signals (pointing two fingertips towards his mask). 'Behind you!' (He points over my shoulder and adds the flourish of an exclamation mark with the wideness of his eyes.) It's like underwater panto. Slightly nervously, I wheel around. And there they are – no messing about – two large adult seals have instantly come over to check us out.

As landlubbers, we're used to seeing seals on beaches and rocks, where they loll around with about as much style and panache as Jabba the Hutt with a hangover, or as shiny heads bobbing around like black fishing buoys on the surface. Underwater they are utterly transformed, moving around with ballerina-like poise and grace. Their dexterity belies their size. And they really are big. As long as me, at least, and a good deal wider – even with my double wetsuit on.

I sense no trepidation from them whatsoever. If humans have ill treated seals in the past – and by all accounts, we have – then this colony doesn't appear to be holding any grudges. Even as I'm thinking about this, another seal arrives with a savage-looking scar around its neck, where something (plastic, fishing net, line or rope) has obviously been caught around its head. Whatever it was has been removed now, presumably by a concerned diver, and the seal seems happy and healthy.

We are out of our natural element and they are very much at home in theirs. They clearly appreciate this fact, and appear to lose all their fear. This is underlined by my next encounter, with a female seal I later learn is well known to Simon by her nickname, Eyeliner. A seal's porthole circular eyes – deep, dark and impossible to read when seen from afar – are so much more expressive when you are suddenly face-to-face in the water. It's impossible to truly fathom what might be going on in such an enigmatic mammal's mind when it looks through a diver's mask, but the thoughts of the seal now peering at me seem to be powered by six parts curiosity and four parts mischief. Her eyes are ringed by black markings, like carefully applied make-up (hence her nickname), and they appear to be sparkling with devilment.

The first seal to really approach us closely, she greets everyone in our dive party individually. Sizing them up, coming in close and nibbling their wetsuits and fins. Eventually it's my turn. After a swim-by and a long stare, she opens her mouth and takes hold of my arm. It's not an aggressive action, though. More a sequence of squeezes than a bite, thankfully, since her teeth are sizeable and sharp.

For a full five minutes or more she stays alongside me. We swim in tandem, twisting around in a strange dance. She chases the bubbles I blow when I breathe out through my regulator, and then flips back around to seize one of my trailing fins as I clumsily try and negotiate the seascape around us. Every now and then she

seems to want a tummy tickle. It's very much like playing with a big, subaquatic Labrador, and I'm completely spellbound. I can't think of any other encounter I've had with a large wild animal that comes anywhere close to this in terms of proximity or engagement. And it's happening right here in England.

Eventually, Eyeliner has had enough of my clumsy dancing, and moves on to tango with someone else. We meet more of her friends and family as the dive continues, but all too soon Simon – who has been regularly checking in to see how much air each of us has left (because it's easy to get distracted from important things like monitoring your gauges when you're playing with a seal) – indicates it's time to surface.

Back on the boat everyone is talking over the top of one another, excitedly gabbling on about their experiences. I ask Steve how it compared to his previous dives, and he tells me it's been the best one yet. Best visibility. Best seal encounters. Best underwater landscape. Bless that easterly – it set us up for an extraordinary day on the wild side of the island, which I'm determined to come back and explore some more one day soon, when the puffins are back.

We do a second dive at another spot further around, in Jenny's Cove, between two fantastic granite features called the Pyramid and the Devil's Chimney, a place that would have been packed with puffins a month ago. The seals are less in evidence during this dip, and instead we swim through shoals of fish and discover colourful urchins and even a tiny nudibranch amid the stunning stone architecture of the Lundy seabed. It's beautiful, but I can't stop thinking of the earlier encounter with Eyeliner. It's an experience that I suspect will give me flashbacks forever, not least every time I hear the weather forecast for Lundy Island – and especially when the wind is blowing from the east.

↑ Playful grey seals find divers' fins fascinating (Simon Barker/Easy Divers)

ESSENTIALS

GETTING STARTED **Easy Divers** (⌖ easydiversnorthdevon.co.uk) in Ilfracombe runs regular seal dives from the end of May to mid October. They fill up fast, however, so book early. You need to hold a PADI open-water qualification or SSI equivalent. The experience includes the boat trip (2 hours each way) and two guided dives, and it is cheaper if you have your own equipment. You can also go along on the boat and simply snorkel or freedive (page 14) with the seals.

If you are already on Lundy Island, it may be possible to join a short, guided snorkel safari. These run several times a week from May until September, and sometimes encounter seals. Each session lasts approximately 1 hour, including kitting up, a pre-snorkel brief and time in the water; the price includes equipment hire (wetsuit, mask, fins, hoods and snorkel). For more, see the island website (⌖ landmarktrust.org.uk) or contact the warden (**e** warden@lundyisland.co.uk).

SPECIAL CONSIDERATIONS The water around Lundy (and elsewhere in the UK) is at its warmest in September and October.

KIT BAG All diving equipment can be supplied by the dive company if you're scuba diving or tour leader if you're snorkelling, but it's always nice to have your own good-quality mask, snorkel and fins – well worth the investment if you like exploring underwater.

GETTING THERE Ilfracombe is accessed via the M5 and A361. Buses, such as the 21A, run between Ilfracombe and other north Devon destinations, including Bideford and Barnstaple.

You can reach Lundy Island on a foot-passenger ferry, the MS *Oldenburg*, which leaves several times a week from May to October from Ilfracombe or Bideford, or by helicopter. Book via the Landmark Trust website; see opposite.

PLACES TO STAY Ilfracombe and the surrounding area offer a variety of accommodation to suit all budgets. Accommodation options on Lundy range from a campsite and bunkhouse, through to unique holiday lodgings (including the possibility of staying in a lighthouse). The island is very popular in summer and accommodation fills quickly – book via the Landmark Trust website; see opposite.

Matt Howard/S

ELSEWHERE Besides Lundy Island, you can also dive with seals around the Farne Islands off the coast of Northumberland, off St Martin's in the Isles of Scilly and around the Inner Hebrides in Scotland.

Elsewhere in Britain, superb scuba diving can be enjoyed all around the coastline of Cornwall, including Falmouth, where there are dozens of wrecks (including a World War I U-boat) and further south around the Manacles, where the reef boasts sensational soft coral and anemones, and you will find the wreck of the SS *Mohegan*.

There are around 400 wrecks along the coast of Anglesey in Wales, including the remains of the *Missouri*, which is in just 15m of water off Porth Dafarch, and a B-17 bomber at North Stack.

Scapa Flow, off Scotland's far northeastern coast, offers arguably the world's best wreck diving experience, around ships scuttled by the German navy at the end of World War I.

EXTRA RESOURCES
🖉 landmarktrust.org.uk/lundyisland
🖉 padi.com
🖉 divessi.com

10 CANICROSS

WHERE	Leigh Woods, Bristol, north Somerset
SKILL LEVEL	Aside from a basic level of fitness and the skills required for typical trail running (where you need to be nimble and reactive enough to negotiate rocks, tree roots and other unexpected obstacles), all the skills that canicross calls upon are things jointly learned between the runner and their dog. The more you run with the same dog, the more a partnership will develop. Dogs can be trained to respond to cues that will direct them to go left or right at trail junctions, to pick up the pace or run to heel during descents.
RISK FACTOR	Running with a dog pulling you along significantly increases your speed, which reduces your reaction time when like a trip hazard rears up. The size and power of the dog, and its level of enthusiasm and experience (or lack of), can all make the risk of you a taking a tumble higher. It's a good idea to join a social/beginners' canicross running group before trying it independently.

↑ Humans and hounds can run in harmony with canicross harnesses (Soloviova Liudmyla/S)

Sharing the thrills, spills and raw enjoyment of adventure activities in wild areas with your best friend is what makes many an outdoor experience worth doing in the first place. This helps explain why canicross events and dog-running groups have been exploding in popularity across Britain in recent years – because there is no better buddy to have on the trail than one with a wagging tail. But, while this might be a sport on the rise, an awful lot of trail runners – even those who have hounds, and like to run with them – still aren't familiar with the word canicross, let alone the finer details of the discipline.

The definition is simple enough: canicross (derived from the words 'canine' and 'cross country') involves running off-road with your four-legged friend. Humans and hounds have, of course, been running together for as long as the special relationship between the two species has existed – and evidence suggests the symbiotic bond between us stretches back many thousands of years, and exists in near enough every culture in the world. But as a refined pursuit, with dedicated gear and well-defined techniques and skills, the roots of canicross lead back to Scandinavia and Canada. Here, in places such as Sweden, where snow sports like mushing (where teams of dogs pull a driver in a sled) are historically huge, a codified form of running with dogs developed as a way to keep the animals fit and the musher's skills sharp during the dry summer months.

In Britain, where winters are more reliably wet than white, and there's no long-standing tradition of dog-assisted snow sports, canicross has nevertheless caught on and been enthusiastically embraced by lots of runners. Hundreds of canicross events now take place across the nation, some of them dedicated exclusively to runners with dogs and others simply with a canicross sub-category. Clubs and training groups have sprung up all over the place too, a few with a competitive edge, but many more socially orientated, formed by people who simply like to run with their dogs as well as with other fleet-footed humans.

At the pointy end of the sport, canicross is very competitive, with elite athletes and their animals running around 5km (3-mile) courses extraordinarily fast in well-organised international races. But even at the most recreational level, there's a lot more to canicross than simply going for a jog with your dog. Special kit is used, and to really enjoy it, both two- and four-legged runners need to learn a few basics. With all this in mind, I reached out to the members of the canicross community around my home in the southwest, and was very quickly embraced by the pack.

A friend who organises trail-running events, including some with canicross categories, put me in touch with a regular entrant (and winner), Cathrine Svendsen. Cathrine, I discovered, competes at an elite level and had just put in a great performance at the Canicross World Championships in France. Instantly warm and welcoming, she introduced me to her local group, Canicross Somerset, who run introductory sessions for complete beginners at Leigh Woods on the outskirts of Bristol. 'Why don't you come out with us?' she suggested. 'We can lend you some kit and, as dogs generally prefer to run in groups, your dog will probably "get it" much faster.'

Cathrine also directed me towards a skills event happening at Charlton Park in Wiltshire, organised by a group called the NATB (New Approach to British Dog Sports), and with my loyal running partner Rosie I make this my first point of call.

DOG DAY AFTERNOON

I've been running off-road for decades, and I enjoy sharing the trails with dogs. In fact, when choosing a canine companion from a rescue centre, where all our animals come from, I always find myself analysing what sort of running I'll be able to do with the dog we're adopting. When I very first started running regularly, in a bid to quit smoking, lose weight and get healthy, my buddy was an Australian kelpie cross. He'd been the runt of an unwanted litter by all accounts, destined for destruction until being taken to a rescue shelter, but he absolutely loved to run. It's no exaggeration to say that dog – Barry – helped me turn my life around, because once he'd become accustomed to going for increasingly lengthy runs, he wouldn't settle for anything less. So I had to keep going out with him, come rain, shine, hail or hangover – whether I wanted to or not.

↑ Rosie running on a canicross harness for the first time (Patrick Kinsella)

Years later, when Rosie first arrived from a kill centre in Spain, via another rescue charity, I must admit to a moment of consternation. She was tiny – much smaller than I expected from the photo and description we'd been looking at – and I just couldn't imagine her ever reaching a size where I could realistically run with her. It was a moot point. My kids were already in love with the little mutt, and it was a done deal. But it turns out I was completely wrong anyway. All she wants to do is run – it's her favourite thing in the world. She's learned to recognise my running shorts and T-shirts (very possibly by the aroma), and as soon as I appear in them she starts spinning in excited, expectant circles, yowling for me to hurry up. It's like a scene from Pavlov's famous experiment, minus all the slobber, because she gets far giddier at the prospect of a run than she does about the promise of food. When I press the button to start my smartwatch, as I do at the outset of every run, the beeping sound is her cue to take off, and she starts dragging me up the road, impatient to reach the real running terrain, the trails. So, in theory, she should be a natural when it comes to canicross. The thing is, she is still pretty small.

↑ Leigh Woods is a verdant sanctuary right on the edge of Bristol (SS)

As we rock up at the NATB event, Rosie and I exchange a few worried looks. Every other dog there is at least twice her size. She could fit through the legs of most without lowering her head. We seem to be surrounded by huskies, malamutes, Alsatians, Weimaraners and other breeds that wouldn't look out of place on the set of *The Hound of the Baskervilles*. There are no other mongrels of indeterminate heritage here, and I think both of us feel a tad intimidated. There's lots of woofing – excited barks, rather than sad howls or warning growls, but it's quite noisy. It's a camping set-up, and some groups of dogs – presumably teams, because they look like actual sled-pulling types – are in cages. Rosie might even be getting kill centre flashbacks for all I know. I very nearly turn around, but then we're approached by a very friendly lady, who can see we're a bit out of place and clearly new, and she points us in the direction of the person giving canicross beginners' sessions, which is what we're here for.

We meet Helen, an NATB instructor who used to compete at canicross for Great Britain. There are several other newbies in the class – mostly inexperienced dog owners with big powerful pups wanting to learn how to tire

↑ Bikejor was developed by mushers in Scandinavia to keep dogs and sled drivers fit during the green season (travelarium.ph/S)

PULLING WHEELIES

If you're not a runner, there are several dog sports you can get involved in. Besides canicross, **mountain biking with dogs** (a sport known as bikejor or canibike) and even **scooting with hounds** (caniscoot) are also popular pursuits. These are better suited to larger breeds of dogs, however – certainly bigger than mine, who loves to run next to my mountain bike, but could never pull it, and I wouldn't ask her to. If in doubt about the suitability of a sport for your dog, check with an organisation such as the NATB or the British Sleddog Sports Federation (BSSF). One activity that can be enjoyed by pretty much every owner and dog – no matter how large, small, fit or fast they are – is '**mantrailing**', which involves a handler and their canine partner attempting to find a hidden person, with the dogs employing their extraordinary olfactory senses. It's basically hide-and-seek, with dogs, but is also a good search-and-rescue exercise. Visit ✆ mantrailinguk.com for more info.

them out while getting some exercise themselves. Although fellow beginners, the others have already invested in their own equipment. Previously when I have been running with Rosie, she has either been off lead altogether (a big no-no in canicross, where canines must be under complete control at all times to avoid chaos) or, when we're by roads or around farm animals and nesting birds, I've had her on a standard collar and lead, which isn't really ideal for either of us.

Luckily, Helen has some sport-specific kit for us to try. This comprises a canicross pulling harness for Rosie, a belt that goes around my waist, and a bungee leash that acts as an umbilical cord between us. Although it looks like a relatively simple set-up, there's a lot going on here. The dog's harness has an ergonomic design with an attachment point either in the middle of the back or, for more powerful pullers, near the base of the tail – definitely not at the neck. This placement is to allow the dog to breathe freely and avoid putting stress on its spine when it pulls. The bungee leash is about 2m long and elasticated, so it can absorb shock, which makes the whole experience gentler for both human and hound. The leash opens in a Y shape and attaches to a belt worn by the runner, which is designed to evenly distribute the power provided by the dog around your hips and bum, close to your centre of gravity.

On a short stretch of trail between some trees, Helen takes us through the basics. To get better at canicross, she explains, you have to constantly keep talking to your dog. 'There are no commands,' she emphasises. 'Just requests and rewards.'

Rosie is clearly a bit baffled by what we're doing and disconcerted by the unfamiliar feel of the harness. Despite my daughters' best efforts, she has always hated wearing anything other than a collar (raincoats are spurned, elf costumes despised – quite rightly too) and this seems a little too close to dress-up for her liking. She doesn't really respond to food prompts either, especially when nervous, and despite Helen's patient efforts I even struggle to get her to break into much of a run. While I learn quite a bit from the session about the basics of the sport and the commands – sorry, requests – to use, I reckon Cathrine is right and Rosie needs some other dogs around her to really start 'getting it'.

DRAG RACE Early the next morning we meet with members of Canicross Somerset in the car park at Leigh Woods. Once again, Rosie is near enough the daintiest dog there, but we have joined a beginners' group, and everyone is extremely friendly – the bipeds make small talk and the quadrupeds sniff and suss each other out. Rosie might be the smallest, but it seems she is the most senior of the newly forming pack and she starts asserting herself accordingly. Again, many of the people are quite green dog owners with large animals, anxious about how to rinse some of the endless energy out of their

↑ Certain canine breeds are especially well suited to canicross (Patrick Kinsella)

→ Elite canicrossers are highly connected to their dogs (Patrick Kinsella)

new companions. We're all virgin canicrossers, except Tim, who is leading the group with his Dalmatian-Weimaraner cross.

The dogs are done with their introductions and starting to get impatient, and everyone is kitted up, so Tim gathers us together, does a very quick briefing, and we set off along a path into the verdant woods. Unsurprisingly, given the size, power and enthusiasm of some of the four-legged members of our posse, we begin at quite a pace. I'm amazed at how disciplined the dogs are, though, especially since they're all just as new to this as we humans are. Perhaps they sense the greater experience of Tim's dog, and they're simply following his lead, but they all seem to be concentrating intently on the single-track trail ahead, and there's no real squabbling or jockeying for position. Clearly the one thing none of them wants is to be left behind by the pack. Tim refers to this as FOMO ('fear of missing out'), and so we all charge along at the speed of the frontrunner.

Although I regularly run with Rosie, my pace is always slightly slower than it is when I run the same route without her. This is because she is typically off the lead, and periodically I either have to pause to pick up poo, or wait until she has returned from some side mission following a scent. With canicross, a central part of the pursuit is harnessing the dog's energy, keeping them under control and sharply focused, and using their pulling power to improve your efficiency and

speed. I'm quite a large lump to tow, and Rosie doesn't have the pulling power that some of these bigger pups possess, but she is enthusiastically charging along the path and I'm getting a very perceptible amount of drive from her. Equipped with the proper canicross rig, my hands remain completely free, which is ideal for my own technique (arm movement is important for good cadence and, when trail running, it's important to keep your hands unimpeded in case you need them to steady yourself after tripping or slipping on an obstacle like wet tree roots or stones).

As I'm chewing on this thought, a woman overtakes me on the left, toe punts an exposed root and falls flat on her face. She's okay, besides some slight bruising to her pride, but blames her dog for going too fast. A short time later, Tim pauses the group at a nice viewpoint, and after we've caught our breath he starts explaining some of the finer points of the pursuit. Clearly it will take a little bit of time, he explains, but dogs are very capable of learning to speed up or slow down, and to correctly turn left or right if you ask them politely (and then reward them with a bit of chicken). Repetition is key, and it's better to make it easy at the beginning, using familiar trails and obvious turnings – don't just run straight up to a T-junction, yell something and then expect them to know which way to go. One of the most crucial requests to master is 'heel', which makes things much safer when you are tackling technical descents.

Rosie is pulling me along gamely, but for a taste of what it's like with a bigger beast in the driving seat, Tim lends me his hound for a few of the uphill sections of the route. The difference is massive – it's the running equivalent of cycling an e-bike. My legs still have to turn, of course, but most of the power is coming from the dog in front of me, who is digging in hard and doing his very best to catch up with Tim and Rosie, just ahead of us.

The switch is only temporary, as it confuses both dogs to be with someone they are not familiar with. Forming a good connection between canine and human is clearly crucial to enjoying canicross success, whether you're just out for a recreational run or competing at an elite level. If the dog doesn't want to run, you should never try and force it – even if it's the day of an event or race. Outside conditions must be right, too. Although it's a dry-season sport by design, canicross events do not happen during the height of summer, due to the risk of dogs overheating. Races are always 5km (3 miles) in length, because that's the maximum distance deemed safe for a dog to run at a fast pace with a person in tow, and most organised social runs are kept to that distance too. But runners need to be able to read and heed the signals their dogs are consciously and subconsciously giving off at all times, not just during races. It's in a dog's nature to try and please – it's our responsibility to make sure they do not damage themselves in the process.

ESSENTIALS

GETTING STARTED There are active social and community canicross groups all over Britain. Peruse Facebook to find one or contact your local event organiser. To find a race, look at the event calendar on ⊘ canicross.org.uk/racecalendar.

SPECIAL CONSIDERATIONS Canicross events typically pause during summer to avoid the risk of dogs dangerously overheating, but you need to exercise caution when training during hot weather too. Running early in the morning is best in the warmer months and, if there are no natural water sources on the routes you're running, bring water for your dog as well as yourself. Learn to read the signals your dog sends you when it's tired or hot, and always prioritise the health of the animal over your fitness or distance goals.

KIT BAG To run properly with a dog you need a canicross harness, leash and belt. Available from numerous online outlets and canicross orgnisations and sites, this equipment makes the experience enjoyable, comfortable and safe for dogs and humans. Aside from this, standard trail-running gear is required, with an extra water bottle for your dog if conditions are hot and dry.

The competitive side of canicross is another world altogether. Although still a niche sport in Britain, it's really big in Scandinavia, France, Belgium and Canada. International events take place regularly, and the UK has some elite performers, including Ben Robinson, who became the fastest person on the planet at running 5km, setting a blistering new world record of 12 minutes 24 seconds with his dog, Blake, at the Canicross World Championships in Sweden. Bizarrely (to my mind, anyway) competitive racing categories are divided by human measurements (gender/age) rather than the dogs used, but the top runners obviously pair themselves with the type of canine considered to be best suited to the sport. Top of the list is the greyster – a crossbreed created originally in Norway in the 1980s for *skikjøring* (sled pulling), which combines the enthusiasm and endurance of a German shorthaired pointer and the all-out speed and explosive power of a greyhound.

Personally, though, I'm quite happy with my mutt. Rosie exhibits the characteristics, traits and physical elements of about a dozen different breeds of dog, but pointer and greyhound are not among them. Yet she has run magnificently today, pulling me along when she felt we needed some extra acceleration, and running to heel during the downhills. She hasn't quite learned her lefts and rights yet, but in all honesty that's far from abnormal in our household, and we can work on that as a family.

GETTING THERE Leigh Woods is a wild area managed by the National Trust and Forestry England just outside Bristol. From the M5 take J19, follow the A369 towards Bristol and the woods are signposted on the left after Abbots Leigh. There's a fee for parking, but entry to the site is free.

PLACES TO STAY There are myriad dog-friendly accommodation options in and around Bristol. You can pitch a tent or bring a campervan to **Basecamp** at Mendip Activity Centre (⊘ mendipbasecamp.com), where friendly dogs are welcome and there are loads of outdoor activities to enjoy.

ELSEWHERE Canicross takes place all around the UK and across the world, but Scandinavia and Canada are the heartlands of the sport.

EXTRA RESOURCES

⊘ canicross.org.uk
⊘ canicross.international/site
⚘ **British Sleddog Sports Federation (BSSF)** thebssf.org.uk
⊘ **New Approach to British Dog Sports (NATB)** natbdogsports.com

11 SAILING

WHERE   Swansea, Wales; north London

SKILL LEVEL Sailing of any sort is a skilled pursuit, but you can learn the ropes in a
friendly and inclusive club environment, or do a series of courses, and
progress your journey within the sport from there, whether you
subsequently choose to sail solo or as part of a crew. Even the most
experienced sailors say they are still learning and that the elements are
the best – but least forgiving – teachers.

RISK FACTOR At beginner level, when done under appropriate supervision with a
club instructor or course leader, sailing is a safe sport conducted in
relatively controlled conditions, with risks carefully managed. As
people progress with the pursuit they can take it in many different
directions, ranging from participating in regattas and races in small craft
to attempting ocean crossings on yachts as part of a team, or even
solo if they have the requisite backing and experience. Generally
speaking, the bigger the challenge and the larger the body of water
being crossed, the more hazardous the activity is, but wild weather
can make any water-based sport dangerous, no matter how sheltered
you think you are. The ability to perform risk assessments and
self-rescues is an essential part of the learning process. It's vital
to wear the right safety gear at all times, including a proper
PFD (life jacket).

↑ Pro solo sailor Joan Mulloy on the bow of a Figaro racing yacht in heavy seas (©EdSmith)

U ntil recently, sailing has always struck me as a fairly inaccessible activity, enjoyed mostly by posh people with names like Tarquin and Piers and plenty of disposable income. Of course the minute I scratched beneath the surface and did some proper research into the sport, I quickly realised that I was largely (if not completely) wrong about this. Certainly some exclusive enclaves still exist within the sailing culture of Britain but, as with many pastimes popularly associated with privilege – from rugby to horseriding and rowing – this is only one small part of a much larger and far more layered and interesting picture.

The first thing to get your head around is that you definitely don't need your own boat – which, when you think about it, immediately makes sailing more accessible than, say, mountain biking, or even SUP. If you're a complete beginner looking for an opportunity to learn how to sail, your best bet is to locate and join a club, and if you look around it's usually possible to find a very welcoming sailing club with a membership drawn from diverse backgrounds. Often these clubs are located many kilometres from the sea. Water is a prerequisite, of course (unless you want to try land sailing; page 66), but it doesn't need to be salty. Lots of excellent sailing clubs are based on rivers, reservoirs and lakes, and many are surprisingly close to, or even right in the middle of, big cities, including London – a place I've spent a large part of my life exploring without ever suspecting it had a significant sailing scene. However, my first real brush with sailing – an experience that would whet my appetite to learn more – was destined to happen just beyond the harbour of a very different city: Swansea, in south Wales.

BAPTISM OF BRINE

I've been on sailing boats a few times, but pretty much only as a passenger. That's not an option here, during an all-hands-on-deck wild-weather trip, and against expectations, my introduction to the sport proper is shaping up to be an exciting and completely hair-raising one. As part of a small group of other landlubbers (mostly media types, thrown in at the deep end to test some Helly Hansen gear in salty surroundings), I leave Swansea Harbour aboard a powerful RIB (rigid inflatable boat). With an extraordinarily skilful skipper at the wheel, the plucky little craft cuts a course through some truly mountainous waves for a good 40 minutes before pulling up alongside a Figaro Bénéteau 3 racing yacht – which I'm told is the sailing equivalent of a Formula 1 racing car. It certainly looks sleek.

A head pops up out the cabin of the Figaro and shouts a friendly hello, and we reciprocate. But then for several moments we all just stare at one another, and then across at the lone sailor on the yacht – who, we soon discover, really is called Piers, and has sailed here from the coast of Brittany, France. Our own bouncing boat ride out across Swansea Bay has been exhilarating enough, but now, somehow, we have to transfer from the RIB to the bigger vessel, while both craft dance dramatically on the back of what seems to me like some seriously massive swell. It feels like we're in the middle of an ocean, instead of on the cusp of the Celtic Sea and the Bristol Channel. A storm had been forecast for this morning, and over breakfast there had been some debate about whether our trip should go ahead. However, happen it has, and here we are, wondering what to do next and trying to keep that breakfast where we not long ago stored it.

Suddenly, Joan Mulloy, the only other person on the RIB besides the driver who isn't part of our press crew, gets up and simply steps from one boat to the other. She makes it look ridiculously simple, but then Joan is a professional sailor who has recently represented her country (Ireland) in the high-profile Solitaire du Figaro, an intensely competitive international race that's widely considered in the sailing world to be the unofficial world championships of solo offshore racing. As we will discover during the day, Joan knows every inch of this boat intimately, and a snarling sea such as this doesn't faze her one bit. She's seen an awful lot worse, as has Piers, a veteran of all sorts of sailing races around the world. The rest of us, however, are extremely green, both in terms of our sailing experience and in the pallor of our faces. Eventually we all manage to make it from the RIB on to the yacht, but with minimal grace and style. Whereas Joan skipped across, we variously trip, flop and roll on to the deck of the bigger boat, and then proceed to crawl around until we each find somewhere to park our posteriors.

Joan is not interested in taking casual observers out for a joyride, however, and she soon starts issuing instructions for us to wind a winch there or hold a rope here, as we hoist the main sail and seek to harness and take advantage of one of

↑ Professional sailor Piers Copham takes control of the Figaro (©EdSmith)   → Piers shows Pat how a winch works (©EdSmith)

↓ Racing yachts going full tilt (SS)

CHOOSE YOUR CHALLENGE

While races such as the Solitaire du Figaro and the Vendée Globe are brutally demanding and too prohibitively expensive for most people to even think about taking part in, myriad more accessible events organised by clubs across the country take place almost every weekend of the year. Some of the most interesting, for adventure-minded people, are the challenges that combine sailing with other pursuits, such as trail running. One of the most famous is the Three Peaks Yacht Race, where crews of sailors/cyclists/runners navigate a yacht between landing points in Wales, England and Scotland, and race to the summits of Snowdon, Scafell Pike and Ben Nevis (⊘ threepeaksyachtrace.co.uk).

the elements, as opposed to simply getting battered around by them. Piers shows me how to operate one of the winches, which is equipped with gears, and then scampers over the top of the boat to attend to the sail. For a few moments it's frenetic, with all of us employed somewhere around the deck of the yacht, busily doing something that we only half understand, but which feels terribly important in the moment. Joan, with her hand steady on the tiller, keeps us travelling in the right direction as the wind fills the main sail and we pick up speed.

SAILING CLOSE TO THE WIND The pursuit of sailing seems to lie somewhere between science and art. At the risk of stating the bleeding obvious, you need to get the wind to work with the sails, which are effectively upended wings. When travelling downwind, the wind fills the sails and pushes the boat along, but when travelling upwind, there is more going on and you have to tack (perform a zig-zagging manoeuvre) to create lift. Pretty much everything depends on the angle at which the sails are positioned, and how tight you have them trimmed – too loose and you lose power, too taut and the same thing happens. According to Piers, when you're racing a yacht like this Figaro, mere centimetres can make all the difference. To a rank beginner thrown in at the deep end, it's all completely mindboggling. And yet, if you have the time and the money, it's possible to acquire a series of qualifications, starting with the Royal Yachting Association (RYA) Competent Crew course and going

↑ Pat helping to trim the sails (©EdSmith)

right through to the Coastal Skipper course, which would equip you with the requisite knowledge to captain a yacht like this in less than 20 weeks. (So long as you passed all the tests of course, and logged the requisite hours on the water, including some at night.)

We're travelling downwind and it's gusting up to 32 knots (60km/hr). Co-skippers aside, we're an inexperienced crew, so Piers has reefed the sail (reduced its size with folds), a technique used to control the power in strong winds. A digital device on the cabin door says we're sailing at 12 knots (almost 22km/hr), which feels fast to me, but the Figaro can go at twice this speed. As I look up, towards the front of the boat, I see Piers holding on to the mast, working away at something. Behind him it looks like the Mumbles hills on the horizon are bouncing up and down violently, except of course it's the yacht that's doing all the moving, as we rise on each wave and then tumble into the troughs, with the prow of the Figaro very nearly being submerged each time. The Helly Hansen kit is holding up well, and thanks to the technical clothing and the adrenaline coursing through my veins I don't feel cold, but on the outside all of us are completely drenched. This is far more full-on and exciting than I'd expected. Despite all the drama, however, Piers calmly carries on with his tasks, and when I look around at Joan, she too seems completely relaxed. I ask about this and she grins. 'Now you're all safely aboard the boat I'm happy,' she explains. 'It was the transfer I was a little worried about. I can't quite believe no-one went in the water! Here, do you want to have a go at steering?'

I take the tiller, which controls the rudder, and listen to Joan's patient instructions about how to keep the boat on a steady course. It's good to have something to concentrate on – it means I don't have to think too much about what she just said and the fact that we're going to have to transfer back on to the RIB at some point. The day has lost none of its temper. If anything the sky is only looking more bruised and angry, and the wind feels feistier than ever. Besides testing the kit in quite demanding conditions, one of the reasons for doing this trip now, in November, is to demonstrate that sailing can be an exciting winter sport, as well as a salubrious summer pastime, and we're certainly getting a taste of that.

Amid all the action, it occurs to me that, when they're sailing this boat solo, skippers like Joan and Piers have to do everything we're attempting to do – pulling ropes, winding winches, setting and trimming the sails – as well as steering, keeping an eye on various gadgets, processing all the information they provide, juggling multiple fast-moving factors, and occasionally snatching some sleep. Sophisticated yachts such as the Figaro have autopilot systems and alarms to help avoid collisions with large vessels, but still, there is an awful lot going on around us right now, and it's very hard to imagine one person coping with it all in the middle of the ocean when they're fresh, let alone while exhausted after several days on the water.

Piers explains that, during big races and ocean crossings, it's quite normal for solo sailors to average around 4½ hours' sleep in each 24, but often this is broken down into 30-minute snoozes. Part of the training process to become an advanced sailor involves lessons from sleep coaches, who teach you that it's beneficial to power nap for anything up to about 40 minutes ('Think 40 winks,' he says), but beyond that you go into deep sleep – which is fine (good, even) so long as you slumber for at least 1½ hours. If you wake up in that period between 40 and 90 minutes, you'll feel terrible and spend ages recovering. Joan tells me that when she did her first big multiday race, her autopilot broke in the first hour and she had to spend the following four days surviving on a handful of 20-minute power naps. 'By the end of it, the ropes were talking to me,' she laughs. But what she is describing is something called 'sleep monsters', which are hallucinations brought on by severe fatigue, and they can be far from funny when you're sailing alone on the ocean.

As Joan finishes telling this story, I look across to see Piers leaning right out over the starboard side of the boat, literally lying face first across one of the two foils that protrude from the hull and are used to lift the yacht out of the water, reducing the water resistance and increasing the speed the boat can travel. I can't work out what he's doing, possibly just larking about, but it looks bloody dangerous, and I briefly wonder whether he's a few feet short of a fathom. Later on, however, during a period of relative calm, I get a chance to chat to our co-skipper properly, as we dangle our legs over the topside and get regularly dowsed by spray.

↑ Piers leans right out over one of the foils of the Figaro (©EdSmith)

Piers proves to be an effervescent fella, bubbling over with contagious enthusiasm about the sport he so obviously loves. The more I talk to him, the more my preconceptions about sailing are washed away over the side. He taught himself to sail as a child in Scotland, improvising with an old rowing boat and a bedsheet for a sail. Eventually an uncle got him a boat called a Puffin. 'It looked like a bath tub with two sails,' he recalls. Now he's a qualified instructor, has completed the Solitaire du Figaro and has his sights firmly set on being on the start line of the 2028 Vendée Globe. This round-the-world solo race is widely considered to be the Everest of sailing challenges, and the costs involved dwarf even the huge sums aspirant climbers pay to reach the top of the world's highest mountain. 'I need to raise at least twice the amount of money I've ever earned in my life,' says Piers, who sails under the name Voiles des Anges (Sails of Angels), a charity that seeks to provide solace to families who have lost children.

Yet, despite all the big cash involved in the yacht-racing side of the sailing world he's immersed in, Piers is passionate about the grassroots side of the sport, and wants to see it made much more accessible to ordinary people. And he is far from alone in wishing to exorcise sailing's exclusive façade.

GOING CLUBBING

Taking the aforementioned crewing courses is one way to get into sailing, but there is another route – a far more accessible one in terms of cost, and arguably an approach that instils in students a more comprehensive understanding of

the way sailboats work – and that is by doing a series of dinghy sailing courses. This way you're master and commander of your own boat (albeit a very small, basic one) right from the beginning, and you have to own all the successes and failures, because there's no-one else to blame. With such courses you start at the very beginning, learning the ropes very literally, plus mastering basic manoeuvres such as tacking and jibing, developing an understanding of the fundamental rules of the water, and performing practical capsize drills – because, unlike a yacht with a large keel, these little boats can and do tip right over.

Despite having spent much of his youth on the water, Piers went and did a Level 2 dinghy sailing course aged 36, to make sure he really understood the basics. 'If I was picking a crew to help me on a yacht, and I had a choice between someone who had done dinghy sailing for a year and a person who'd just done a competent crew course,' he tells me, 'I'd go with the dinghy sailor every time.'

Once back on terra firma – after an exciting, but thankfully untraumatic transfer back on to the RIB and a thrilling, wave-jumping return journey into Swansea Harbour – I dig deeper into the dinghy sailing world and the question of accessibility of the sport in general. I meet with Tony Wood, a highly experienced sailing instructor who was, until recently, the RYA Development Officer for the southwest, covering a patch that extended from Gloucester across to north Dorset and down to the Scilly Isles, overseeing some of the country's best coast and seascapes.

'There are some clubs out there that want to remain very exclusive, and others that are the complete opposite, and strive to be as welcoming as possible,' he says. 'The RYA had a massive accessibility drive in Britain around the 2012 Olympics, when the sport was in the public eye. We went to great lengths to appeal to new people. Back then, the average annual cost of joining a sailing club was £99, which compared to, say, gym membership, is very cheap. And you get loads for your money too, not just the sailing, but use of equipment, social facilities, access to very reduced-price courses. At places like Dartmouth Sailing Club, they have stand-up paddleboards, kayaks and all sorts of kit you can use, and as a result they have 1,200 to 1,500 members.'

In many urban areas, access to the water and sports such as sailing can be truly transformative, especially for young people. 'In a place like Plymouth, where the city is really built up and there isn't much access to green areas for kids to go exploring, we tried to push the concept of the "blue playing field" that exists right in front of them,' Tony tells me, but he admits much more remains to be done. 'Parents need to be aware that the facilities and opportunities are out there, and the sport needs to feel more friendly to everyone. Britain has a phenomenal record in competitive sailing. It's the most successful nation at Olympic level, with names like Ben Ainslie being the best known. He won his first silver medal aged 19, and then racked up four consecutive golds. And Ainslie began by sailing dinghies. But imagine the talent we're missing out on, and the experiences all kids could be enjoying.'

LONDON AHOY!

'Yes, sadly, sailing still has that whiff of elitism about it,' sighs Peter Edel, Commodore of King George Sailing Club (KGSC) in northeast London, when I ask him about the accessibility of the sport in the capital. 'Luckily,' he continues, sounding much more upbeat, 'I do think it's gradually going away, as that generation…well, moves on.'

At the tender age of 33, Pete is exceptionally young for a sailing club commodore – very possibly the youngest in the country. The vast majority, he points out, are over 50, greying, white British males. Like Piers and Tony, he too is passionate about eradicating the old snobby reputation of sailing and embracing a far more inclusive approach. The KGSC utilises the 170ha blue playing field that is the King George V Reservoir, the largest of a chain of reservoirs in east London. Sailing on a drinking-water reservoir that's also a site of special scientific interest (SSSI) and a habitat for wild birds isn't without its challenges, but the club and their training partners, the London Watersports Company, offer dinghy sailing courses to anyone who wants to do them, in a catchment area that includes some of the poorest neighbourhoods in the country.

They work closely with Greig City Academy in Haringey, north London, a state school with a brilliant outdoor pursuits program that allows pupils from disadvantaged backgrounds to experience sports such as sailing. More than 50

↑ The very down-to-earth Gary from the London Watersports Company at the tiller on King George V Reservoir (Patrick Kinsella)

ESSENTIALS

GETTING STARTED For aspirant sailors, there are two main ways to learn the ropes. You can either start by taking dinghy lessons with a local club such as the **King George Sailing Club** (⊘ kgsc.org.uk), during which you will be taught how to sail your own small craft, or if you'd rather go down the yachting route, you can do a 'Competent Crew' course through various RYA-affiliated providers.

Unsurprisingly, there is also a huge crossover between boat sailing and windsurfing (and wingfoiling and kitesurfing; page 272).

SPECIAL CONSIDERATIONS Not only are most modern sailing clubs very open and welcoming to all-comers, the sport's governing body has gone to great efforts to make the pursuit very accessible to people with physical and/or mental challenges. The RYA's Sailability program offers experiences and instruction to individuals and groups with disabilities and special requirements, ranging from paraplegics to people with PTSD, depression and schizophrenia. Time spent on the water, and skills learned while sailing, can be more than simply therapeutic, they can be completely transformative.

KIT BAG The fundamental equipment required for sailing will be provided by the club, although sometimes you do need to pay for boat hire. Wearing sailing-orientated weather-proof clothing – made by brands such as Helly Hansen and Gill – will make the experience a lot more comfortable, especially on a racing yacht in winter, but when

↑ Dinghy sailing on the King George V Reservoir in London (Patrick Kinsella)

languages are spoken at the mixed-sex school, and 70% of pupils are eligible for free school meals, but thanks to the Greig Trust, the fund-raising efforts of the kids themselves and the leadership of Jon Holt (founder of the Scaramouche Sailing Trust and head of outdoor education at the academy, who was named International Sailor of the Decade in 2020), they own an ocean-racing yacht, the *Scaramouche*. Every single child has the opportunity to learn how to sail on dinghies, and in 2017 they were the first state school to enter a team in the illustrious 695-nautical-mile (1,287km) Fastnet Race, in which they finished in 142nd place in field of 368 competitors. The captain of the team, sixth-former Montel Fagan-Jordan, was named Young Sailor of the Year in January 2018, an award previously given to Ben Ainslie.

It's a truly extraordinary story, which completely confounds my preconceptions of the sport, and it all begins with dinghy sailing. Which is exactly what I do. I arrange a taster dinghy sailing session on the King George V Reservoir with London Watersports Company's Stuart Philbey and Gary Bennett, and immediately get hooked. Next on my to-do list is a Level 1 dinghy sailing course with my kids at my welcoming local club in Seaton, east Devon. I can't believe I didn't do this years ago. Sometimes barriers to entry are entirely in the mind.

sailing dinghies and small boats you can just wear an old wetsuit. A PFD (life jacket) is absolutely essential, and devices such as PLBs (personal location beacons) need to be used on open water.

GETTING THERE The King George Sailing Club is located near Chingford railway station, which is serviced by regular trains from London Liverpool Street.

PLACES TO STAY Chingford is close to Epping Forest, where there are various accommodation options ranging from boutique hotels to camping grounds such as the **Lee Valley Almost Wild Campsite** (visitleevalley.org.uk/lee-valley-almost-wild-campsite), which offers everything from wild camping to safari glamping tents, right on the edge of London.

ELSEWHERE There are many great sailing clubs around the country, including the **Exe Sailing Club** (exe-sailing-club.org) and **Dartmouth Yacht Club** (dyc.org.uk), which both offer dinghy sailing and more. But look at a map of your local area, seek out the blue bits and search for sailing clubs – you'll find one.

EXTRA RESOURCES The **Royal Yachting Association** (RYA; rya.org.uk) is your one-stop shop for finding courses, clubs and information about sailing, and it's also the governing body for wind- and kitesurfing, as well as wingfoiling.

12 FOREST BATHING - SHINRIN-YOKU

WHERE	Pound Wood Nature Reserve, Thundersley, Essex
SKILL LEVEL	No previous knowledge or skill is required to enjoy forest bathing.
RISK FACTOR	Besides the possibility of minor stings from woodland flora or fauna, there's virtually no risk involved in forest bathing in Britain. Elsewhere, local environmental factors should be considered.

Essex isn't, perhaps, the first place you would think about going to reconnect with nature, or to experiment with an activity that has its roots deep in Japanese culture. And yet, on a regular basis, small groups of people come to Pound Wood Nature Reserve, between Basildon and Southend-on-Sea, to practise Shinrin-Yoku. If those words sound entirely unfamiliar, you might not be much enlightened by the translation either, which is 'forest bathing'. Despite how it sounds, this does not mean that gangs of people are marauding around the woods, parks and nature reserves of Essex in bikinis and budgie smugglers – at least not in the name of forest bathing. Neither does it have anything whatsoever to do with wild swimming. In fact there is no need to get wet at all. What you 'bathe' in is the atmosphere of the forest, taking a deep dive into the natural environment, absorbing the sights, sounds, smells and textures of the woods.

↑ Shinrin-yoku engages all your senses (SS)

Conceived in Japan in the 1980s, Shinrin-Yoku is as much a philosophy as it is an activity. Essentially, it involves taking a slow, meditative meander around a forest (or any green space), stopping regularly and opening your eyes, ears and hands to consciously soak your senses in the natural surroundings. Of course, humans have been doing exactly this for millennia – once upon a time, having your mind sharply tuned in to the movements, colours, noises and aromas around you in the outdoors was the only way to survive, and such skills were passed down through generations. In that sense neither forest school or forest bathing are new ideas, but centuries of social evolution, industrialisation and modern life have, for most people, severely dampened the ability to interpret, or even recognise, the signs and indicators constantly being transmitted by the elements and the flora and fauna all around us. And when you first dip your toe into a forest bathing experience, the sudden realisation of the extent of that loss is almost scalding. Fortunately, one of the lessons that can be learned during such an experience is that it doesn't take too much effort to slip back into a more receptive mode.

Recent events and restrictions have emphasised just how important and valuable time spent outside your four walls can be for mental health, but long before global pandemics hammered this home, the ideas behind Shinrin-Yoku had been spreading beyond Japan to places where populations were living work-orientated lives in heavily built-up environments. It was especially enthusiastically embraced in places like Scandinavia, but also Britain, where forest bathing has become particularly popular around the bigger urban jungles. Which is why a nature reserve not far beyond the M25, within earshot of London Southend Airport, is actually the perfect place to explore Shinrin-Yoku. So here I am.

DECOMPRESSION SESSION

After stressing about the opaque toll requirements of the Dartford Tunnel beneath the Thames, and negotiating the endless roundabouts, one-way systems and cavalier drivers of suburban Essex, I'm in serious need of some calming mindfulness by the time we meet up with Ruth, who will lead me through my inaugural forest bathing experience. Although, truth be known, I'm not even sure what my brain thinks about mindfulness. I'm naturally a little bit skeptical about such things, but I do massively enjoy spending time outside, in forests or on mountains, moors and seashores – hiking, biking, trail running, paddling, swimming or simply dawdling and daydreaming – and I am coming into this with a wide-open mind. Or at least that's my intention.

My octogenarian dad, on the other hand, whom I've brought along for the ride, suffers from no such ambivalence. I am so confident that he will be disparaging about the idea of forest bathing that I deliberately haven't fully explained what we've signed up to do. As far as he is concerned, we're just going for a nice walk in the woods, with a guide. However, he is the person who instilled in me a love of the outdoors as a child – with cycling and canoeing adventures, and annual walking and camping holidays – so I'm intrigued to see whether his almost compulsory male-of-a-certain-vintage cynicism will be overcome by what, I hope, will be a thought-provoking experience. Poor Ruth doesn't know what she's in for.

There are six of us in the group, with just one other guy, and later Ruth explains that women outnumber men on all her sessions. Blokes, it seems, tend to favour challenge-based outdoor therapies, such as the Wim Hof method for freezing your goolies off. After clearly emphasising that Shinrin-Yoku is not a miracle cure for anything and will not by itself prevent heart attacks or protect you from disease or depression, Ruth explains that she will issue us with a number of invitations throughout the session, which we can either accept or disregard. Nothing is compulsory. If anyone is uncomfortable with any of it, they can simply ignore the suggestion and do their own thing for a bit.

'Bloody hell – she's not going to ask us to strip off and run around the woods is she?' asks Dad, in what he thinks is a whisper. (He has forgotten his hearing aid, so everything is a near-bellow.) I grin with nervous embarrassment. Truth is, I have no idea what she might invite us to do.

Our first task is actually to ask the forest for permission to be there. We're each sent off to find a tree and have a chat to it. This should be interesting. I walk into the woods, find a swaying sweet chestnut tree and ask how its day is going. There's no reply, so I close my eyes, put my forehead against the trunk and try some human-tree telepathy. The chestnut is no chatterbox, but it doesn't seem to object to me being there, and I don't feel quite as daft as I thought I might. Looking around, I see Dad has found himself an ash tree, and is making a game attempt at talking to it. Bless him. The sad thing is, if it replied, he probably wouldn't hear it. Then his phone rings at top volume, and everyone's bubble is burst – not least because he answers it. I mouth an apology at Ruth, confiscate the miscreant's mobile and we carry on.

MAKING SENSE OF IT ALL The next invitation is to look for movement as we walk along a section of path. When you start to pay proper attention to it, motion is absolutely everywhere in what at first appears to be fairly still forest. There's the obvious stuff, such as trail runners, cyclists and dogs zipping past, but then there are lots of more subtle, small movements. Leaves shiver on an ash tree, making the dappled light dance on the floor. A squirrel dashes along a branch and a caterpillar spins in mid-air, dangling from a single thread of silk. One of the women with us points to a tree stump writhing with the mesmerising movement of thousands of carpenter ants. Then Ruth calls us back by banging together two clap sticks, and we share our observations.

We're then encouraged to find a bit of space, shut our eyes, look skyward, hold our arms out and splay our fingers, to see what we can feel. There's sun on

↑ Paddy Kinsella using his remaining senses while forest bathing in Essex (Patrick Kinsella)

my skin, and the gentle stroke of a faint breeze. Something tiny scampers along my arm. Ruth suggests we stick our tongues out to see if that heightens any of the sensations. Weirdly it does, probably because of the concentration of nerve endings on that peculiar sensory organ. I feel like a snake, licking the breeze and tasting the air. I sneak a peek, and everyone is stood there like rude schoolkids, with tongues poked out – even Dad, with his eyes obediently clamped shut.

We keep our eyes closed as Ruth redirects our attention to sounds, suggesting we focus on one far away first, and then one nearby. The not-far-distant buzz of the A127 is hard to ignore for the background component of this exercise, but then I push that away and eavesdrop on a conversation between two birds of the forest – a pair of song thrushes (I think). It sounds simultaneously lyrical and urgent, and I become totally absorbed in their exchange, as the roar of the road (that mad world we'd been part of mere minutes ago) gradually diminishes. Dad's tinnitus has robbed him of the ability to hear birdsong without the absent hearing aid, but when we all compare notes he talks about the rustling of the leaves. Others mention the fluttering of insects.

Little beakers are distributed, and during the next section of walking we're instructed to fill these with anything with an aroma, from blooming wildflowers to bits of tree bark found on the forest floor. As Ruth is explaining what to do, a labradoodle bounds up and goes around the whole group, sniffing our legs and giddily looking for attention. The dog's owner has overheard part of our conversation and as he passes he quips: 'If you want any tips on smelling stuff, watch her, she's an absolute champion!' He's joking, but of course it's true; numerous dogs lollop past us during the day, tongues out, noses to the ground and ears twitching – for all their domestication, canines are far better tuned in to all of their senses than humans, because we seem to have put most of our faith in eyesight. And, true to form, off we go, looking for things that might have a scent, rather than tracking them down with our olfactory organ. To be fair, the fact that we're bipeds does make exploring with nose to the ground a bit tricky.

It's May, and the woods are awash with a fantastic flood of bluebells, but no-one feels right decapitating these or any other wildflowers, so instead we root around on the ground for fallen bouquets, variously adding leaves, bark and pinches of soil. Some give their concoctions names – neither of us go that far, but as we compare perfumes, Dad sparks a conversation about how odours can transport you through time, and talks about certain smells instantly taking him back to his childhood on the banks of the River Shannon in Ireland. He genuinely seems to be warming to this.

And then the invitation to strip off really does come. Fortunately, it's only from the ankles down, for those who want to remove their shoes and socks, and try a bit of barefoot walking through the woods. I love this part. As a trail

↑ With Ruth, going barefoot amid the bluebells (Patrick Kinsella) → Losing your shoes turns a walk in the woods into a tactile experience (Halfpoint/S)

runner, I've experimented a lot with 'barefoot running' – this doesn't literally mean running with no shoes at all (although some people do), but instead you wear minimalist footwear, with very thin soles and no padding or drop between heel and toe. Such shoes encourage runners to land each stride on the front or ball of their feet, rather than the heel, and it's often considered a more natural and efficient way to run, and indeed walk. It's much more tactile too, with the thin soles facilitating what's known as 'trail feel', where you literally sense and 'read' the surface beneath your feet. In order to avoid injury, you pay close attention to each and every foot placement, steering clear of sharp sticks and stones, so instead of just ploughing along the trails there's a much more conscious mental engagement with the environment. And so it is with barefoot walking. Instead of looking straight ahead, we really explore the floor with our eyes before taking each step. It sounds ponderous, but quickly becomes second nature and progress is no slower than when we had our shoes on. One of the sensations that really

↑ Relaxing in leaves while forest bathing (Patrick Kinsella)

stands out for me, with completely naked feet rather than just thin soles, is the change in temperature you feel when walking on different surfaces, from the coolness of the green moss to the warmth of the dark tree bark that holds on to the heat of the sun.

With shoes back on, we're paired up and encouraged to remove something far more confronting than footwear: our sight. In what starts as a trust exercise but develops into a really revealing form of exploration, Ruth tells one member of each pair to close their eyes, while the other leads them to a tree and then leaves them alone to explore it with their hands. Obviously, I'm with Dad. Resisting the temptation to take him back to the stump with the carpenter ants swarming all over it (which would have been hilarious, but not really in the spirit of the moment), I guide him to a gnarled old oak tree, and leave the two elders to convene for a while. When it's my turn, he takes me to a trunk that I feel (literally) belongs to a youngish beech, because the bark is relatively smooth and the leaves soft and slightly furry. I've been reading about beech recently, learning how they form communities of friends and families in the forest, and share resources when one of their number is struggling. In this way, even if a beech tree is cut down, its mates sometimes keep the stump alive for decades – centuries even – by donating water and nutrients through their interconnected root systems. Frankly, I find this information mindblowing, and I enjoy my time with this tree, contemplating its social life and friendship group.

THE SEED

The idea behind Shinrin-Yoku was developed in Japan in the 1980s by the government department in charge of land, forestry and fishing. There was a growing concern in the country at the time that a large percentage of the population was becoming increasingly stressed out by their urban existence - that people's body clocks had become synced to their job, and they had entirely lost touch with the natural world. In the same decade, the word *karoshi* - which literally means 'overwork death' - was introduced to the Japanese language and recognised by the Health Ministry. In a country where the biggest religion is Shinto - an ancient belief system that links divinity with nature - the sudden need to have a word to describe people dying at their desks was a red flag. Through various programs they started busing city-based folk out into the Japanese countryside and holding Shinrin-Yoku sessions, where people could learn or remember how to tap into nature and use time spent relaxing in the wilderness to decompress from the mental pressures of modern life. And it worked. The stats they collected showed such fresh-air therapies reduced people's blood pressure and improved their perceived levels of happiness.

Our final invitation is to find a spot amid the trees where we can lie down among the leaves and look at the forest from an entirely new perspective. And not just look, but close our eyes and let our other senses explore too. We spread out, and I note that Dad doesn't dither around this time; he walks straight off into the trees. I wonder whether it's to answer a call of nature, but apparently not – at least not in the sense I feared. He's really into it now, and when Ruth calls us back, this time by playing a gentle refrain on a flute, a tune that wends through the woods like a will-o'-the-wisp, I have to go looking for him. I find him sat with his back to a tree, eyes shut. Initially I think he's asleep, but no, he's just soaking up the surrounds and deep in thought.

When we reach the glade where she's waiting, Ruth has poured us each a little bamboo cup of green tea, which is the traditional way to conclude a Shinrin-Yoku session. Before dispersing, each member of the group offers their thoughts on the

ESSENTIALS

GETTING STARTED Ruth runs regular Shinrin-Yoku sessions at places including Pound Wood Nature Reserve and Hatfield Forest. You can book and find out more by visiting ⊘ forestcloudsnaturetherapy.co.uk.

SPECIAL CONSIDERATIONS The activity is both meditative and dynamic, but there's no necessity to be bendy and contort yourself into eye-popping poses, so people of all ages and levels of fitness can take part.

KIT BAG Bring appropriate footwear, layers (including waterproofs) and some water. Avoid wearing strong smelling perfume.

GETTING THERE Leave the M25 at junction 30 or 29, and take the A13 or A127 respectively to towards Southend-on-Sea. Pound Wood Nature Reserve is accessed via St Michael's Road, Thundersley, Benfleet, Essex SS7 2UW.

PLACES TO STAY There are various hotels and B&Bs in nearby Southend-on-Sea including the charismatic **Hamilton's Boutique Hotel** (⊘ hamiltonsboutiquehotel. co.uk) located in a Georgian terrace on the seafront.

ELSEWHERE Organised Shinrin-Yoku sessions take place at many Forestry England woodlands and National Trust properties across the country at locations including Alice Holt Forest in Surrey, Rendlesham Forest in Suffolk, Thetford Forest on the seam of Suffolk and Norfolk, the Forest of Dean in Gloucestershire, Salcey Forest in Northamptonshire and Whinlatter Forest and Arnside Knott in Cumbria.

experiences we've just shared. People give thanks to the forest for hosting us, and to Ruth for being our guide. Several mention the respite from physical or mental discomfort they get by practising forest bathing. When it's Dad's turn, I'm fidgety. God only knows what he's going to blurt out. But when it comes, his feedback is glowing. He has spent much of the quiet, reflective time thinking about Mum, who we lost last year. They always loved the outdoors and spent lots of time walking in woods and wild places together. He's not a spiritual person and has no religious beliefs, so the loss has been brutally final – she has simply gone, and he knows he'll never see her again. But here, in the verdant, totally non-denominational chapel of the forest, he has been with her in thoughts at least.

There is a caveat, of course. As we get back in the car and brace to take on the traffic, he turns to me and says how much he enjoyed the experience. 'But if you tell any of the lads I've been out talking to trees, I'll bloody kill you!'

EXTRA RESOURCES

◊ forestryengland.uk/blog/forest-bathing
◊ nationaltrust.org.uk/lists/a-beginners-guide-to-forest-bathing

Nature & Therapy UK

Shinrin Yoku & Nature Therapy

1:1 and group forest bathing walks
1:1 and bespoke group Ecotherapy sessions
Practitioner training - International Forest Therapy Diploma
National directory of Practitioners

www.natureandtherapy.co.uk
info@natureandtherapy.co.uk
+44 1364 652162

UNIVERSITY OF PLYMOUTH

CPD CERTIFIED
The CPD Certification

MODERN SCIENCE, ANCIENT WISDOM

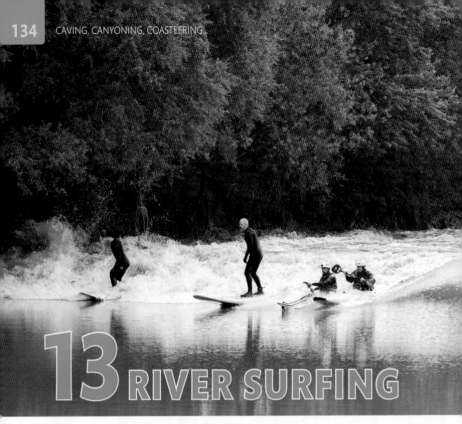

13 RIVER SURFING

WHERE   The River Severn, Gloucestershire

SKILL LEVEL   Surfing is a skill people spend years perfecting, and river surfing has
certain idiosyncrasies that make it uniquely challenging. Crucially, you
only get one chance to catch the wave. If you fail, or fall straight off,
then you'll have to wait until at least the next tide to have another go,
and potentially for several months, until everything aligns once again
for the bore to run sufficiently high and in daylight hours.

RISK FACTOR   The Severn bore can be big, and when a good wave is forecast it gets
busy around the popular put-in places – not just with surfers, but
also kayakers, bodyboarders, SUPers and other water users.
Collisions and occasional injuries do happen, and some people wear
helmets to protect themselves from boards and boats, plus debris in
the water (flotsam and jetsam ranges from large logs to free-range
fridges) and rocks in the river. Behind the wave a huge volume of
confused and fast-moving water continues rushing up the river for
hours, going against the tide, which creates whirlpools that can get
hold of surfers, especially on the wider, lower reaches of the river. It's
essential to avoid parts of the bank with overhanging trees, where
inflowing water can pin people to submerged branches.

↑ River surfers are often joined by kayakers riding the Severn bore (Oliver Edwards)

The rush experienced when you catch a wave is one of the most exhilarating sensations you'll ever get in the outdoors. The sudden thrust of acceleration that kicks in when you're no longer driving and nature has taken over is incredible. Suddenly, you're in the powerful hands of the elements and all you can do is hang on and enjoy the ride, steering here and there if you have the requisite skills, and trying to stay upright on the rolling break for as long as possible. I've felt this often as a sea kayaker and surfskier, and occasionally on a SUP, but as someone who can (at best) be described as a beginner boarder, it's an experience I've only had a handful of times while surfing. And usually it's fairly short-lived, and comes only after multiple attempts and many missed waves. All of which makes the prospect of river bore surfing, when you only get one chance to catch an exceptional wave, both daunting and exciting.

While salty surfing is enjoyed by millions of people around the coastlines of all ocean-facing nations, river surfing is a far more niche pursuit – mainly because it can only be done in a few places around the planet, when several factors align and the conditions are right, which occurs on a couple of consecutive days a month during daylight hours. If you're lucky. Unlike boardriders on the sea, who can hang out on a break for hours, choosing waves from multiple sets and staying upright for a minute or two, river surfers ride a singular wave caused by a bore, which is the leading edge of an incoming tide, created as the surging seawater rushes up an estuary against the outflowing current. In particular places – where the tidal range is high, and the estuary is shaped like a funnel and faces the right way – and at certain times (around the full moon, especially during the equinox), these waves can be big.

But it's not just the size and rarity of the wave that makes this such a unique and intriguing pursuit, it's the fact that good surfers can potentially ride it for miles as it rolls up the river. And one of best places in the world to experience river surfing is on the Severn in Gloucestershire, where the second biggest tidal range on earth pushes a bore up the Bristol Channel into an estuary that's uniquely shaped, positioned and proportioned to turn it into the perfect wave. I'd heard about this phenomena a few times, but a conversation with a photographer friend, Ollie, who'd been shooting some of the Severn surfers while working on a project about the bore, got me totally hooked. I was eager to experience it, but two things were standing in my way: I didn't have a board, and I can't really surf.

MEETING THE MUDDY BROTHERS

I've always intended to learn how to surf properly, but the east Devon coast I call home faces the English Channel, and with little swell it's far better suited for SUPing, swimming and kayaking. I've rented and borrowed boards many times, and even taken a lesson or two while visiting Cornwall and north Devon, but although I can occasionally stay on my feet for a few fleeting seconds, Kelly Slater I'm definitely not. However, with the spring equinox rapidly approaching – a time when the bore runs at its best – and all the websites forecasting a four-star wave during daylight hours on a couple of consecutive mornings when I could feasibly be in the right place at the right time, I decide to go for it. Time and tide wait for no-one.

Ollie introduced me to several of the Severn regulars, who are collectively known as the Muddy Brothers. They're a loose knit-bunch of blokes (mostly), with one common denominator: the full moon makes them do something slightly unusual on surfboards. My first conversation is with Ben Rogers, who lives on the east of the Severn and crafts surfboards for a living, including some specifically designed for riding the river.

Ben has been surfing bores on the Severn and elsewhere for 15 or 16 years. 'There are quite a few misconceptions around it,' he tells me, when we chat on the phone. 'Sometimes it can be dribbly, other times it can be great. Lots of people do the bore once, get a good ride or a crap one, depending on their luck, and then they never do it again. For a few years I didn't catch any decent waves, but then I came back with a board I'd made myself and it was fantastic. Around 2015, when we had the supermoons, it got a bit crazy. The wave was regularly running high, like a 6ft wall of whitewater. It was great, but there were a lot of people on the water – kayakers and surfers – and some of them were getting it wrong. One time a windsurfer turned up, and he ended up crashing into a friend of mine and smashing up his ankle. But it's calmed down a bit now. And the regulars have their secret spots.'

Another veteran is Tom, an artisan cider-maker based on the west bank of the river. For a few years he organised festivals for surfers coming to do the bore around the autumn equinox, a time when the wave runs reliably big. When we talk, he explains the dynamics of the wave. 'Below Newnham, in what we call

↑ Waiting for the wave on the River Severn (Oliver Edwards)

the Lower Severn, the aftermath of the wave can be quite dangerous,' he warns. 'The massive influx of water creates big whirlpools, and it can be hard to get out. Above the first couple of bends, when the river narrows, it's safer, but then you have the crowds. There's just one wave, and I've seen up to 40-odd people lining the river waiting to catch it. But it's all good fun.'

And then he says the magic words: 'Are you going to come and have a look then?'

FIRST MUD We arrange to meet at Tom's mate's place, on the morning after the spring equinox, when the first four-star wave is forecast. Steve, a welder, surfer and artist, lives on a boat at the Bullo Pill, right on the edge of the river, in the perfect spot to assess the wave as it rolls past. After driving for two hours in the pre-dawn darkness, I cross the Severn Bridge just after sunrise. Way below me the estuary looks immense, intense and intimidating. The water is a swirling mess of milk-chocolate brown brine. I'm only planning to watch today, but I shiver slightly at the thought of anyone getting into that.

Arriving at the rendezvous spot, I find Steve standing on the bank, surveying the river. Minutes after we make our introductions, he points to some wash whipping around a bend further downstream. 'Here it comes,' he says, with the kind of nonchalance you'd expect from someone who has been doing this caper for over 20 years. Although we're a fair way from the bridge, far further up the funnel neck of the estuary, the waterway still yawns wide here and for a moment I can't see what he's looking at. But then I spot a rapidly approaching, rolling ridge of water, spanning the entire width of the river. Right in the middle of it, where the wave is cresting, sits a lone kayaker, moving at pace despite only putting in the occasional stroke. The Severn is so broad here it's hard to get a sense of scale and

LIFE'S A BORE

The tidal range of the Bristol Channel can exceed 15m, which is enormous and explains why the bore wave is so special on the Severn. Many things combine to determine how large the wave will be each month, but the most important contributing forces are the lunar cycle and how that interacts with the tide. The largest waves happen around the full moon during the spring and autumn equinoxes. Besides the tide, factors that influence the size and quality of wave include wind direction, the level and flow rate of the river after rain across the catchment area, and the lay of the land around and beneath the river itself. The estuary constantly shape shifts, and the depth and width of the lower river changes, with sandbanks forming and then disappearing. Water runs fastest around the outside of bends, where the river is usually at its deepest, but surfers have to be very careful not to get snared in trees overhanging from the riverbanks, and often the wave is bigger when the depth is shallower. It takes a lot of experience to pick the right line.

speed, but as soon as he passes the paddler seems to disappear; he's completely hidden by the height of the wave.

The bore wave moves at around 12km/hr, and it's quickly out of sight. In its wake, a vast volume of water continues to surge upstream, and a second kayaker, who has long since lost his morning race with the elements, is getting bullied by it. He looks like he knows what he's doing, though, so we retire to Steve's boat for a brew. Tom arrives in time for coffee, and we talk while Steve gets his wetsuit on. I start getting fidgety, but the lads – both old hands – insist we have plenty of time. Because the river takes such a serpentine route inland, the wave takes an hour to reach the put-in place Steve has in mind for this morning, whereas we can drive a more direct way and overtake it. 'I used to ride it here, then hop in the car and get on and off it all the way to Gloucester,' grins Steve. 'I'd take three days off work. It was exhausting!'

Suitably caffeinated, we jump in our vehicles and drive through Newnham to a spot just past the Severn Bore pub, near Minsterworth. Tom gets his wetsuit on and we wander down to the riverbank. One other surfer drifts downstream on a SUP, wearing a helmet, and there are a couple of kayakers on the water. 'Oh no… we've got bloody canoes!' says Tom, but he's laughing. As Steve and Tom limber up and get in, a few more spectators join me on the bank, including another one of the regular bore riders, who soon spies the approaching wave.

After passing the pub, the bore is re-energised by a shallow section before Minsterworth, and as I watch, the wave rises and crests as it rushes towards the figures in the water, who all start paddling frantically to pick up momentum before it reaches them. The helmet-wearing SUP surfer gets collected first, and it looks as though he'll get tipped straight over the front of his board, but he recovers and gets to his feet. Steve is right next to him, and has to pull hard right to avoid a collision. And then they're past me, beyond the trees and obscured by the wave.

Twenty minutes later, Tom and Steve reappear, buzzing, having caught the wave for a thrilling 500m run. Their excitement is infectious, and instantly we make arrangements for tomorrow, when an even bigger wave is promised because the autumn equinox tide will be at its peak.

GIVING IT A WHIRL The following morning we meet at Steve's place again, an hour later to allow for the tide. When I arrive, Tom is already there and both he and Steve are visibly excited. 'The wave's just gone through, and it's *much* bigger than yesterday,' Steve enthuses. I wander down to the bank while the coffee pot boils, and witness a massive whirlpool in the middle of the river. It's a violent-looking vortex, which I wouldn't want to be anywhere near if I was in the water. Steve hands me a steaming mug and recounts a time a few years back, when he got caught in just such a whirlpool after the wave had gone through, and had to sit tight on his board, spinning for 10 or 15 minutes until it released him. Neither the anecdote nor the caffeine does anything to calm my nerves. But before I get halfway through my brew Ollie arrives and it's time to go, if we want to overtake the wave.

What with the whirlpools and the whopping wave, I start to wonder whether this really is the best time to surf my first bore, but I'm here now, wetsuited and booted and with a new toy to try out. Straight after watching the action yesterday, I'd gone out and scored a board. Ben, the Muddy Brother boardmaker, had told me to go with something long and buoyant that I wouldn't be too precious about,

↑ During the spring and autumn equinoxes the bore wave is bigger (Patrick Kinsella)

so that's exactly what I did, hunting down a cheap-and-cheerful 8ft foamie from Devon-based beach brand Two Bare Feet. Steve stifles a pretend guffaw when I get my virgin beginner board out of the car, but he's only messing with me. His own river steed – a seasoned single-fin bearing the scars of many earlier adventures – is a rescued castaway that had been destined for the dump.

Before meeting them, I'd worried the locals might sneer, or even snarl, at obvious newbies like me, turning up with bargain boards and encroaching on their surf and turf – something that certainly happens on many beach breaks. But my experience was completely the opposite. They were super-welcoming and helpful every step of the way, and Steve talked at length about how sad it was that many surfers had forgotten how to share waves, which is how the sport had started.

And now my Muddy Brother amigos have some sage advice for me. 'Stay well back on your board,' Steve says. 'It's really easy to get thrown straight over the front when the wave catches you. Most importantly, though, mind out for the trees on the left with branches dangling in the water. You do not want to get pinned to those by the force of the water that follows the wave.'

True – I definitely do not want that to happen. In kayaking parlance such dangers are called strainers, and getting caught in one can be deadly. 'If you come off the wave and find yourself getting pulled towards them, paddle out into the middle of the river,' Steve continues. 'We keep an eye on each other here, and will make sure you don't miss the get-out.' This is comforting, as I'm definitely feeling out of my depth. 'And if you do end up among the trees, get your ankle leash off as quick as you can,' chimes in Tom. 'Forget the board, save yourself.'

RIDE BEFORE A FALL It's nearly action stations, so thankfully I don't have time to dwell too deeply on all this. We make our way down the muddy bank and wade into the water until we're waist deep. It's not as cold as I feared it might be on this fresh March morning in my 3.5mm wetsuit, but I'm glad I grabbed some neoprene gloves from my gear drawer at the last moment. We're joined by two kayakers in nimble little river-running boats, and four other surfers who have drifted downstream from a put-in point further up. Steve instructs me to lie on the board and checks I'm positioning myself right, and the swift current promptly takes me 20m downstream. Paddling back to the others is a good warm-up, though.

There's a bit of nervous banter between us, and a few spectators join Ollie on the bank. One of them spies the early signs of the wave and a ripple of excitement spreads across the water. Several surfers are just about visible in the distance, riding the wave by the Severn Bore pub. None of them stay on for long, but a speedboat jumps ahead of the wave and zooms past us, with more surfers in the back. The white wash of the wave is soon visible, kicking up along the sides of

↑ Preparing to board the Severn bore (Oliver Edwards) → As the wave approaches, you have find some room and paddle hard (Oliver Edwards)

the river, and then we see the wall of water rearing up and racing towards us. Even allowing for the fact that it was always going to look bigger from water level than it seemed while standing on the bank yesterday, this morning's wave is a whopper. 'Paddle, paddle, paddle!' shouts Steve, as we all turn our boards and boats in synchrony and do exactly as he says.

Facing away from it, I hear rather than see the breaking wave as it catches me. Following Steve's advice, I've deliberately positioned my weight well back, but I still feel my legs being lifted and only narrowly avoid getting nose-dumped. I hang on for dear life, and the board finally levels. Amid all the exhilaration, acceleration and chaos, I manage to recall another tip I'd been given, this time by Ben: 'Stay prone on the board for a while and enjoy the ride,' he'd said. 'Don't try and stand up too soon, otherwise you'll fall straight in and regret it.' I heed his wise words and stay horizontal for the first 50m or so, enjoying experiencing the full force of the famous water beneath me. And when I do eventually attempt to get to my feet, Ben's warning proves prescient, because I only get about halfway up before the bore bucks me, and I fall off.

As the wave barrels onwards, with some of the better boarders still riding it, I feel the awesome power of the flow that follows the breaker pushing me upstream. I see the trees Tom and Steve warned me about, languidly dangling their lethal limbs in the water, and steer well clear of them. Tom, it turns out, is behind me, having been thrown off early on, and we both drift and paddle to the get-out place, around 500m from where we put in. Steve is there waiting, well pleased with his ride. As we wait for others ahead of us to scramble up the steep bank, the chat is all about how spectacular the wave was, with the consensus being that it was around 2m tall.

↑ Bore master Ben Rogers makes it look easy. (Oliver Edwards)

I may not have been upright for very long, but I've been well and truly bitten by the bore and I'm absolutely fizzing with adrenaline. While we stash our boards in the bushes and run up the road to get the vehicles, I can't stop babbling, and start formulating plans to return. First though, I promise to polish my general surfing skills. And before that, I've arranged to meet Ben and some more of the Muddy Brothers at their favoured watering hole, located where the Stroudwater meets the Gloucester to Sharpness Canal.

SEVERN LEGENDS I've been chatting to the guy sitting next to Ben in the Stables Café at Saul Junction for a good 15 minutes before realising I'm talking to river royalty. A railway engineer by trade, Steve King holds the record for surfing the Severn bore, having ridden the river wave for an extraordinary 9¼ miles (just shy of 15km) in a legendary run that happened on a misty March day in 2006, and was serendipitously recorded.

Steve grew up on the banks of the Severn – his grandparents used to operate a ferry service across the river. One of the two main pioneers of the pursuit, along with a guy called Dave Lawson, he has been boarding the bore since 1981, and has an intimate knowledge of where you need to be at any point in order to keep momentum. Because catching the wave is only the beginning; once you're up and going, it takes technical skill and local nous to stay on it, as the shape, width and depth of the river changes, affecting the height of the swell as it sidles around broad bends and surges through tight straights. It demands real endurance too – Steve's record run lasted one hour and 17 minutes.

↑ Ben Rogers, with one of the river-specific boards he crafts, and Steve King, who holds the record for surfing the Severn bore for over 9 miles (Patrick Kinsella)

'I had to swap sides around 15 times,' he tells me. 'You need to know where to put yourself – I was constantly looking around and ahead of me to see what the water was doing, and what was coming up ahead.'

Steve's 15km epic was an exceptional run, and the fact it was captured and measured by a photographer and boat pilot who were there to document the antics of a very different surfing celeb, visiting Californian shortboarder Jon Rose, is even more amazing. Rose had engaged Steve as a local expert, and he was catching the wave for short periods at different places, hopping on and off the boat in between rides, while his guide simply stayed on the swell the whole way.

ESSENTIALS

GETTING STARTED To find out when the wave will run, and how large it will be, check the calendar on the informative website ✎ severn-bore.co.uk, which indicates the size with a star system (five starts being the biggest). Popular put-in places include Epney and Arlingham on the east side, and Newnham, the Severn Bore pub and the Denny on the west bank, but the bore wave behaves in different ways depending on a range of factors. Talk to locals and listen to their advice.

SPECIAL CONSIDERATIONS The Muddy Brothers and other regular Severn bore surfers are a welcoming lot, and I saw no sign of the kind of protective localism you can encounter at some surf breaks, but you do need to be considerate of others when you're on the wave, especially around the equinoxes, when it can be really busy. Kayaks can easily get spun broadside, when they will potentially take out several surfers, so paddlers need to be as competent as they are confident, and smaller boats are best. Likewise, people should park sensibly and safely, and not encroach on local people's property just to get a little closer to the river. Some of the best put-in spots require a little bit of a hike in.

Before getting in the water, plan your exit strategy. Look at where you can get out of the river in order to return to where your vehicle is. Be mindful of overhanging trees (remember the water level will rise with the wave) and other potentially dangerous obstacles. Choose a safe spot rather than a quick spot to get out. Good surfers might find themselves 1.5km or more upstream, and the current does not change direction for ages after the bore has gone through. Always get out on the same bank as you launched from, otherwise you could face a massive walk out, or a very long wait until it's safe to cross over again – because the water can be extremely turbulent for some time after the wave.

KIT BAG Most people surf longboards on the river. Extra volume and buoyancy is ideal, because of the water's low salinity. Ben from Leaf Longboards (✎facebook.com/LeafLongboards) produces boards specifically designed for bore surfing, with more float

These days, Steve is content with rides of 2 or 3km, but that is still a huge distance to cover on a board. He has also surfed numerous other bore rivers around the world, from France to India and Brazil. 'I never surf in the sea,' he says, grinning. 'I like rivers.' I tell him that I'm a convert, and that I'll definitely be back to surf the bore again. 'Let me know when you're coming,' he replies, generously. 'You can camp in my field.'

It's hard to imagine this happening elsewhere – a rank outsider, and a total rookie at that, rocking up to a premium surf break and being so warmly received by local legends. It's almost overwhelming. But mud is thicker than saltwater, clearly – these guys are living proof of that – and I can't wait for the next full moon.

than usual. Because river boards need to be better at going straight, rather than carving left or right, you don't require much rail or rocker.

Besides the board, you need a decent wetsuit, and neoprene booties and gloves in the colder months (remember, you'll need to walk back to your start point). Some surfers wear whitewater kayaking helmets to protect their heads from collisions with boards, boats, debris and rocks.

GETTING THERE Take the M5 towards Gloucester. For west bank put-ins, cross the Severn Bridge via the M48, then go right along the A48 towards Newnham. The A38 runs east of the river, but you'll need to use backroads to reach put-in points. Look out for vehicles carrying surfboards and kayaks.

PLACES TO STAY There are multiple B&Bs, hotels and holiday lets around Gloucester and along both banks of the Severn, but an ideally situated camping spot is **The Anchorage** (theanchorage.site), right on the riverbank by Bullo Pill, just south of Newnham on the west side.

ELSEWHERE Besides the Severn, there are several surfable bore waves on other rivers in the UK, including the Trent, the Dee and the River Kent as it runs past Arnside in Morecambe Bay (always research local conditions). Overseas, famous bore waves occur on waterways including the Dordogne and Garonne rivers in Bordeaux, France; the Hooghly River in West Bengal, where the wave is known as the 'Baan' (after the autobahn, because of how fast it moves); the Amazon in Brazil; the Petitcodiac in New Brunswick, Canada; and on the Turnagain Arm near Anchorage in Alaska.

EXTRA RESOURCES *The Severn Bore*, by Fred Rowbotham, is still considered the ultimate book to read if you want to understand the extraordinary natural phenomenon that creates the wave. severn-bore.co.uk is an excellent digital resource.

14 MOUNTAINBOARDING

WHERE	Maisemore, near Gloucester, Gloucestershire
SKILL LEVEL	Mountainboarders use similar skills to snowboarders and skateboarders, but you don't need to be an expert at either to have a go, and there are some differences in the techniques employed. At a beginner level anyone can try mountainboarding. A good sense of balance and a reasonable level of fitness is useful, especially when attempting longer runs, but you really only require a positive attitude.
RISK FACTOR	As with any land-based board sport, the possibility of crashing is always a factor, whether it's from a wipeout during a turn or trick, or a collision with an object or another boarder. Minor scrapes and bruises are the most common injuries, but mountainboarding typically takes place on grass and dirt, which is more forgiving than concrete. Head protection should be worn at all times to avert the risk of a more serious incident, especially when boarding at speed or attempting any sort of jump or trick. Knee and elbow pads are a good idea, as are wrist protectors.

In a quiet, bucolic corner of Gloucestershire, amid a patchwork of rolling green hills, lies an activity centre dedicated to a niche adventure sport that has been threatening to break through for years. Mountainboarding, or dirtboarding as it's sometimes known, is most easily described as snowboarding on wheels, with icy slopes substituted for grassy hills, dirt tracks and rough trails. Comparisons with skating are inevitable too, since the boards do look like oversize longboards, with chunky all-terrain wheels and a bit of extra bounce in the trucks (the baseplate, hanger and axle system that attaches the wheels to the board and allows you to steer). But mountainboarding also shares crossover skills and attributes with aquatic board sports such as surfing and wakeboarding.

People take up mountainboarding for all sorts of reasons. For snowboarders, it offers the chance to keep their carving skills sharp all year round, as they can hit the slopes on a mountainboard in the green season just as often as they can strap on a snowboard in the cold white-weather months, and keep practising their tricks and turns. For surfers not lucky enough to live near the ocean, the attraction is similar; using a mountainboard is a brilliant way to work on your balance – you are simply swapping swell for gravity as the means of propulsion. Skateboarders who park their little wheels to try the chunky tyres and longer base of a mountainboard are perhaps driven by a different desire – chasing the same sense of freedom road cyclists and runners experience when they first trade tarmac for backcountry trails, and take their hard-earned skills into a wilder setting.

BOARDING SCHOOL

I'm no powderhound, but whenever I have been lucky enough to hit the snowy slopes, my weapon of choice has always been a board rather than skis. I've had

← Getting some serious airtime on a mountainboard (Richard Humphrey Photography)

the odd lesson over the years and I'm able to stay vaguely vertical on most green, blue and even the odd red run. I have taken the occasional wrong turn from the lift and mistakenly ended up on a few blacks – including one particularly hair-raising, nerve-rattling experience on the famously ferocious slopes of the Eiger, the ogre of the Bernese Oberland – but so far I've escaped with just a few bruises to my posterior and pride.

I've long wanted to spend some time perfecting my technique and improving my feel for the sport, but living in the southwest of England and lacking the resources to jet off to the Alps every winter, I just don't experience enough snow time to get really good on a board. At least that's the excuse I've been using for as long as I can remember, but as it turns out I have been ignoring a resource that's virtually right on my doorstep. Because just up the M5, close to the border with Wales and less than a 2-hour drive from my house, is a place called Bugsboarding, which is Britain's premier mountainboarding centre, and the perfect place to shape and sharpen your board-riding skills.

Not that mountainboarding is merely a dry-season substitute for snowboarding. Far more than that, it's an off-road and very exciting form of skateboarding – one that you can take up when you're well beyond your teenage years and not feel like a complete tool. But it has also evolved into a defined sport in its own right, and one that can be enjoyed year round, in a massive variety of locations. However, the bloodline of the pursuit, and the design of the equipment, can definitely be traced directly back to frustrations born from the seasonal nature of snowboarding, the unreliability of winter conditions in many places, and the desire of boarders to keep riding when there's no snow to glide across.

SKATE MINDS

As with many modern pursuits, there's plenty of debate about the beginnings of mountainboarding. Several websites purporting to tell the history of the sport claim it was invented in the early 1900s by a mysterious 'James Stanley', after he arrived at the Matterhorn intending to go snowboarding, only to find the slopes bereft of slippery white stuff, and proceeded to attach wheels to his board instead. I don't know whether there's any truth in this story whatsoever – there doesn't seem to be any solid evidence to support it – but the dates are definitely spurious, since snowboarding itself wasn't a thing until the 1960s. But even the more verifiable versions of the mountainboarding backstory are almost as unbelievable as this apparently apocryphal origin tale.

According to the folklore that swirls around the sport, the very first recorded mountainboarding run happened in the summer of 1978, when an American called Mike Motta rode his Franklin skateboard down a tobogganing hill known as Seven Bumps in Malden, Massachusetts, for a $1 bet. As the story

goes, Mike only made it halfway down the run, and the bet was never paid out. But from this decidedly inauspicious start, an exciting new outdoor pursuit did eventually evolve.

An 'All Terrain Dirtboard' was reportedly patented in 1989 by Supercruiser Inc., a company owned by visionary filmmaker Morton Heilig, who pioneered the idea of virtual reality (VR). But the term 'mountainboarding' was popularised by a guy called Jason Lee, who played a much more feet-on role in the development of the sport as it exists today, with riders using dedicated boards designed specifically to go off road.

Weirdly, just as mountain biking was invented simultaneously in several different countries at around the same time, with innovators using improvised shock absorbers and adapting frames and tyres for off-road riding, so the concept of mountainboarding appears to have occurred to a trio of entirely separate people, based on three different continents, during the same year: 1992.

Even more bizarrely, the British chapter of this story centrally involves celebrity vet and TV presenter Joe Inglis, who – when he's not giving out advice to pet owners on *The One Show* or *Good Morning Britain* or acting as *Blue Peter*'s resident vet – is a highly accomplished skier, surfer and boarder (and a one-time UK Mountainboarding Champion). In the early 1990s, along with a friend called Jim Aveline and brothers Dave and Pete Tatham, Inglis began working on a prototype of a snowboard with wheels that could be ridden along rough downhill tracks and hillsides, and in 1992 they launched the 'noSno'. Their design featured a truck system that allowed the rider to steer the board and travel at pretty high speeds while remaining stable, and they even introduced the concept of a hand-operated hydraulic disc brake.

Almost simultaneously, in the United States, snowboarding buddies Jason Lee, Patrick McConnell and Joel Lee, fresh from a 1992 winter season at Heavenly Mountain in northern California, started their own quest to develop a board that could be used on mountain trails in the green season. Within a year they had invented the 'frame board', which featured rudimentary foot bindings and also had a truck design with springs that enabled the rider to steer and carve, and Jason Lee had coined the term 'mountainboarding'.

Meanwhile, thousands of kilometres away in Australia, a frustrated surfer came up with a remarkably similar concept, albeit for very different reasons. John Milne's contraption was a board with three wheels, which he developed for use when the waves weren't coming to the party. Like a surfboard and a skateboard, it had no bindings and the rider had to steer by positioning their body and weight in a certain way.

If necessity is the mother of invention, then – to me – this strange tale of coincidental but seemingly unconnected creation points pretty clearly to the need for an off-road board sport that isn't reliant on increasingly unreliable winters. So, why is mountainboarding still such a niche activity that most people seem to be completely unaware of? Surely there should be mountainboarders on hillsides and trails all over the place during the green season. To find out more, I took a long-overdue visit to Bugsboarding to have bash at it myself.

GETTING THE BUG

Crossing the River Severn, I drive deep into the folding green hills of Gloucestershire, entering the verdant valley region that stretches between a trio of designated AONBs (Areas of Outstanding Natural Beauty): the Cotswolds, the Malvern Hills and the Wye Valley. It gets pretty remote and rural once I'm beyond the village of Maisemore, but just as I start to wonder whether I've taken a wrong turn, the distinctive sign for Bugsboarding looms to my left. I follow the waymarkers, passing through a sprawling ranch-style farm, until I get to the UK's top mountainboard centre, which occupies a huge hillside with rails, jumps, tracks and all sorts of alarmingly adrenaline-orientated architecture built all over it. Here I'm greeted by Buggs himself, along with his wife and wingwoman Nina and a mad ball of effervescent energy called Freya – a friendly little dog of entirely undeterminable origin.

↑ Buggs setting up the boards (Patrick Kinsella)

Buggs is a farmer by calling, but over two decades ago he was convinced by AJ Watkins, an old school friend and co-founder of Bugsboarding, to convert part of his expansive property into a mountainboarding centre. The partnership is perfect – AJ rode mountainboards at an elite level for many years, and works closely with Maxtrack, the company that distributes MBS mountainboards (one of the sport's leading brands) in Europe. He set up and still runs the MBS Pro Rider team, and many of Britain's best board athletes use the facilities here to train. If you come along for a lesson, there's even a chance that a legend of the sport might end up teaching you – the Bugsboarding team includes Joe Dickson, one of the UK's top riders and a British Elite Freestyle Champion. As Buggs says: 'There

WHILE YOU'RE THERE...

Although the Bugsboarding centre has been built with board riders most prominently in mind, Buggs and Nina also welcome mountain bikers to the site, where they can test their skills on the cross track and safely practise jumps over the Big G Airbag. Cyclists need to bring their own bikes, but the centre does also hire out grass sledges, on which you can bomb down the hill at exhilarating speeds in any weather, and dirt scooters, which are easier to master than mountainboards and brilliant fun to ride down the boardercross track in particular. Mountainboards are continuing to evolve, and recently Bugsboarding hosted an e-boarding event.

↑ The Bugsboarding trailer (Patrick Kinsella)

aren't many places around where you can be a complete and utter beginner, and be learning how to do a sport just metres away from where a world champion is perfecting their skills. But that's exactly what happens here.'

The varied gradient of the hill is ideal, with gently sloping sections for newer riders and steeper parts for those that know what they're doing. Beyond the learners' area there is a 400m-long, purpose-made technical boardercross race course, which runs down the back of the hill and features multiple steep-sided bends and berms, for use during training and when there are competitions taking place, which is regularly during the season. All down the hill there are ramps and jumps of various sizes, and one of the most eye-catching features is the 'Big G Airbag', named after a friend of the centre called George, and used by some of the more experienced riders to practise their big jumps and most impressive aerial moves.

At the very heart of the centre, though, is the main slopestyle course, which was built by AJ, Buggs and former World Champion Leon Robbins, and is rated among the best on the planet for mountainboarding. It offers riders the choice of multiple different lines and boasts features ranging from 7.6m tabletops to kinked rails and quarterpipes. This is where the MBS Pro Team hone their skills, and the resulting visuals are so impressive it has been used in lots of large-scale photoshoots and adverts.

ON A ROLL After showing me around the course and talking me through the history of the centre, Buggs opens up the humongous HGV trailer that stands loud and proud at the top of the hill. In complete contrast to the picturesque pastoral surrounds, this trailer is covered in colourful urban-style graffiti, and right next to it is the Bug Shack, a café-style hangout where spectators can sip hot and cold drinks while watching riders doing their thing on the courses and ramps outside. I'm here on a weekday towards the end of the season, but during summer weekends Bugsboarding buzzes with riders racing down the slopestyle and boardercross courses, and flying through the air while practising tricks on the ramps and rails. Today, though, I have the place (and Buggs' expertise) all to myself.

Inside the trailer there's a treasure-trove of mountainboarding booty, from hundreds of boards to spare trucks, helmets, safety gear and other paraphernalia. Buggs gets a couple of boards off the racks and talks me through the various features as he sets them up. The wheels are larger than I expected, and they're mounted on trucks positioned much further forward than on a skateboard. They can also be used with several different pneumatic tyres, according to the terrain you're intending to roll over – ranging from slick road tyres for travelling fast on concrete, to much chunkier 9in freeride tyres for landing tricks and super-grippy 8in T3 tyres with mega-knobbly tread for tackling rougher tracks.

Like me, Buggs rides goofy – with his right foot forward, closer to the nose (front) of the board, and his left foot further towards the tail (back), controlling most of the steering. I'm not generally left-footed, but I am left-handed and there seems to be a correlation between being a lefty and riding with a goofy stance. As with snowboarding, there's no pronounced pros or cons to being goofy or regular, so long as your board is set up correctly. The bindings are similar to the ones you find on a snowboard – you just slide your feet into the hoops and tighten them up with a ratchet system – but you don't require boots as warm, chunky or rigid as a snowboarding boot, and most riders don't strap in anywhere near as tightly as they would on ice and snow, because you need a little more movement in your feet to work with the steering.

Once I'm padded up, with my lid on, Buggs begins to take me through the basics. Many of the main principles are the same as snowboarding, but with big wheels attached to the board your centre of gravity is a bit higher and of course you don't use the edge of the board to carve or slide when turning, slowing down or stopping – instead, turning techniques are more akin to those used when skating a longboard, and to stop completely you have to pull a big power slide, grabbing the edge of the board and using your weight to lean into the hill. When he's done explaining, Buggs bounces his board until the nose is facing downhill and sets off, weaving a broad S shape down to the bottom, chased all the way by the irrepressible Freya. I follow suit, and I'm delighted to make it most of the way down before over-egging a turn and ending up on my backside. Getting up again without undoing the bindings and taking your feet out is always a good abdominal workout, but you can use the gradient to help.

↑ Buggs demonstrating on the beginner slope (Patrick Kinsella)

While there is no lift at the centre, there is a pick-up truck waiting for us at the bottom, with a custom-made rail to hang our boards on, and I spend the rest of the afternoon shooting different lines on the hill and then shuttling back up to the top again. Soon enough, one of Buggs's buddies arrives with his young son, who proceeds to show me how it's done when it comes to tackling some of the small jumps. I'm happy to leave the bigger ramps to the experts, but getting to grips with the friendlier features of the slopestyle course is great fun, and I put in a couple of runs on the boardercross course too, on a board and then a dirt scooter.

Big jumps and aerial tricks are never going to be my thing – I'm far too old and fragile for those sorts of shenanigans – but as I get more confident and my turns get tighter and more controlled, I start dreaming about taking a mountainboard on longer stretches of downhill trail. This is definitely where I see the future of the sport, especially as average temperatures continue to rise year after year, and downhill resorts get less natural snow. Mountain biking in the green season has transformed the fortunes of many alpine-style resorts in places on the frontline of climate change, like Australia, where the lifts now run all year round, instead of for just a few months, and even famous winter destinations like Whistler concentrate as much on wheels as they do skis and snowboards these days.

I think of the wild trails around my local area that I could explore on a mountainboard and find myself making enquiries about the cost of a rig. Surely there's room for one more set of small(ish) wheels in the garage? My wife probably won't even notice. Hmmm, perhaps trying this new sport was more dangerous than I thought…

↑ A skilled mountainboarder takes a turn on the downhill track (Richard Humphrey Photography)

ESSENTIALS

GETTING STARTED Bugsboarding is located just outside Maisemore, near Gloucester (♥ GL2 8HP). The season runs April–October, and during these months the centre is open Saturdays, Sundays and school holiday from 11.00 to 17.00 (⊘ bugsboarding.co.uk).

SPECIAL CONSIDERATIONS Mountainboarding is a brilliant all-family activity, as is dirt scooting and grass sledging, so consider bringing the whole gang along to try something new.

KIT BAG Although you will be wearing a helmet, knee and elbow pads and wrist protectors, it's worth pulling on a pair of hard-wearing trousers and a long-sleeve top to give yourself a little bit more cover in the event of a spill. Footwear needs to be reasonably substantial (don't turn up in flip-flops or sandals), but you don't need a chunky boot with the kind of thermal protection that a snowboarding boot boasts – trainers or lightweight boots are fine. If you get hooked, all the gear you need to go mountainboarding independently (including boards) is available for sale at Bugsboarding.

GETTING THERE To drive to Bugsboarding, head towards Cheltenham on the M5, take the turning for Gloucester and follow the A417 across the River Severn; pass through the village of Maisemore and keep going until you see a sign for the mountainboard centre on your left, opposite a lay-by. The closest train station is in Gloucester, which is 6km from Bugsboarding.

PLACES TO STAY Country camping and caravan spots are available in the fields adjacent to the riding area at the Bugsboarding centre throughout the summer, with electric hook-ups an option and great views all round. Combining a night or two camping with a couple of days' board hire is a very economical way of maximising your time.

ELSEWHERE Besides Bugsboarding, mountainboarding tuition and board hire can be enjoyed at several other locations around the UK, including **The Edge Adventure** in Much Wenlock, Shropshire (⊘ theedgeadventure.co.uk) and the **Mountainboarding and Gravity Centre** on the Gower Peninsula, south Wales (⊘ brdsports.co.uk).

EXTRA RESOURCES

The **All Terrain Boarding Association** is the national governing body for mountainboarding in the UK ⊘ atbauk.org

⊘ mountainboarder.com

↑ Bugsboarding caters for beginners through to boardmasters (Christoph Riddle/S)

15 CANYONING & GORGE SCRAMBLING

WHERE	Bannau Brycheiniog/Brecon Beacons National Park, Wales; the Lake District National Park, Cumbria
SKILL LEVEL	Gorge scrambling is accessible to everyone with average fitness levels when done with a professional guide. Canyoning is another level up; it's more technical, involving the use of ropes, harnesses, helmets and other gear typically associated with rock climbing and water sports. Canyoning routes almost invariably involve abseils/rappels, ropework, jumps, slides, swims and downclimbs. Again, done with a professional guide, canyoning can be enjoyed by anyone with reasonable fitness, if they're confident with heights. To do either gorge scrambling or canyoning independently, however, you require extensive experience, technical climbing skills and a good knowledge of how to negotiate fast-moving water, and need to be capable of performing risk analysis in a dynamic environment where water depth changes rapidly.
RISK FACTOR	Under the supervision of a professional guide, the risks involved in both gorge scrambling and canyoning are carefully managed. Independent exploration of a canyon or gorge should only be done by people who are experienced and knowledgeable about the route being undertaken, and have all the right equipment in good working order. Routes vary enormously in terms of difficulty and technicality, with risk levels rising rapidly along with the grades – especially in certain circumstances – up to and including danger of death. Jumps are always optional, but these pursuits take place in dynamic terrain where water levels and flow rates are constantly changing, and new obstacles can be encountered each time the route is undertaken. Risks include falling, hitting the floor or submerged objects when jumping, getting caught in flash floods, hypothermia, rockfall, concussion and drowning.

Water is very good at finding the fastest and most exciting route down any given mountain, hillside, cliff or crag, and following high-flowing streams as they plunge over drops and rush through narrow gaps has spawned an especially exciting adventure sport. It goes by different names depending on where in the world you are – in the United States they call it cayoneering, in South Africa they say kloofing, while in Britain, continental Europe, Australia and New Zealand it's known as canyoning. At entry level – where anchored ropes, technical downclimbs and abseils are not required to shoot the route – the pursuit can be referred to as gorge scrambling. But it should not be confused with ghyll scrambling (page 226), which specifically involves going up a watercourse, against the direction of flow, usually in Cumbria. Canyoning always

← Ivy leaping from Loonies Weir high jump (Patrick Kinsella)

involves descending routes, using ropes and other equipment, while gorge scrambling can be done in either direction.

However you refer to it – and we're sticking to gorge scrambling and canyoning for the purposes of this chapter – the activity involves starting at the top of a water-carved ravine and following the flow, leaping from ledges into plunge pools, swimming across stretches of water, downclimbing crags, sliding and scrambling over rocks, and abseiling beside (and sometimes within) waterfalls as you go.

Canyoning could be described as a hybrid sport, using a mixture of skills employed in other outdoor pursuits. You can envisage it as gravity-assisted wild swimming, or whitewater kayaking without the boat, or perhaps semi-aquatic scrambling, with some rock climbing and rappelling thrown in for good measure. But really it has evolved into a very distinct activity in its own right, with defined grading systems and a set of self-imposed rules to protect both the participants' safety and the environment it takes place in. A culture and community has grown around it, with governing bodies set up to encourage good practice and promote the sharing of information about canyoning routes, and specific equipment developed to make the experience safer and more enjoyable.

On all levels, the activity is challenging, thrilling, occasionally chilling, and delivers a completely unique experience every time you head out – or so I've been told by keen canyoners. To find out for myself I took a trip to south Wales to join a guided experience through one of the most extraordinary hydraulically hewn aquascapes in the country: the canyons, gorges and waterways of the Brecon Beacons, now officially named Bannau Brycheiniog.

CHASING WATERFALLS

Not for nothing is the southwest corner of Bannau Brycheiniog/Brecon Beacons National Park known as Waterfall Country. In this sensational spot – which has the biggest concentration of cascades and caves in Wales – the Mellte, Hepste, Pyrddin and Nedd-fechan rivers rush through gorgeous gorges and charge over multiple majestic waterfalls before splicing together to form the River Neath. There are well-signed trails leading to the most dramatic drops, including the famous Four Waterfalls Walk, which takes amblers to a quadruplet of cascades: Sgwd Clun-Gwyn, Sgwd Isaf Clun-Gwyn, Sgwd y Pannwr and Sgwd-yr-Eira. You can walk right behind the veil of tumbling water at Sgwd-yr-Eira ('fall of snow' in Welsh), which has made it an extremely popular place to visit. In fact, unless you arrive really early, or come out of season (when the falls are most energetic), the car parks and paths around here can get seriously congested.

But there is an entirely different way to explore Waterfall Country – one that allows you to see it from liquid level and literally immerse yourself in the elements that have created this stunning terrain, while staying away from the madding crowds. You can get a wetsuit on and do a canyoning trip. Although, actually, while many guiding companies do describe their offerings as 'canyoning adventures', because the use of ropes is not permitted in the ravines of Waterfall Country, they are more like gorge-scrambling experiences. But gorge scrambling – being a kind of canyoning-lite – is the ideal introduction to the sport, and since I'm going into this one with my teenage daughter by my side, it feels like the perfect starting point.

We meet Rob, an Adventures Wales guide, in a car park near Pontneddfechan, beneath the iconic limestone edifice known as Dinas Rock, a popular spot for sports climbers and gorge explorers alike. Besides Ivy and me, there's a family of four on the trip – a mum and dad, with two teenage kids. Rob gives the main briefing in the car park, as gathering in groups on the waterside is not good for the sensitive flora that clings to the banks. He lets us know what we've signed up for today, which is a circular gorge-scrambling adventure along two rivers, a route graded as 2C G II in the ACA system used in the UK, which translates as 'Basic canyoning, with waterfalls and deep pools, suitable for general audiences and doable in half a day'. Rob also explains how best to jump into plunge pools from height (feet first, legs closed, arms crossed over the front of your body – not holding your nose, unless you fancy punching yourself in the head when you hit the water) and how to safely deal with swift-moving water: float on your back, with your feet pointing downstream, so they meet any rocks or obstacles first, rather than your head.

GRADES & COURSES

In the UK, canyons are usually graded according to the ACA (American Canyoneering Association) system, which gives a number first, describing the technical difficulty of the route, followed by letters depicting the average aquatic volume and risk factor, with the latter going up to XX 'Double Extreme, with risk to life'. The French grading system (FFME) is also often used; this begins with an indication of the vertical difficulty of the route (V1 being easy, V7 extremely technical) followed by an assessment of the aquatic difficulty (A1 to A7), the commitment level (I being quick and easy, VI being hard and long) and the quality of the experience (one to four stars).

To advance your capability and experience, consider taking a UK Canyoning Association (UKCA ⊘ ukcanyoning.org) course, which will equip you with the knowledge and skills required to explore gorges and canyons independently. Reputable providers include **Vertical Skills** (⊘ vertical-skills.co.uk), which conducts in-depth multi-day courses, workshops and assessments in Yorkshire and Cumbria, training people how to safely tackle technical canyons and swiftwater, and teaching them skills including rope handling, knots, rigging, setting anchors and abseiling. You can also do a Canyoneer Initiation (CAI) course while having an exciting canyoning experience with Lakes-based **Mountain Rat Adventures** (⊘ mountainratadventures.co.uk/canyoneer-initiation).

After climbing into our 5mm wetsuits, donning a helmet and PFD (personal flotation device), we walk beneath Dinas Rock to the banks of Afon Mellte. Here Rob introduces us to 'the shocker', which basically involves plunging into the river's icy embrace in order to get some water into our wetsuits, so our body heat can start to warm it up. This is just a little leap, so we can do it in whatever style we choose. Rob leads with a sketchy somersault and we follow with an array of graceless star jumps, bombs and bounds. It's August and the day is warm, but this water has come straight down off the Beacons, and it still has the chill of the hills.

We swim, paddle, clamber, amble and scramble down the river, passing beneath a bridge, until we meet the confluence with Afon Sychryd. Here we bust a left and go upstream for a while, pausing at waterfalls that gradually grow in height, to leap into plunge pools and slide down chutes on the less vertical cascades. At one waterfall, Rob lies in a gap in the rocks, so the water builds up behind him, and then suddenly releases it to send us one by one zooming down the sluice with extra velocity. In between the cascades, we swim sections of still water, or float on our backs staring up through the verdant foliage to the bright blue sky.

Although the rivers are much less trafficked than the trails, gorge scrambling has become a very popular pursuit in Waterfall Country, and a code of conduct has been agreed between activity providers and custodians of the land and wildlife. Rob explains how it's important we stay in the water as much as possible, to avoid treading on the fragile flora on the exposed boulders and banks. The riverside is densely populated with trees, which throw dappled shade on the clear water in the pools between the falls. Incredibly, the whole valley was once heavily industrialised, with silica mines and gunpowder works along the banks. This all stopped after World War I and, while there are lots of reminders of the industries that once dominated (and contaminated) the river, nature has almost entirely taken back control, smothering the remnant metal and concrete structures built and then abandoned by humans.

As the gorge walls get steeper and craggier, we pass a famous climbing route called Mortal Kombat and the jumps grow progressively bigger. However, the biggest of all lies in wait back on the waterway where we first got wet. After scrambling around a right-hand bend, swimming across a lovely canyon lagoon and enjoying several exciting leaps from a multi-tiered cascade called Sychryd Waterfall, we exit the smaller river and hike over the hill. The day has well and truly warmed up by now, and we sweat in our wetsuits while walking along the forest footpath. I for one have built up an appetite too. Fortunately, there are blackberries aplenty to scrump along the way, and Rob points out some sorrel to add to our foraging feast.

Our destination is Loonies Weir, where the concrete remains of an old gunpowder works on the banks of Afon Mellte, above a plunge pool, offer gorge

↑ It's possible to walk behind the cascade of Sgwd-yr-Eira waterfall (Billy Stock/S) ← A group gorge scrambling in Bannau Brycheiniog/Brecon Beacons National Park (Adventures Wales)

scramblers the choice of two launch pads: a mid-height hop or an 8m-plus jump from the very top. Everyone in the group has a crack at the smaller option, and then Rob asks for volunteers to go first off the big one. Ivy's hand shoots up in the air, and before long she joins it, plummeting through the blue sky into the clear water below. The other teenagers won't be outdone, and they're quick to follow in her aerial footsteps, and then I take the plunge too. The leap floods our systems with adrenaline, and soon the four of us are competing with one another to see who can do the most impressive, or daft, jump, while remembering Rob's earlier advice to always land feet first – ideally with your legs together, lest your voice go up an octave or two. I do alright with this, until getting overexcited and ill-advisedly attempting a somersault, which ends in a face flop and cheeks that are bright red from the force of the impact as much as my embarrassment. But at least it gives Ivy a good laugh.

Owing to sensitive environmental concerns along Afon Mellte, and in the interests of keeping landowners onside, we have to climb back over the hill to return to the car park, instead of following the river. While it's frustrating not to be able to complete a neater loop route, it's extremely important to be mindful and respect the agreements that are in place around gorge scrambling and canyoning, because the pursuit has faced plenty of negativity in the past, especially in areas like this where it is very popular, and the last thing any of us wants is for it to be prohibited. And anyway, it transpires I missed loads of big blackberries on the walk in.

GRAND CANYONING

Gorge scrambling in Waterfall Country is a brilliant introduction to the sport, but I'm keen to have a crack at canyoning proper and for that I look further north, where ghylls, thrills, cascades and gorges aplenty wait to be explored in the water-sculpted landscape of the Lake District. Here, in another seemingly remote car park that gets surprisingly busy, I meet a second canyoning guide, also called Rob. (Apparently some people involved in the sport have different names, I just haven't met them yet.)

The thing about real canyoning is that it's always done in alliance with gravity, and to descend a ravine, you first have to climb to the put-in point. From Hardknott Pass car park, we begin with an hour's uphill hike, while wearing wetsuits – to the amusement of walkers we pass en route. Rob is thinking about water levels and as soon we get a visual on the ghyll (stream) we're planning to descend, he assesses the flow. These calculations are crucial. If there's too much juice in the sluice, the waterfall we'll encounter halfway down will be too feisty to abseil, but if there's not enough water then some plunge pools won't be deep enough for us to jump into. As we cross the embryonic River Esk via a delightful

→ Pat abseils through a waterfall while canyoning in the Lake District (Henry Iddon)

dry-stone bridge, Rob grins. Conditions are perfect for our planned route, which has a similar technical rating to Afon Sychryd/Afon Mellte (2C G III), but is longer, with some optional abseils and larger jumps.

The steepest part of the climb awaits, and by the time we reach the put-in, I'm virtually steaming. Rob assures me I won't be overheating for long, and he's not wrong. A narrow cleft in a split rock marks our intended entry point into a fold in the hillside carved over millennia by a mountain stream that, further down, will become the real river. The chasm looks cold, and deep, and hectic – with water cacophonously cascading into it. There's more kit to put on before we take the plunge. Rob has climbing harnesses designed specifically for canyoning, which don't absorb water, and we each step into one of these before donning a PFD to help with buoyancy (handy for some of the bigger jumps, because you don't go as deep). As with any sport that takes place around swift water, defensive swimming techniques are an important part of canyoning. The biggest priority is head protection – helmets are always worn and you lead with your feet, whether you're jumping or floating.

Rob sets off. I squeeze through the narrow portal in the rock behind him and drop into a thigh-deep stream on the other side. It's a shock. This water flows straight off the flanks of Scafell Pike – England's highest mountain, which has been peering down quizzically at us during our approach – and the sun hasn't touched it this morning. A short scramble starts the blood flowing again, and then it's time to get properly submerged. The first jump is a gentle introduction to what lies ahead, and it allows Rob to remind me how to leap into rockpools without breaking myself. Elbows need to be tucked in tight to avoid collisions and knees should be slightly bent, to absorb the impact if you hit the bottom or, worse, land on a submerged boulder. It's good advice. While our first jump isn't big – around 2.5m– it's into a reasonably shallow pool and my feet do sense the stony bottom.

The second jump, which we have to use a rope to access, is higher and more 'technical'. That essentially means that if you don't land in the right spot (between the submerged rocks in the pool below, rather than on them) then, technically, you're in strife. Rob points out my landing zone (which is quite generous) and the areas I should definitely avoid, and I take the 5m plunge into the deep, dark water.

There's no jumping down the next section, where a waterfall with an awkward, twisty entry point charges off a 10m drop. This requires an abseil. When Rob has fixed a natural anchor and is ready with the rope, I pass it through the belay device on my harness and edge towards the torrent of water rushing through the funnelneck gap at the top of the fall. The force is terrifying – it spins me like a conker on a string and pummels the wind from my body as I drop off the lip. Halfway down, the cascade spits me out on to a dripping rock to the right, from where I drop on to a small ledge.

This is fantastic – I feel like I'm really canyoning now. I give the rope a tug and Rob follows me down, performing a face-first Aussie-style rappel (show-off), before pulling the rope through. Together we leap off the ledge into the pool below – like wetsuit-clad versions of Butch and Sundance – and continue through the canyon to the third major jump, which Rob calls Lemon's Leap. This is a big, dramatic 7m drop through foliage into a narrow pool. It looks gnarly, but the water in the landing zone is deep and rock free, and it's quite simple.

But next comes the canyon's crux move – the place where it gets a bit scary. Rob gives me a choice: the chicken run, where you clamber down the edge of the ghyll and do a straightforward jump, or the more 'exciting' option from a higher point – around 10m up – where you take a run up and launch yourself as far out as you can, in order to clear the underhanging rocks that protrude below. I eyeball the stony elbow that juts out from about 3m beneath the more elevated launch spot. It looks every bit as unyielding as you'd expect a piece of Eskdale granite to be, and certainly not the sort of surface you'd want to bounce your bum off mid flight.

There is only one choice, really, so on the top level I pace out my run up, like a nervous footballer lining up a penalty kick. Rob advises me to throw everything at my outward projection. 'It feels like you're going to hit the other side', he says,

↑ Pat leaping off the canyon's crux jump (Henry Iddon)

helpfully. 'But don't worry, you won't.' And again, he's right. Sprinting up, I launch from the wrong foot but still manage to clear the rocks and plunge into the pool. I'm not feeling the cold anymore – adrenaline is keeping me toasty.

In total, we scramble, crawl, slip, slide, jump, plunge, paddle and float our way down the Esk for four hours, pausing briefly like trolls beneath the dry-stone bridge we'd crossed earlier, before finishing at a wonderful wild-swimming hole known as Paradise. There are several leaping points into this plunge pool – including one from an overhanging bough of a tree. For the finale, we swim to the other side and climb to the loftiest launch spot of the day, a 14m bank,

ESSENTIALS

GETTING STARTED

You can experience gorge scrambling in Wales with Adventures Wales (⌛ adventureswales.co.uk), Adventure Activities Wales (⌛ adventureactivities.wales) and Seren Ventures (⌛ serenventures.com).

Reputable guiding companies leading canyoning experiences in the Lake District and Yorkshire include Mountain Rat Adventures (⌛ mountainratadventures.co.uk) and Vertical Skills (⌛ vertical-skills.co.uk).

SPECIAL CONSIDERATIONS

Recreational and commercial canyoning in the UK can attract criticism from landowners, conservation groups and even other outdoors users, so it's extremely important to respect guidelines designed to minimise the impact on flora and fauna, leave no trace on the environment, and avoid negatively affecting other people's enjoyment of the outdoors. Responsible guiding companies adhere to codes of conduct created with local authorities, landowners, and environmental and land-management agencies. Independent canyoners are asked not to park or camp in sensitive areas, to avoid canyons where companies are guiding clients at busy times, to get changed discreetly and pack out everything they take in. The placing of bolts and anchors is something that should only be done by highly experienced canyoners, and only where it's permitted. The situation is especially sensitive in Wales' Waterfall Country, where Afon Sychryd and Afon Mellte flow within Fforest Fawr UNESCO Global Geopark (⌛ fforestfawrgeopark.org.uk), a Site of Special Scientific Interest (SSSI) and a Special Area of Conservation (SAC). Here an agreement has been established between experienced providers, under the umbrella of South Wales Outdoor Activity Providers Group (SWOAPG), Brecon Beacons National Park Authority (BBNPA), Natural Resources Wales (NRW) and landowners. More information is available on the SWOAPG website (⌛ swoapg.com).

KIT BAG

Companies offering gorge scrambling and canyoning as a guided experience will supply all the requisite kit (helmet, PFD, static or semi-static ropes made from a hydrophobic fibre, climbing harness, wetsuit, etc). You will need swimwear, and it's

which I later learn is the highest cliff jump in the Lakes. The water is deep in Paradise, but clear enough for me to see the two rocks Rob is telling me to avoid. There's enough freefall time on this drop for fearsome thoughts to flicker through my mind, but I land in the sweet spot. And then go and do it again. And again.

Months later, I find myself back on this same waterway (albeit a different section) exploring ravines carved by the Esk from the perspective of a ghyll scrambler (page 226), which looks like a similar pursuit, but has its own set of rules, conventions and traditions. But for now, I'm a convert to canyoning.

wise to wear cheap shorts over the top of expensive wetsuits. Five Ten make specialist canyoning shoes, but grippy trainers are fine (open-toe sandals are not).

GETTING THERE Reach Dinas Rock car park via the A465, which runs between Hereford and Swansea. There's a train station in Merthyr Tydfil, from where buses serve Pontneddfechan.

Approach the parking point below Hardknott Pass by coming via Eskdale, leaving the M6 at junction 36 when coming from the south, or junction 40 when approaching from the north.

PLACES TO STAY A wide range of accommodation is available across Bannau Brycheiniog/the Brecon Beacons, but for something different, close to Dinas Rock, try **Waterfall Country Pods**, which offers little glamping pods in woodland near Pontneddfechan, in the Neath Valley (⊘ waterfallcountrypods.co.uk).

The National Trust's excellent **Eskdale Campsite** (⊘ nationaltrust.org.uk/holidays/eskdale-campsite-lake-district) near Boot, Holmrook, is an ideal starting point for a canyoning adventure on the Esk.

ELSEWHERE Besides Wales' Waterfall Country and the Lakes, there are excellent gorge scrambling and canyoning routes in Snowdonia (⊘ adventureactivities.wales), Yorkshire (⊘ mountainratadventures.co.uk), Devon (⊘ adventureokehampton.com) and elsewhere. See the ⊘ canyonlog.org map for more.

EXTRA RESOURCES

⊘ ukcanyoning.org

⊘ canyonlog.org

⊘ swoapg.com

⊘ waterfallcountry.wales

⊘ breconbeacons.org

16 COASTEERING

WHERE	Pembrokeshire Coast, Wales
SKILL LEVEL	Low – when done with a guide, you just need to be physically capable of swimming short distances and scrambling over rocks; jumps are optional (but fun). When done independently, more skills are required, especially in relation to risk assessment and management.
RISK FACTOR	Low–high. On a guided experience with a reputable company, the route and risks will be regularly assessed and well managed. When done independently, however, there are multiple factors to consider (tides, water depths, rips, rock and cliff condition, escape routes, weather and so on) and therefore the risk factor is much higher.

I t's not often you can pinpoint the precise place where a sport was born, but Pembrokeshire, on the extreme southwestern edge of Wales, is where the pursuit of coasteering was pushed out into the world. It may not have been conceived here – people all around the world have been independently, accidentally even, enjoying coasteering for as long as they have been exploring rocky rugged shorelines – but this is arguably where the activity was christened, and it's certainly the spot where, in the mid 1980s, someone first recognised the potential for it to become a popular commercially guided adventure. It's also rare to actually meet the person responsible for pioneering

↑ Taking the plunge from a Pembrokeshire cliff (Patrick Kinsella)

a pursuit, and I'm excited at the prospect of chatting to that aforementioned someone, but just in case you have been living in one of the few caves yet to be visited by a crew of swashbuckling coasteerers, I should start with some definitions.

The sport of coasteering sees wetsuit-wearing participants clambering and scrambling along a section of shoreline, variously climbing along cliffs, leaping from rocks into the sea, and swimming across coves and through semi-submerged caves, tunnels and arches. The focus activity area is the exciting and ever-changing intertidal zone, between the high and low tide mark. Coasteerers will typically (always if they're being guided) be wearing some safety gear – including a helmet, a PFD (personal flotation device) and footwear offering some grip and protection. But, joyously, there are no ropes required, which imbues the whole experience with a wonderful feeling of freedom. The barriers to participation (for a guided outing) are also very low. You don't need any technical rock-climbing skills or prior experience whatsoever, nor do you even have to be a particularly strong swimmer – thanks to the PFD – so it is open to almost everyone with a basic level of fitness. And yet, for those who actively like to push and petrify themselves when they're exploring the outdoors, the thrill factor can usually be dialed right up with the inclusion of some big gnarly jumps.

An outdoor activity that looks and feels super extreme, but remains accessible to almost everyone – sounds like the perfect adventure sport, right? Well that's exactly what Andy Middleton thought when he bought the Twr-y Felin Hotel in St Davids in 1986, turned it into an adventure base, launched his company (TYF) and began offering an activity he'd been enjoying for decades as a guided experience. There are plenty of arguments about the sport's true origin story, but it's fairly well accepted that Andy pioneered coasteering as a commercially led activity here on the Pembrokeshire coast. Incredibly, it took many years for other operators to start doing it, but over the last couple of decades the pursuit has exploded in popularity around Britain and well beyond, with outdoor providers seemingly leading trips around virtually every piece of pretty coastline on the map. Now I'm going back to where it all started, to meet the man who came up with the plan, and explore the craggy cliffs and surging seascape that inspired him.

LAUNCHING POINT

Andy built his company on three main pillars, the first two of which are a commitment to environmental engagement and sustainability, and a belief in the transformative power of outdoor pursuits and adventure sports. TYF, a name that sprouted from people's inability to pronounce Twr-y Felin, soon morphed into an acronym for 'To Your Future' – which imbues these values and works as everything from a post-adventure drinking toast to a mission statement and design for life.

TYF was an early embracer of zero-emission experiences – none of the company's activities involve any motorised transport, including getting clients to and from the start and finish points. Andy and his guides have taken over 200,000

people on coasteering trips with a large percentage of those never having done anything remotely similar before, and he chuckles while recounting some of the correspondence he has received over the years, including complaints from parents about the adventure setting levels of expectation in their kids they couldn't keep up with. He's visibly proud that after all those trips, taking so many inexperienced people into technical terrain and encouraging them to jump off high ledges into a wild sea, they've never had a serious injury.

The third pillar is family. TYF is a big name on the outdoor scene in Wales – the company was a founding member of the Pembrokeshire Outdoor Charter and is prominently involved in the National Coasteering Association – yet it retains the feel of a family business. A large team of guides and instructors are now employed offering all kinds of outdoor experiences, but the name Middleton runs through TYF like the writing in a stick of seaside rock. Andy's children grew up jumping in and out of the sea along this coastline and they remain heavily involved. It's his daughter Bonnie who welcomes us in to the adventure centre.

Embracing the spirit of this, my eldest daughter Ivy has been invited along to accompany me on this escapade – which should act as a litmus test for just how transformative an experience coasteering really can be. Not so long ago Ivy was my ever-enthusiastic outdoor buddy, up for anything that involved a bit of adventure but, since adolescence kicked in, that has changed dramatically – especially if the activity at hand involves getting up early. Today, however, I've managed to convince her to arise before noon on a sunny summer Saturday and shake off some of her teenage insouciance with the promise that we will be doing some proper scary jumps. The sort of frankly terrifying leaps that are being played on a loop on screens in the TYF base, where we wriggle into wetsuits.

Sid, our extremely effervescent guide, has confirmed there will be ample opportunity to get adrenaline flowing through our veins if we're willing to take on the big drops. But, true to the zero-impact ethos of the company, our coasteering trip begins with a hike from the TYF base, through the back streets of St Davids (Britain's smallest city) towards the cliffs at St Non's Bay. Ivy is horrified – less by the prospect of the walk than the thought of being seen with her old man waddling around in public, half-clad in a wetsuit. (And I don't blame her – it is quite the sight.) But, after I placate her with reassurances that the chances of us bumping into anyone she knows are slim, we join our group and set off.

With Sid, there are eight of us in the group, including a family of three from France who cheerfully admit they are straying completely out of their comfort zone. We walk out of town and past St Non's Chapel, believed to be the birthplace of St David in the 6th century, en route to the cliffs where Andy first tested the water on those very first guided coasteering trips nearly 40 years ago. He's been exploring the shoreline here from a young age, he tells me, but when this stretch

↑ Andy Middleton came up with the concept of coasteering as a guided activity (Patrick Kinsella)

← Gearing up before hitting the water (Patrick Kinsella)

SEA SIDE

The **Pembrokeshire Coast National Park** (⌀ pembrokeshirecoast.wales) is Britain's only coastal national park. It sprawls across 620km² (240 square miles) of sensational saltwater-flecked terrain, but is never more than 16km (10 miles) wide, even at its fattest point. The park boasts over 1,000km (600 miles) of public footpaths and bridleways, including the 299km (186-mile) Pembrokeshire Coast Path, which hugs the cliffs below which coasteerers can commonly be seen (and heard) exploring the intertidal zone.

PLUNGING INTO THE PAST While Andy and TYF arguably turned coasteering into the popular pursuit it is now, the activity has a long history. It has been documented since the late 19th century, when pioneering climbers such as Dr Tom Longstaff were taking on sea-level horizontal traverses at places like Baggy Point in north Devon. Alpinist Arthur Andrews, who was very active around the coast of Cornwall in the early 20th century,

↓ The picturesque Pembrokeshire Coast National Park offers a plethora of adventure opportunities (Ian Fletcher/S)

is often seen as the real father of coastal climbing and coasteering, having famously set himself the challenge of traversing the entirety of Britain's coast in the intertidal zone. Exactly how much of that he achieved is unknown, but he was certainly the first person to scale the Bosigran Ridge in Cornwall, now better known as 'Commando Ridge' because it has been used as a training ground for elite soldiers since the 1940s.

Famous expedition-length coasteering routes including the epic **Exmoor Coast Traverse** (Britain's longest climb, first done over four days in 1978 by Terry Cheek, Trevor Simpson, Graham Rogers and Robert Simmons) and the **Traverse of the Gods** at Swanage, Dorset, a difficult multi-pitch climbing adventure that finishes with a wild swim across Black Zawn, first done by John Cleare and Rusty Baillie in 1963. However, many of these historic and longer adventures involve ropework, placement of protection and Tyrolean traverses – coasteering, as it's typically understood now, involves more scrambling and free climbing (without rope or harness).

of the coast path opened in 1972, when he was 12, it was suddenly easy to get all the way along the cliffs. Not that he wanted to do that on the path – Andy was much more interested in the challenge of traversing the intertidal zone, where no two trips are ever exactly the same. With friends, he named features along the route we're about to take, and some of them, such as Babylon Bay and Jumps Bay, have stuck.

It's a bluebird day, with barely a cloud in the Celtic sky, and by the time we reach the cliff edge we're sweltering in our wetsuits and more than ready to plunge into the beckoning blue sea below. It does look quite a long way below, though, and the access route Sid seems be indicating down the drop is indistinct at first glance. Multiple groups do this journey each day, but you wouldn't guess it from here – which is quite refreshing, and gives us the feeling that we're properly exploring. After Sid's safety talk, we don our lids and start descending, gingerly picking our way down the crag, edging around rocks and passing blooming wildflowers until we reach a ledge – the launch point for the first leap of the day.

It's a relatively gentle drop of 2 or 3m, straight into a pool of gin-clear water with no submerged boulders to bash into if you get the entry point wrong – the perfect plunge point for Sid to talk us through the basics of how to jump. As he makes clear, you can do whatever sort of leap you want to – and, as confidence grows during the trip, people do perform some increasingly ambitious and amusing mid-air stunts – but the most important thing is to hit the water feet first. Ideally with your legs closed. As the launching points get higher, the consequences for getting this golden rule wrong are amplified, and face plants and partially completed star jumps are evermore painfully punished. The other big things to avoid are jumping into shallow water and hitting rocks, either on the way down or beneath the water. This sounds obvious, but the environment coasteering takes place within is extremely dynamic, with the height of the drops and the layout of the landing zone constantly changing, depending on what the moon is up to and where the tide cycle is at. And this is where having a guide with good local knowledge is absolutely invaluable.

JUMP-START Standing on the ancient terra firma of the Treginnis Peninsula – some the oldest rocks in the country – we form a line, like large lemmings, and leap one after the other into the wonderfully cool embrace of the Atlantic-fed Celtic Sea. For this initial plunge, we all perform a classic tombstoning-style jump – entering the water feet first as instructed, with hands crossed and body straight. It means you get a bit of depth and your wetsuit takes in some water, which shocks at first but warms you later. Bobbing back to the surface, we give the 'I'm okay' sign (a hand tap on the head) and swim free of the landing zone to make room for the next plummeting person.

Once we're all in the water together, Sid draws our attention to a bunch of translucent globes floating around us, each about the size of a grape. As it turns out, these are sea gooseberries, little jellyfish, and there are hundreds of them. Thankfully, they are harmless, and don't have a sting. As we hang on to a rock, rising up and down with the swell, Sid tears off a strip of green seaweed and pops it into his mouth. It's sea lettuce, he explains, encouraging us to give it a go and describing how nutritious it is. Soon another variety is added to the marine menu, pepper dulse, which is red and tastes deliciously garlicky, with a hint of heat. To my astonishment, when I look around Ivy is enthusiastically chomping on this surprise sea salad. All that excruciating time spent around the table trying to get her to eat greens… I should have just pushed her into the nearest rockpool. I'm learning lots of surprise lessons here.

And this sets the tone for the whole trip. I fully expected the thrills and spills of the jumps, and they don't disappoint, but I hadn't realised how much hands-on and educational engagement with the environment we would have, foraging for wild sea snacks, and encountering marine life. Along the way, Sid talks to us about the plants, birds, fish and marine mammals that inhabit this Celtic coastline, living among rocks that date back 600 million years. Seals are often seen sunbathing along the shore here, and lolloping around out to sea, and dolphins are not uncommon visitors, but it's actually the smaller stuff seen close-up that captures the imagination the most in a situation such as this – like the vibrancy of the seaweed and anemones, and the intricate intestinal patterns visible inside the see-through sea gooseberries and moon jellies that give them an almost alien appearance.

↑ Sid serves up some pepper dulse, straight from the rocks (Patrick Kinsella)

Lying on our backs and kicking with our feet, we float out through a narrow gap between a couple of rocks – a manoeuvre known as a zawn swim – and clamber out on to another ledge. This time Sid challenges us to plunge in and try and swim underwater to the rock opposite. With the PFD doing its job and pulling you towards the surface, it's near impossible, but eventually I manage to dive in deep enough to make it across. Ivy gives me a mid-leap thumbs up as she takes a turn, doing a bomb rather than a dive or a tombstone jump, and she pops up with a broad grin plastered across her face. The jumps keep getting higher and a tad more technical, with one requiring a run up in order to reach the landing zone, but she rises to the occasion each time, bounding off the rocks, and bobbing up to the surface beaming and buzzing with the adrenaline. In between plunges, we pause to play around in a place where the rising and falling swell has created a little standing wave that it's possible to bodysurf on briefly before you're propelled into a pool formed by rocks. These discoveries are all the more special because the conditions are only right for a short period of time, before the tide rises or falls a fraction more and the phenomenon disappears.

It's great fun while it lasts, but when we move on and enter a cave, the experience reaches a new layer of extraordinary. The doorway to this fissure in the face of the cliff feels tiny but, as Sid leads us in, the sunlight seems to follow, and the water turns turquoise around our semi-submerged bodies. It's dark inside, but shards of light pierce through the gloom like laser beams. It feels utterly surreal, as though we're in a cathedral being lit up by a celestial torch shone through stained glass. Everyone starts talking in hushed tones, and then conversation stops completely as we get deeper into the cave and darkness envelops our upper bodies altogether.

↑ Coming up for air after a jump (TYF)

It could be confronting, but instead feels calm. As we bob around in the near-luminous green water, eyes adjusting to the inky air, Sid tells a tale about Sam, one of the head guides at TYF, who had a life-affirming moment of clarity in this cave – an epiphany of sorts, where the magnificence of his surroundings almost overwhelmed him and chased away feelings of doubt he'd been experiencing about what he was doing with his life. Andy subsequently recounts the same story to me, evocatively describing it as a 'numinous experience'. When I finally meet Sam, he laughs it off as a bit of TYF folklore that has gained a life of its own. But he does finish by saying: 'It is a pretty special place, though, hey?' I can't argue with that, and Ivy was completely spellbound by this part of the trip in particular.

Finally we reach the crescendo of the coasteering experience. The biggest, baddest leap of the day, from a sheer cliff face into a deep blue hole. There are several possible launch points, and no-one is under any pressure to prove anything. As Andy says, when you're coasteering everything comes down to choice, and two people on the same trip can opt for completely different jumps. 'It's like having a green run and a black run right alongside one another,' is how he describes it. Ivy seems to know exactly what run she's on, and it isn't green. She heads straight on up to the highest ledge that Sid allows her on to, and barely hesitates before flinging herself off. I get a pang of pride, not so much because she's brave (or daft) enough to push it to the max, but because she's properly thrown herself into the whole experience, and is so obviously loving every minute of it. I've got my adventure buddy back.

And then I see her grinning face and raised eyebrows, and realise she has deliberately set the bar as high as she can, and I am going to have to jump straight off the tallest ledge too. Damn.

↑ The Pembrokeshire Coast cliffs are punctuated by secret caves (Patrick Kinsella)

ESSENTIALS

GETTING STARTED TYF (⊘ tyf.com) runs two kinds of coasteering trips all year: 'Discover' for young families (with kids aged 8–12) and 'Explore' for adults and over-13s. The Explore adventure lasts 3½ hours and you are in the water for 2 hours.

SPECIAL CONSIDERATIONS While coasteering can be enjoyed almost anywhere with a rocky coastline, it's vitally important that you don't jump blindly into water where the depth is unknown (and remember it will change by the hour, according to the tide, so a jump that's safe one day will not necessarily be safe the next, or even later on the same day). **Tombstoning** – where people leap into the sea from rocks, ledges, piers and other platforms in a straight-body position – is a very popular element of coasteering and is often done as a stand-alone activity, but it can also be extremely dangerous if you don't know the local conditions and tide times. Also be aware of rips, and make sure there is somewhere safe to get out of the water once you have jumped in.

KIT BAG You will need a wetsuit that you're not too precious about (it will get ragged around on barnacle-covered rocks), swimming shorts (to protect the wetsuit) and shoes with good grip. Neoprene gloves can be useful (for protection against the cold and the barnacles). Wear a PFD (personal flotation device/life jacket) and a helmet. When coasteering independently take a first-aid kit, throw rope and a means of communication.

GETTING THERE Head towards Haverfordwest on the A40, or Fishguard on the A487, then keep going west, following signs to St Davids. Haverfordwest and Fishguard both have train stations, and bus T11 travels between them, going via St Davids.

PLACES TO STAY There is accommodation around St Davids to suit all budgets, including hotels, B&Bs and campsites including coast-facing **Caerfai Bay Park** (⊘ caerfaibay.co.uk).

ELSEWHERE Commercially guided coasteering trips are now offered all around Britain (and the world). Elsewhere in Wales, **Anglesey** (⊘ angleseyadventures.com) and the **Gower** (⊘ savage-adventures.com) are well-regarded. Outside of Wales, southwest England is particularly good, and some of the best experiences are found in **Dorset** (⊘ jurassicwatersports.co.uk), **south Devon** (⊘ sea-n-shore.com) and at **The Lizard** in Cornwall (⊘ lizardadventure.co.uk). In Scotland, notable coasteering locations include **Skye** (⊘ skyeadventure.com) and **Arbroath** (⊘ verticaldescents.com).

EXTRA RESOURCES
⊘ coasteering.co.uk
⊘ nationalcoasteeringcharter.org.uk
⊘ nationalwatersafety.org.uk/advice-and-information/coasteering-and-tombstoning

17 STAND-UP PADDLEBOARDING (SUP)

WHERE	Norfolk Broads, Norfolk & Suffolk; Jurassic Coast, Devon
SKILL LEVEL	The standing up part of stand-up paddleboarding requires a bit of balance, but it's perfectly acceptable to start your SUP journey on your knees, and kneeling on a board on flat water is easy. Transitioning to a standing stance is simple enough in calm conditions, once you've practised it. In lumpier conditions – with waves, swell or fast-moving water – more advanced SUP skills are required, which can only be acquired with on-water experience. Once on your feet, there are myriad paddling skills to learn, which will enable you to become a better, more efficient SUPer. To go on a guided SUP experience, however, you just need a willingness to learn and to be comfortable in the water (everyone falls in at some point).
RISK FACTOR	All water-based activities contain an element of risk, but undertaken with a qualified instructor, stand-up paddleboarding is very safe. However, when SUPing independently on open water, it's essential you paddle within your limits, take appropriate safety precautions and check (and understand) the weather forecast and tidal conditions. The RNLI and Coastguard rescue lots of ill-prepared and inexperienced SUPers every year. Look out for strong offshore winds (which can blow you out to sea scarily quickly) and – especially when paddling in unfamiliar locations – be mindful of submerged objects and rip tides. A PFD (life jacket) should be worn, along with a leash connecting you to the board (always stay with your board, even if you're unable to get back on it, as it acts as a giant flotation device and makes you easier to find during a rescue). Paddle with people, or at least let someone know your plans. Taking a phone or other communication device in a waterproof case or drybag is a good idea. If an electrical storm is taking place anywhere nearby, stay off/get off the water – you don't want to be stood up on a board with a metal or carbon paddle in your hands when lightning strikes.

Stand-up paddleboarding, or SUP as it's invariably abbreviated to, has been one of the fastest-growing adventure pursuits to arrive on the outdoor scene for decades. When SUPs first started appearing at beaches and on lakes and rivers, many other recreational water users looked at them with a mixture of bemusement, amusement and scorn. Kayakers and canoeists often either dismissed them as gimmicky or seemed genuinely confused about why anyone would choose such a cumbersome method of paddling, some surfers resented their presence and I heard swimmers laughingly call them 'Jesus boards', because, viewed from sea level, the paddler appears to be standing or walking on water.

← Stand-up paddleboarding near Horning (Visit the Broads)

This derision didn't last long. The activity picked up momentum miraculously fast and now, if you visit any stretch of coastline around the UK – or anywhere else – on a calm summer's day, there will be a fleet of SUPs out on the water. Take a stroll along a riverbank or canal towpath on a half-decent morning, or wander around a lakeshore where paddling is permitted, and again, you'll almost certainly see paddleboarders. One of the wonderful things about the activity is that – unlike many outdoor pursuits – it's not dominated by any particular narrow demographic. You see just as many women out on boards as men, and the age range is super diverse, from proper youngsters to silver-haired SUPers. Exact numbers are hard to come by, but it's pretty obvious stand-up paddleboarding has overtaken sea kayaking, canoeing and whitewater paddling in terms of popularity and participation. Andy Gratwick, the Head Coach of the British Stand Up Paddle Association (BSUPA), tells me they have 105 recognised schools nationwide in Britain, and he estimates that around 30,000 paddlers get a structured lesson through their schools network each year. 'And we are by no means the whole market,' he adds. 'So maybe triple this number.'

Although prices have gone down as more budget-orientated brands have jumped into the market to surf the success of the sport, a SUP set-up still isn't particularly cheap – for a reasonable quality board, paddle, PFD, pump and the various paraphernalia that goes with it, you'd be lucky to get much change from £500, and the better brands (which make longer-lasting, more performance-orientated boards and paddles) are much more expensive. And that's before you've invested in a wetsuit, without which SUPing beyond the summer months can be pretty uncomfortable. Neither is SUPing particularly beginner friendly – at least, not without some tuition. It's one thing kneeling on a board and doing loops on a sunny day when the water is like a millpond, but to perfect your paddling style properly takes plenty of practice, and only then can you stand up and go in a straight line without constantly changing hands, let alone venture out in less benign conditions, or explore more exciting waterways.

So, how did this awkward-looking activity get so popular so quickly, and appeal to such a broad range of people – especially in a country not exactly known for its endless summers?

GETTING ON BOARD

I first got into stand-up paddleboarding while living in Australia, where prevailing conditions lend themselves perfectly to the pursuit in so many places. But I still didn't invest in my own set-up and take up SUPing seriously until I was back in Britain, and some of the best paddling I've ever done has been while stood up on a board, exploring the coastline, canals, rivers, lakes and hidden aquatic corners of the UK.

I'm lucky enough to live on the World Heritage-listed Jurassic Coast, in the bite of Lyme Bay, where Dorset and Devon meet. Facing out towards the English Channel, this is not a surf-stroked shoreline, and instead of sand we have pebbles, which means the larger crowds stay away and we don't get great clouds of grit

WHAT SUP?

SUP boards come in all shapes and sizes. Most people now opt for inflatable models (which are excellent), but you can get high-performance rigid boards. Beginner and bigger-framed paddlers, and people who really struggle with their balance, are best on larger-volume boards such as 10ft 10in models. Most people will find a 10ft 6in board ideal for general use after they've paddled a few times. You can get boards sized and shaped specifically for various uses – larger boards with minimal drag for touring and expedition use, for example, and sleeker rigid models with a narrower nose for racing. There are also oversize boards that accommodate several people (Go Paddle have one called `Big Clive', which can carry 4 adults, or 2 adults and 6 kids). SUP yoga is a thing, with some brands making bespoke boards for this activity. Go Paddle even offers a SUP-based escape room experience.

making the sea murky. On a calm day the clarity is akin to gin, and you can see straight down through 3 or 4m of water to the sea floor. We're not that far from famous features such as Durdle Door (an iconic landmark to paddle through) but even on the local beaches around Lyme Regis, Seaton, Beer and Branscombe there are myriad bays and beaches to explore, many of them accessible only from the sea and littered with ammonites and other fossils. The coastline is punctuated with sea caves and arches that you can paddle into or go under, and the place echoes with yarns about smugglers and other salty shenanigans. Seals and dolphins are occasional visitors, and there's a plethora of other sealife to spot and enjoy. Basically, I'm totally spoilt, and to live here and not SUP would be borderline criminal.

One of the most appealing aspects of stand-up paddleboarding is the unique perspective it provides of the aquatic terrain you pass through and over. I've paddled kayaks and canoes for decades (and still do) but, while sat low in a boat, you can't easily appreciate the waterscape that's directly beneath and around your craft. When you are fully stood up on a board, by comparison, your gaze is often drawn straight down past your paddle, and when conditions are calm and the visibility is good, staring through the translucent water to the rocks, weeds and wildlife that populates the sea, as you skim and float above it all, creates the illusion of flight. When wispy white clouds are also reflected in the water, it all becomes pretty trippy – like you're surfing sedately through the sky.

If you want to get a closer look, simply jump off the board into the water. Most SUP boards have bungee cords or webbing at one end, and these can be used to stash a snorkel and mask – so long as you keep your ankle leash on (so the board doesn't drift off towards the horizon while you're underwater), this is a really fun way to explore the coast. And, unlike trying to re-enter a kayak or canoe from

the water (which requires quite advanced skills) remounting a SUP is simple, meaning once you've finished snorkelling you can clamber back on board and resume your paddle. When I want to encourage the kids to put their screens down and get out into the fresh air, the one thing that guarantees success is a promise to take the SUPs and snorkels out for a play.

Getting your SUP to an interesting launch point is so much simpler than carrying a kayak or a canoe, too. Virtually all inflatable boards come with some sort of bag, and the best roll down into a backpack with a proper harness that makes lugging them relatively easy – especially compared to carting a big, heavy rigid boat around. Okay, so you have to blow the board up when you get there, but modern dual-chamber pumps are so efficient and fast that this takes very little time and only a modest amount of effort.

Transporting the board and kit further afield is also relatively hassle free – it's possible to lob the whole lot in the back of a standard-sized car and take it all over the place, so you can explore other coasts, lakes and river systems while you're on holiday, or make a dedicated trip to see somewhere from the perspective of a paddleboard. With this in mind, I recently packed up my SUP set-up and went to check out a wet and wild corner of the country that I've always wanted to explore – the Norfolk Broads. This is one of Britain's best-loved freshwater aquascapes, a place where the conditions are absolutely ideal for SUPing, and where the surroundings and wildlife are brilliantly different to those on my doorstep.

↑ SUPing along the Jurassic Coast in Seaton, East Devon (Patrick Kinsella)

PADDLE BROADING

The Broads National Park, or Broadland as some locals refer to it, is Britain's biggest protected wetland – it's a sprawling network of rivers, canals, marshes, meres, fens, dykes and broads, full of history and home to a massive diversity of water-based wildlife, including otters and herons. There are more than 200km (125 miles) of lock-free waterways to explore here, and what better way to nose around them than on a stand-up paddleboard? Most people chug about the Broads in powerboats, but these are pretty expensive to hire, can be a headache to moor and can restrict where you go. On a SUP, you can paddle almost silently along the surface and access lots of little waterways, all while emitting zero pollution and witnessing wild animals in their natural habitat without disturbing them. If you have your own board and gear, it's possible to paddle the Broads independently, virtually for free (there is a toll – page 190), and there are numerous campsites on or near the banks – not to mention waterside pubs and inns – many of which offer paddler-friendly accommodation and facilities.

SUPing on the Broads is also absolutely ideal and super safe for beginners, because the water is typically flat and there are no tides, currents or waves to worry about. The biggest safety consideration is boaters and other water traffic, and in the height of the season it can get extremely busy, but it's also well managed. Another benefit of SUPing here, where the chances of falling in are comparatively small and there's always a stretch of water sheltered from the wind, is that it's possible to comfortably paddle all year round. In fact, some of the best experiences can definitely be enjoyed well outside of summer, when the worst of the madding crowds have gone home and the wildlife is more relaxed and active.

To get a taste of what SUPing the Broads is like out of season, I caught up with Katie Baxter from Go Paddle, who has been taking people paddling on this extraordinary waterscape since 2020. We meet on a crisp November morning at her HQ in the marina at Horning, a beautiful Broadland village in the heart of the national park, perched right on the banks of the River Bure. Wisps of mist hang ethereally on the water, but there's no breeze at all, and with wetsuits, bright cags and bobble hats on, we're both toasty and nicely visible to boaters. Heading out of the harbour, we turn right along the Bure and paddle past the Ferry Inn, one of many waterside pubs in the Broads that offer overnight moorings to boats (of course, when you're travelling by board, you don't need to worry about such logistics, it's easy enough just to pull up at a pub or café and hop on to the bank with all your gear). It's a bit early for a drink now, though, and we've only just started, so we continue along the river.

As we paddle Katie explains how her guiding business is getting busier all the time, as more visitors want to explore the Broads by board and locals like to learn how to paddle properly. Go Paddle is a certified BSUPA school and she is a fully qualified SUP coach, so beyond taking out groups of complete beginners, which is a large part of what she does, Katie can also provide instruction for those who want to improve and perfect their paddling technique and advance their SUPing skills so they can purchase or hire a board and get out on the water independently. I've been SUPing for years, but I'm largely self taught and I lean perhaps a little too much on skills acquired while canoeing, so it's great to get some advice from a proper SUP expert.

'This section of the Broads is the perfect place to learn how to SUP safely,' Katie tells me. 'The water is typically flat around our base at Horning, and that isn't always the case across the whole Broads, which cover such a big area. We're very lucky. It allows us to help people find their balance in relatively calm conditions, always a bonus for first-time SUPers, and means we can concentrate on paddling technique, which is excellent for building people's confidence.'

SUP SCHOOL The first step for anyone is learning how to transition from a kneeling position to a standing stance – which is best done in one movement if possible, placing your palms either side of the carry handle in the middle of the board and pushing up, so your feet end up where your hands were. Once upright, you should stand with your knees very slightly bent and your feet facing forward. It's important to keep your head up and look forward too, focusing on where you want to go, rather than gazing at your feet or the board beneath you. You should hold the paddle with one hand firmly clasping the top of the T grip, and the other roughly one third of the way down the shaft (to gauge this, a good tip is to hold the T grip with one hand and raise your arms above your head – if your elbows are forming right angles, your hands are positioned about right). The top hand provides most of the control (and it's important to keep hold of that T, so you don't whack yourself or anyone else in the face with it), while the bottom hand supplies the power.

You may need to adjust the length of your paddle, which is best done before you get on the water. To find the correct length, put the blade tip on the floor, while the shaft is vertical, and reach up with your arm – you should be able to just comfortably hold the T grip with a bent wrist. In terms of technique, there are several basic paddle strokes to master, including forward, reverse, sweep and draw strokes. At first, when going forwards, you will need to change arms and paddle on alternate sides every few strokes, in order to avoid going in a big circle. Over time you should try and master the J-stroke, which is like a forward stroke but with an outward kick at the end, so you can paddle in a straight line without constantly changing sides, which is a far more efficient way to SUP.

↑→ In Norfolk you can paddle past waterside pubs and through nature reserves such as Bure Marshes (top: travellight/S; left: Jim Laws/A) → Katie boarding on the Broads (Patrick Kinsella)

BROAD STROKES Katie is an enthusiastic ambassador for her sport, and in between sharing her coaching expertise she explains all the places in the world she's explored by SUP. A couple of little boats bimble past, and the occupants wave good morning, but we virtually have the river to ourselves as we paddle with the Bure Marshes National Nature Reserve on our left and the riverside cafés, bars and marine buildings on our right. This is the more built-up part of the route Katie would typically take guided paddles on, and in summer it would be a whole lot busier.

Once we get to the sensationally positioned Swan Hotel, where the river wends left and a pretty paddleboat lies moored, we turn around to retrace our paddle strokes, and then continue east to explore the wilder section of the river. For a while we're accompanied by one of the Broads rangers, who chugs alongside us in a lovely looking wooden patrol launch. The rangers are a common sight on the

ESSENTIALS

GETTING STARTED To try SUPing on the **Broads** with Katie or one of her instructors or guides, contact Go Paddle (⚲ gopaddle.co.uk).

To try SUPing in **east Devon**, contact Seaton-based SB Watersports, which offers lessons, guided trips along the coast and board hire (⚲ sbwatersports.co.uk).

SPECIAL CONSIDERATIONS To use any craft, including stand-up paddleboards, on the waterways of the Broads you are required to pay a toll. Short Visit Tolls can be purchased in advance from the Broads Authority office in Norwich by phone (☏ 01603 756080), or by post (Yare Hse, 62–64 Thorpe Rd, Norwich NR1 1RY), or from various outlets in the area. For more, see ⚲ broads-authority.gov.uk/boating/owning-a-boat/tolls/short-visit-toll. The price for canoe, kayak or SUP is calculated for short-term visits (£8.50 for seven days/£17 for 14 days at the time of writing) or annually (£37.78). However, if you're a member of British Canoeing (⚲ members.britishcanoeing.org.uk), the toll is waived (carry proof of your British Canoeing membership with you on the water – your digital or physical membership card – because Broads rangers will check).

KIT BAG SUP Instructors typically supply everything you need except, perhaps, footwear and swimmers. Wear light shoes with some grip that you don't mind getting wet, or neoprene booties (going barefoot is risky because you could fall or stand on something sharp). Independent SUPers require a board, pump, paddle, leash and PFD at the bare minimum. You'll also need a spray vest in summer and a wetsuit for colder months.

GETTING THERE To drive to Horning, head northeast from Norwich on the A1151 and turn right on the A1062 at Hoveton. The closest train station is Hoveton &

waterways here, ensuring boaters observe speed restrictions and generally keeping an eye on things. Katie knows this ranger well, and we have a long friendly chat about the wildlife he has seen on this section of the Bure, which includes otters. Eventually we part company, and then, rounding the bend towards Ranworth Marshes, Katie and I enter an entirely different environment. The buildings and roads rapidly disappear and all we can hear is the swoosh of our paddles through the water and the chatter of birdlife in the rushes. To our right, Katie spots a heron, which takes off gracefully as we approach.

The whole experience is so utterly different to the SUPing I do at home, and when we get back to the marina it's nice not to be covered in salt for a change. Katie has a busy day ahead of her, but I could happily paddle here for days. And I intend to do just that, in the springtime, with lightweight camping kit stashed on my board and an itinerary as open as the Broadlands waterscape.

Wroxham, which is 5km away – there is a bus, but there's also access to the River Bure in Hoveton, so if you have your own board you can paddle it.

PLACES TO STAY The **Swan Inn** (⊘ vintageinn.co.uk) in Horning offers single, double and twin B&B hotel rooms with great views over the River Bure.

Camping is available at The Dog Inn at Ludham Bridge, on the River Ant, which joins the River Bure. Further up the River Ant there are wonderful waterside campsites and glamping facilities at Canal Camping in Dilham (⊘ canalcamping.co.uk). Further south, Three Rivers Camping & Caravaning site is located on the Broads in Geldeston, on the Norfolk-Suffolk border beside the River Waveney, and it offers SUP hire (⊘ threeriverscamping.co.uk).

ELSEWHERE You can SUP all around the UK coastline, but be very mindful of weather conditions and tides when on the open sea. Protected bays and coves are best for beginners. Canals can generally be paddled at any time, but sadly SUPing (along with kayaking and canoeing) is heavily restricted on the rivers of England and Wales – in Scotland outdoor access is much better, and you can paddle most rivers and lochs. Besides the Norfolk Broads, another wonderful waterscape to explore on a board in England is the Lake District, and in Wales Bala Lake/Llyn Tegid is an excellent spot, where you can typically enjoy calm conditions. Read *Paddling Britain* by Lizzie Carr for dozens more excellent ideas about where to go SUPing.

EXTRA RESOURCES
⊘ bsupa.org.uk
⊘ britishcanoeing.org.uk
⊘ norfolkbroads.com
⊘ nationalparks.uk/park/broads

18 SCRAMBLING

WHERE	The Glyderau, Eryri/Snowdonia, north Wales
SKILL LEVEL	Scrambling adventures range widely from Grade 1 routes, which are accessible for most hillwalkers and anyone with a reasonable level of fitness and a head for heights, through to extremely exposed and vertiginous Grade 3 routes where advanced technical rock-climbing skills and equipment are required. In this chapter we are talking about Grade 1 scrambles, where ropes are not generally used.
RISK FACTOR	The risks associated with scrambling range from minor falls to death. There is rarely a safety rope involved on a Grade 1 scramble, so even though the route may be deemed easy, the consequences of making a mistake can be very serious. Research the route thoroughly, or go with someone who knows the area well. Climb within your limits and remember it can be very tricky to retreat down a route if you decide you've taken on more than you can handle halfway. Always check weather forecasts carefully – bad conditions will make every scramble harder, especially on polished rocks. Aside from falls, additional risks come from loose rocks being knocked down from above (on certain routes, helmets should be worn).

↑ Andy scrambling up the north face of Tryfan (Patrick Kinsella)

In simple terms, Grade 1 scrambling is rock climbing minus some of the degrees of difficulty and all of the ropes. It's like free climbing or soloing (where no protection is employed), but on routes that are – in theory at least – far less tricky and technical than the sheer cliff faces and crags that trad and sport climbers hang out on. (Grade 2 and 3 scrambles do usually require the use of a rope.) A classic scrambling route is usually more of a journey than an all-out battle against gravity. You typically traverse quite a lot of ground, scrambling up and over several sections of near-sheer rock while ascending a peak and traversing a ridge or series of summits before taking a more circuitous route back to your starting point, rather than simply slinging a rope off the top and abseiling down.

Grade 1 scrambling is an activity that feels delightfully free, because you're unencumbered by a climbing harness, gear rack and ropes. There's also a visceral pleasure to be had in taking on tough terrain with your bare hands, and many people find the fizzy frisson that flows through the brain as you fight an instinctive fear of falling while scampering up an exposed rockface extremely thrilling. The foot- and handholds are usually much more solid and easy to find than those on more technical climbing routes, but the drops are just as dramatic and dangerous, so you need to stay very focused, choosing your line carefully and risk assessing each move, because any significant mistake could lead to a potentially catastrophic outcome.

Looked at another way, scrambling at Grade 1 level is akin to extremely steep hiking on rocky terrain, where all limbs are required in order to make any progress. Most hillwalkers will have already inadvertently done a bit of low-level scrambling, especially regular peak baggers, who often find themselves clawing and crawling their way up the trickier sections of a summit approach. But 'real' scrambling routes, the kind that have been assigned a grade and which appear in dedicated guidebooks about the pursuit, can be found in various craggy areas around Britain – such as north Wales, the Lake District, Dartmoor and scattered right across the Scottish Highlands and islands.

One spot where scramblers are spoilt for choice is Eryri/Snowdonia National Park, home to classic routes including Crib Goch – the sensationally scary way to get to the summit of Snowdon, or Yr Wyddfa as it's properly called in these parts. And this is where I'm heading, although not to visit the tallest peak in Wales. Instead, for my first foray into proper Grade 1 scrambling, I'm going to attempt the Cwm Bochlwyd Horseshoe in the Glyderau, which takes in the summits of Tryfan and Glyder Fach and is considered by many to be the best route in north Wales.

SCRAMBLING ON THE SHOULDERS OF GIANTS

Prior to heading to the Himalaya, the 1953 British Everest expedition (the first to definitely reach the roof of the world) led by Colonel John Hunt and including Edmund Hillary and Tenzing Norgay, needed a place with highly technical terrain to train together. With the entirety of the British Empire available to them, they chose the Glyderau, a group of bristly, gristly granite mountain peaks in Snowdonia, dominated by the shattered-stone trio of Glyder Fach, Glyder Fawr and Tryfan. In the midst of winter, betwixt the broken boulders and vertiginous

↑ Wild goats scramble all over the Glyderau; beyond this billy is Tryfan's South Ridge (Patrick Kinsella)

crags of this wild arena, they tested the techniques and the gear that would, a few months later, help Hillary and Norgay get to the top of the planet. And the Himalaya connection to Tryfan runs even deeper, because this was where George Mallory – who famously lost his life on Everest in 1924, just 245m below the summit – experienced his first British rock climbs. Mallory named the 'Western Cwm' on Everest after the cwms (Welsh for 'valley') where he learned his craft.

Standing in a lay-by off the A5, by the south bank of Lyn Ogwen, I contemplate this part of the peak's past while looking up across the sheer flanks of Milestone Buttress and along Tryfan North Ridge towards the 917.5m (3,010ft) summit. I won't lie – I'm a bit intimidated by a combination of the mountain's reputation, near-vertical rocky visage and the thought of the challenge that awaits me if and when I get to the top. But more of that later.

Fortunately, standing beside me is Andy Collins, a veteran RAF physical training and adventure instructor with 15 years' service under his belt, who now works as a mountain leader and fitness coach, using these mountains as an outdoor gym for beasting his clients. Today, I am his sole victim. I've been told by the friend who introduced us that Andy takes no prisoners, but underneath my nervousness, I'm really looking forward to the scramble. This is a challenge I have wanted to try for years, ever since visiting the nearby Pen-y-Gwryd Hotel, which housed the 1953 Everest expedition party during their training and where the signatures of Hillary and Norgay (who visited during the tenth anniversary celebration of the climb), plus a host of other top mountaineers, can still be seen scribbled on the ceiling of the front bar.

↑ Hobnail boots hang from the ceiling in the Pen Y Gwryd Hotel, which hosted the 1953 Everest expedition party while they trained on Tryfan (Patrick Kinsella)

MAKING THE GRADE

Notable scrambling routes are graded according to their degree of difficulty, with the easiest routes being Grade 1, and the hardest Grade 3 (or Grade 3S for severely hard routes). Sometimes + or − signs are used to give additional clues to how hard a scramble is. (It's also worth noting that some Scottish guidebooks use a grading system that goes up to Grade 5.) There is a massive degree of difference between a Grade 1 scramble (such as Tryfan North Ridge and Bristly Ridge, covered in this chapter) and a Grade 2 scramble, like Aonach Eagach, let alone a Grade 3 epic like the Cuillin Ridge. Beginners should stick to Grade 1 routes until they have considerable experience, and be aware that above Grade 1, the distinction between scrambling and rock climbing becomes blurred, and many routes will require the use of ropes at least on some sections. Do your research thoroughly.

Despite his fearsome reputation, Andy turns out to be an exceptionally affable guy, full of endless, highly infectious effervescent enthusiasm about the landscape he lives and works in. Throughout the day, whenever we meet anyone he greets them in Welsh, which is widely spoken as a first language here, and his passion for getting people into the peaks is constantly on show. Well, almost constantly. When a couple in shorts and trainers ask him some questions and start to tail us along our intended route, he makes it abundantly clear that he thinks it's a very bad idea for them to follow us. He has undertaken a rapid risk assessment and concluded that they would be a danger to themselves and others on certain sections of the mountain, and even I can see they have completely inappropriate footwear on, and neither is carrying any extra layering or emergency provisions in case something goes wrong. It's a grey autumn morning with wispy clouds and mist sticking stubbornly to the hills, and although the mountain forecast suggests this might clear later, conditions can change in a heartbeat on the higher reaches of the Glyderau, which is an unforgiving place to get lost when you're poorly prepared. Andy already has one amateur to keep an eye on, he doesn't want responsibility for any more.

Although very popular with peak collectors and scramblers, Tryfan is not a mountain to be trifled with. No matter what approach route you take – even the easiest, via Bwlch Tryfan – it's famously impossible to get to the summit without using your hands as well as your feet. And we're not using the easiest approach. Once the ill-equipped couple have taken the hint and disappeared along another path, Andy leads me up a route with a series of introductory scrambling sections, some of them reasonably tricky, requiring a knee brace or a sequence of climbing moves. It's important, he stresses, to always keep three solid points of contact with the rock as you move one hand or foot to the next hold.

CANNON FODDER As we ascend, Andy constantly regales me with folkloric stories. He wants me to know the Welsh words for the features around us, and feeds me a stream of fascinating facts about the cliff face we're climbing, which is made of rhyolitic volcanic rock, with brilliant white streaks of quartz, covered in an abundance of flora such as bilberries and sphagnum moss. We gobble a few of the tasty berries and he demonstrates how the spongy moss can be used to quench your thirst by squeezing a great handful of it while I drink the water that comes oozing out. It has a pleasant peaty aftertaste. This moss also has antiseptic qualities, I learn, which were discovered during the Crimea War. But, even while he is waxing lyrical about our surroundings, I'm acutely aware that Andy is keeping a very close eye on how I'm coping with the climbing.

Apparently happy with my performance so far, Andy announces that we're going to raise the bar a bit. There are myriad routes up this mountain, some where the rock underfoot has become polished by their popularity and others where the way is rougher, tougher and much less travelled. Andy picks a new line and the scrambling becomes a tad trickier and – far more confronting than the climbing – the exposure (in terms of how high up we are, and the drop immediately below the section we're ascending) increases tenfold. So long as I focus carefully on placing my foot- and handholds, and avoid looking down too often, I find I can remain in the zone and not keep worrying about how far I'll fall if I mess up. Andy's constant commentary and instruction also helps keep such thoughts at bay.

We're well above Milestone Buttress now, with the famous climbing area of Tryfan Bach off to our left, and soon arrive at the iconic Cannon Stone, a rocky protrusion that pokes prominently out of the side of the North Ridge. I venture out along the granite-grey barrel of the cannon and peer over the edge, down to the waters of Llyn Ogwen way below. It's startling how much elevation we've gained in a short space of time. As soon as we set off again, along a steep section of quite intense scrambling, a pungent aroma wafts across the rocks. 'Goats!' announces Andy. Sure enough, directly above us, standing atop a boulder, exuding an imperious air along with a distinctive whiff, is a male goat, with great big horns and a gaggle of females and youngsters around him. We edge on upwards along the crest of the North Ridge as the foot-sure feral animals nonchalantly nibble at the undergrowth on brutally exposed outcrops, and happily hop across the most harrowing of drops, from one splintered stone to another.

A second cannon-like stone platform provides a few more photo opportunities, and then we reach Notch Rocks, a nuggetty section of scrambling that needs to be negotiated at the very top of the North Ridge, just below the summit. This leads us into a gully ascent, and when I poke my head over the final part of the

crest Andy is waiting with a big grin. 'Congratulations,' he enthuses. 'You've climbed Tryfan. Now we're going to meet Adam and Eve, or Siôn a Siân, as they should be known.'

FREEDOM FLIGHT On the summit of Tryfan stand two flat-topped stone monoliths known as Siôn a Siân to Welsh speakers, or Adam and Eve to most English-speaking visitors. According to folklore, whoever dares to jump across the gap between them is granted the freedom of the mountain, and this leap of faith has become a very popular tradition for climbers and scramblers – another test of their mettle (as if the nerve-wracking ascent isn't tough enough). As we stand and contemplate the challenge, a couple of fellow climbers sit crouched between boulders, eating their lunch. 'Just in case you're about to suggest it, there's no bloody way you're getting me to do that,' the woman informs her partner.

'Are you going to give it a go, then?' Andy asks me. It's not really a question, and we can't hang around up here for too long, so I shed my backpack, hand my camera to Andy and clamber up on to the shoulders of the pillar on my right. Getting up there is tricky enough, and then, completely exposed to the elements, I immediately get buffeted and bullied by the wind. The gap isn't actually as large as I feared it might be, but it's the sheer drops on all sides and the jagged limb-snapping terrain that surrounds the rocks that makes the jump so confronting. You really would not want to get it wrong, or slip when you land. I gird my loins and go for it, and my feet find their target without any drama. Phew. I'm glad that's done. 'Hold on!' shouts Andy. 'Can you do it again? I want to make sure I get the shot.'

From the sensational summit, we downclimb the South Ridge, go up and over Far South Peak and cross Bwlch Tryfan (a pass in the saddle between Tryfan and Glyder Fach) en route to our next scrambling challenge: the brilliantly named Bristly Ridge. This route to the top of Glyder Fach is actually regarded as a technically trickier scramble than Tryfan North Ridge (although both are Grade 1s), and it takes us through the even more imposing-sounding Sinister Gully. I've been growing in confidence throughout the day, and Andy encourages me to lead for this section, which gives me another boost. It's quite a claustrophobic squeeze in parts, and there's a tricky overhang to be negotiated at the end, but we get through the gully without any worries and continue up and over the twin heads of Great Pinnacle Gap.

The rest of the route to the top is easy, but we stop off for some obligatory photos at the Cantilever, a great slab of flat rock improbably balanced across other boulders like a stone diving board, which everyone who makes it this far pauses to pose on the end of. The summit plateau of Glyder Fach is a magical mess of splintered stone shards, sharpened by the elements, but the 994m (3,261ft) peak

---

↑ Leaping between Adam and Eve (Siôn a Siân) rocks atop Tryfan is a rite of passage for scramblers (Andy Collins)

← Canon Rock is a prominent feature on Tryfan (Andy Collins) ← Andy scrambling up Sinister Gully, on Bristly Ridge (Patrick Kinsella)

itself is just a jumble of rocks. We ascend them and then continue to clamber over the much more evocative crown of spiky stones called Castell y Gwynt (the Castle of the Winds), which would have offered a panoramic view of the Glyderau and across the whole of Snowdonia, had the mountain mist not chosen that moment to descend upon us. No matter, the ethereal whirl and swirl of the moisture-laden air only adds to the otherworldly atmosphere. Unfortunately, it also adds to the slipperiness of the rock surface, and having not put a foot wrong during the most

ESSENTIALS

GETTING STARTED For a breathtaking bespoke adventure experience in the Glyderau or elsewhere in Eryri/Snowdonia, contact Andy Collins on Instagram or Facebook: Challenge Snowdonia/Sialens Eryri.

SPECIAL CONSIDERATIONS Scrambling is a potentially dangerous pursuit, where local knowledge is required, along with technical expertise. Downclimbing a route can be harder than climbing up, so don't scramble yourself into an emergency situation. If you're new to the sport and/or the crag, it's highly recommended you scramble with a professional guide who knows the area well.

KIT BAG While you don't require a climbing rope or harness for Grade 1 scrambling, you do need good shoes with great grip – approach shoes are ideal, offering a mixture of rigidity, robustness and traction. Take extra layers, including a waterproof shell, and a mobile phone in case you need to call for assistance. A whistle, map and compass should also be carried, along with a first-aid kit. On some routes it's wise to wear a helmet.

GETTING THERE The Cwm Bochlwyd Horseshoe route starts and finishes at the shores of Llyn Ogwen, by the side of the A5 between Betws-y-Coed and Bangor. The Ordnance Survey grid reference is 📍 SH 661/602.

↑ Castell y Gwynt, 'the Castle of the Winds' (Patrick Kinsella)

technical part of the adventure, both Andy and I take a tiny tumble during the steep, but much easier descent along Gribin Ridge.

The mist lifts as quickly as it fell, and our walk out is beautiful, with the clouds parting to reveal Tryfan in all its glory, towering above Llyn Bochlwyd, the watery feature this horseshoe route encircles. To Andy's absolute disgust, some guidebooks and websites refer to Llyn Bochlwyd as Lake Australia, because of its shape. The real name translates as the Lake of the Greycheek and, of course, it has an origin story, which he recounts as we walk back towards the road. It's said that a legendary grey stag prowled these peaks and valleys, and although many skilled hunters attempted to track it down, the wise animal eluded them all by swimming out into the middle of the lake with just its cheek turned sideways to the surface, so it could breathe.

Before meeting the road by the banks of Llyn Ogwen, where we'll turn right and wander back to our cars, we stop to splash water on our faces and take a drink straight from the water of Nant Bochlwyd, which rushes right out of the llyn. Andy looks up at the peaks of Tryfan and the Glyders.

'Mi oedd y mynnydd yn hael,' he says, with a smile, before translating for me. The mountain was kind to us today.

PLACES TO STAY For a real taste of the mountaineering history of the area, book a room (or at least call in for a drink) at the **Pen-y-Gwryd Hotel** (⏚ pyg.co.uk), where members of the 1953 Everest Expedition stayed while training for their historic adventure to the top of the world. The PYG is scenically situated between Yr Wyddfa/ Snowdon and the Glyderau.

ELSEWHERE Eryri/Snowdonia offers myriad sensational scrambling routes, but there are many more fantastic options elsewhere around the UK, especially in the Lake District and Scotland. Some are legendary, with names familiar to all mountain-minded folk, such as Striding Edge and Jack's Rake in the Lakes; Aonach Eagach high above Glen Coe; and, most notorious of all, the Cuillin Ridge on the Isle of Skye, generally regarded as the holy grail of British scrambling and a huge challenge even for highly accomplished rock climbers.

EXTRA RESOURCES

Scrambles in Snowdonia by Steve Ashton, updated by Carl McKeating and Rachel Crolla (published by Cicerone) is a great guide to scrambling in north Wales.

⏚ thebmc.co.uk/hill-skills-scrambling
⏚ ukscrambles.com

19 BOULDERING

WHERE	The Plantation, Stanage Edge, the Peak District, Derbyshire/ South Yorkshire
SKILL LEVEL	Bouldering can be enjoyed by complete beginners and extremely experienced climbers – it all depends on the boulder and the 'problem' you choose to tackle.
RISK FACTOR	While it typically takes place much closer to the ground than other forms of rock climbing, bouldering does not involve any ropes and there is always the risk of injury (ranging from bruises to broken bones and potentially worse) if you fall and land awkwardly, even if you hit the crash mat or your spotter takes some of the speed out of your plummet. Do a mental risk assessment before you start to climb, taking into account the landing zone and checking there is a safe route down.

On almost every day of the year, the trails leading out of Hollin Bank car park in the heart of the Peak District are busy with gigantic shield beetles, or at least that's how it looks from afar. Closer inspection reveals these curious figures to be a particular species of human – the common boulderer – complete with crash mats strapped to their backs, scurrying to and fro along well-trodden paths into and around an area known as the Plantation. Tucked in beneath the towering crags of Stanage Edge, a legendary escarpment constantly covered in trad climbers from dawn to dusk, the Plantation is a verdant fern-filled place, where great chunks and lumps of gritstone that have rolled off the edge of the High Peak plateau over many millennia form a playground for this specific kind of rock hound.

While trad climbers scale long vertical routes up tall crags and cliff faces, belaying one another with ropes, wearing harnesses full of gear and placing protection as they ascend (in the form of cams, nuts and hexes that are wedged into cracks and crevices, and connected to the rope via a quickdraw), boulderers don't wear a harness, use a rope or carry any kit other than the aforementioned crash mat, a pair of climbing shoes and a perhaps a chalk bag.

More broadly, this minimalist rope-free form of climbing is known as 'free soloing', and some nutters... sorry, free-soloists, such as Alex Honnold, will tackle terrifyingly long and high routes in this way, with zero safety net. Bouldering, however, is a much more popular form of ropeless climbing, which typically takes place relatively close to the ground on a large rock, rather than a tall crag. A crash mat is usually placed below the route to provide some protection should the climber peel off, and a partner (or two) often positions themselves to 'spot' the climber, which means breaking their descent and helping them land feet first in the event of a fall.

Alongside sport climbing, bouldering became an Olympic pursuit at the Tokyo Games in 2020, and lots of trad and sport climbers enjoy it because it enables them to hone their skills at a lower level, unencumbered by a heavy rack of gear. However, some climbers – such as

← A climber tackles a problem in the Peak District's Plantation bouldering area (SS)

my companion today – concentrate almost exclusively on bouldering and free climbing. There is a simple purism to the pursuit – it is literally you versus the rock. Boulderers call the route they are attempting to climb a 'problem', and outside of competitive events they will typically take a calm, cerebral approach to solving each one. This process can take many hours, days or even months – with the climber repeatedly tackling the problem from the beginning and (ideally) progressing a little further with each attempt. Once they have solved one problem, they will go in search of another, slightly harder one, to work on.

Really good bouldering areas offer a multitude of problems for climbers to get stuck into, but they are few and far between. Fontainebleau in France is one such area, considered to be one of the best bouldering sites in Europe, and the Plantation, in the English Peak District, is another. This is the home of British bouldering, and it's here I have come to meet Charles Cooper, a boulderer and freelance climbing instructor who has agreed to help me find my ideal problem, and (hopefully) assist me in solving it.

99 PROBLEMS

When I first contacted Charles, he replied with an email that came through under the pseudonym John Bachar, which confused me no end. It turns out that this *nom de guerre* is a respectful nod to a legendary American free soloist of the same name, famous for both his hair-raising, ropeless rock-climbing exploits and his equally frightening fitness regimes, which involved things like performing endless two-finger chin-ups and dangling from wobbly rope ladders by his arms for ages. As a result of all this brutal training, Bachar was incredibly strong and capable of performing seemingly superhuman acts of ascent on very tricky climbing routes, but in 2009 he fell to his death while free soloing Dike Wall near Mammoth Lakes, California.

Charles explains all this as we walk through the ferns, from the car park to the Plantation. Hauling the bouldering mat on his back, like a tenacious tortoise on a mission, he tells me about some of his own free-climbing adventures, and describes the feeling of freedom that climbing without a rope creates. Mercifully, he stresses that we'll be staying pretty close to the ground today, before rather less reassuringly describing how his worst climbing injury happened while bouldering. 'I missed the mat,' he explains. 'Broke my arm in three places, and still had to drive home in a manual car.'

Like the man whose name he has incorporated into his email, Charles is wonderfully wiry, without an ounce of spare fat on him. He too trains daily, performing pull-ups and fingerboard exercises inside, and attempting to solve new problems on bona fide boulders whenever the northern weather will allow him. Charles is based on t'other side of Snake Pass, in Saddleworth near Manchester, and there is some superb bouldering near him at Buckstone Edge, where he often takes his climbing students. Today, however, we've chosen to meet at the

WEASELING

Another adventure pursuit that finds a natural home in the rock-strewn surrounds of England's Peak District is weaseling, an activity which combines elements of bouldering, potholing and even parkour, and is sometimes described as 'above-ground caving'. Participants squirm, squeeze, climb and clamber their way through tunnels, cracks and openings in boulder fields. Generally suitable for all age groups, it's very inclusive and great fun.

Peak weaseling spots include the Roaches and Higgar Top. Helmets and grippy shoes should be worn, and until you know what you're doing it can be more rewarding to go with a guide, such as Dan Crawford, owner and operator of Sheffield-based DC Outdoors (⊘ dcoutdoors.co.uk). Weaseling can also be enjoyed elsewhere, from Okehampton on Dartmoor (⊘ adventureokehampton.com/activities/weaselling) to Inverness in Scotland (⊘ iye.scot/weaseling).

↑ Children enjoying a weaseling adventure at Burbage North in the Peaks (Dan Crawford DC Outdoors)

Plantation because of the sheer number of problems that can be confronted here, of various levels of difficulty, and because there's a wet-weather option fairly close by at Rubicon. Oh, and because it's the absolute 'Mecca of hard bouldering', as Charles recently described it to me, with over 200 problems to keep us busy.

His use of the word 'hard' has created a ripple of concern in my mind, but at least our worries about the weather seem unfounded, for the moment. We're here in the middle of a deep drought and although heavy rain and thunderstorms have been predicted, there's no sign of it breaking yet. It's perishing hot, though. The ground is like concrete, making the mat even more essential than ever, and the humidity is high – consequently we're both wearing shorts, a choice of attire that I will soon bitterly regret.

GROUNDED While looking around for a suitable rock we can both have a go at climbing, Charles points out an arête (where two rockfaces meet in a point) named 'Careless Torque', which features an infamous route that is, apparently, considered the hardest bouldering problem in the Peaks, if not the entire country. Right enough, the faces on either side of the boulder's distinctive arête look seriously smooth and completely unclimbable to me, and there's a horrible landing area beneath it to boot, with rocks and stones forming a minefield of bone-breaking obstacles. But chalky handmarks on the gritstone give away the fact that it has been climbed (or at least attempted) recently.

Charles eyes the arête quizzically, like a cryptic crossword addict contemplating the first clue of a new puzzle, but thankfully we start with something many multitudes of degrees easier. Or, at least, that's the way it looks. The face of the boulder we have selected to climb is sloped at what feels like a generous angle, lulling me into a false sense of confidence. But when we examine the problem in more detail, it turns out the crux (most difficult) move is the very first one. In order to get both feet off the ground you need to push up from a foothold that's little more than a blemish on the rockface, while using one finger rammed into a tiny hole to pull your body weight up enough to reach a second sketchy handhold and get your other foot on another small crack. This single-finger hold is known as a 'mono', and dedicated climbers will spend hours hanging from 'fingerboards' to gain the strength and endurance required to use them. There is another boulder right behind us that we could use to push off from, which would make the start a whole lot easier, but Charles tells me this is considered 'cheating', so that's out.

Charles considers the problem for several long minutes, rubbing his hands together in what seems like an expression of excitement and anticipation, but is actually a warm up. From his pocket he produces something that looks like a crude weapon and starts whacking the rock with it, aiming for his intended hand placement points. This improvised tool is a chalk ball in a sock, and the fine dust

↑ Charles pointing to Careless Torque – a brutally hard bouldering route (Patrick Kinsella)
→ A crimp hold (Patrick Kinsella)

that settles on the rock after each explosive strike will help him maintain grip. He rubs more chalk on to his hands, places his first foot on the rock, rams an index finger in the hole above and springs into action, with me standing below, arms outstretched in the spotting position. After nailing the first move he makes short work of the rest of the route, scampering up to stand triumphantly atop the first successfully bagged boulder problem of the day.

Then it's my turn. And things quickly turn ugly. I can reach the finger hold alright, but I could never be described as wiry and I haven't spent years strengthening my hand and arm muscles like Charles has. I know I need to 'trust my feet' – this is a mantra chanted by all kinds of climbers, because using your big leg muscles to ascend is the most efficient way of fighting gravity – but the first foothold feels so sketchy. I grit my teeth and attempt the move multiple times, but just can't seem to get off the ground. In a final attempt I push down hard on my right foot, which slips off the hold and scrapes my leg right across the cheese-grater-rough rock, resulting in several lumps of skin being left on the gritstone. I'm attempting a problem that's beyond my rookie level here, but the biggest lesson is this: never wear shorts while bouldering. Especially if you're not very good at it.

SIDEWAYS & UPWARDS We move on. I'm bleeding and a bit disappointed in myself, but Charles soon finds a totally different problem to take my mind off the early defeat. Unlike most forms of rock climbing, bouldering isn't necessarily all about going upwards. Problems can be approached from all angles, including from a sitting position (which will up the grade of a climb) and sometimes they involve going sideways rather than skywards. We pause at a low-lying chunk of rock with a long, distinct crack, and Charles proceeds to smash out a horizontal traverse, using mainly his arm muscles to scramble right along the length of the boulder, keeping his feet off the floor at all times. Again, he makes it look easy, and again I struggle to complete more than a fraction of the problem before my arms get totally pumped (full of lactic acid) and become useless. I'm starting to feel very weedy now, but Charles reminds me how much strength training he does each week, and I simply have to console myself with a promise to toughen up and get fitter for next time.

The next boulder we attempt to climb seems intent on compounding my misery. Again, the very first move seems to the hardest of all and, while Charles completes it relatively easily, I'm unable to escape terra firma. There is an alternative approach to this one, though, involving a running start with a leap from a smaller stone next to the big boulder, which propels you right over the early tricky move. Charles demonstrates the dynamic start, and I follow him. I land it, almost topple backwards, but then manage to get my balance and find a handhold. The rest

↑ It's important to trust your feet when bouldering and climbing (Patrick Kinsella) ← Charles doing a horizontal traverse (Patrick Kinsella)

GRADING PROBLEMS

There are two widely used grading systems that indicate the difficulty of bouldering problems: the Font Scale and the V Scale. Born in the wondrous boulder forest of Fontainebleau in France, and commonly used in the UK and Europe, the **Font Scale** is simply numerical up to six, at which point letters start to get introduced (with a 6A problem being easier than a 6C), occasionally with the addition of a '+' sign to indicated an extra layer of difficulty. Used mainly in North America and Oceania, the **V Scale** is purely numerical and the higher the number the harder the problem is (the V comes from 'Vermin', the nickname of a pioneering climber called John Sherman who created the scale to describe bouldering routes in Hueco Tanks, Texas, in the late 1980s).

of the route is simple enough and soon I'm sitting beside Charles on the top of the rock. As pleased as I am to have nailed it, and as much as Charles reassures me that this jump-start was a legitimate approach, I have a nagging feeling that I've cheated my way around this particular problem, and that I'm yet to solve one properly.

For the last foray of the day we fight our way through some thick ferns and move into a different part of the Plantation, where we find a classic freestanding boulder that I really like the look of. It's splattered in chalk from hundreds of hands that have preceded us, and there are multiple problems to be approached

↑ Fontainebleau, France, is a legendary bouldering area (Elena Ska/S)

on its various faces, ranging from severe to simple. On an easier route the first few moves are doable, which gives me confidence, and finally I nail my first successful ascent. The first problem I solve is a pretty simple one, granted, but then I move on to a far trickier route, and manage to scale that one too. My style is far from textbook, and I use my knee to jam a move at one point (taking yet more bark off my bloody legs), but then I give it another go and climb the route in a much cleaner and more efficient fashion. After my earlier dejection, I'm suddenly full of enthusiasm, and we spend ages tackling and talking about different problems, working away at them until a solution becomes apparent.

One route eludes me, though. But only just. Like many bouldering problems, there is just one crux move that you need to crack before you can solve it, and it defeats me each time. A lot comes down to confidence, and with each attempt I complete the early moves with increased assurance and ease, and commit myself more to reaching the final elusive hold. But each time, I peel off the rock and tumble down on to the mat below, with Charles taking some of the velocity out of my fall with his outstretched arms. It's no good. And, as the long-threatened storm starts to break, there's electricity in the air. We need to get back to the car.

On the lengthy drive home, my mind keeps gnawing on that last problem. I'm convinced I was so close to solving it. I replay each move in my mind, and obsess about what I could have done differently to complete the last one. I know I'm going to have to come back to the Plantation to get it done. And this is how it hooks you. There's always one more problem to puzzle upon.

↑ Pat attempts to solve a bouldering problem in the Plantation (Charles Cooper)

ESSENTIALS

GETTING STARTED If you're heading to the Peak District and you're new to bouldering and would like someone to show you the ropes, or lack thereof, contact Charles Cooper (**e** jonbachar929@gmail.com, 🐦 @Charles80641832).

SPECIAL CONSIDERATIONS Always check there is a safe route back down from the top of a boulder before you climb it (remember – downclimbing is much harder than upclimbing).

KIT BAG Bouldering is a very gear-light pursuit. Besides climbing shoes, all you really need is some chalk and a bouldering mat. Larger, thicker mats are best for high boulder problems, but they are obviously heavier to cart around.

GETTING THERE Stanage Edge and the Plantation are above the Peak District village of Hathersage, about 13km from Sheffield city centre. There's a train station in Hathersage, bus routes serve the area and there are three car parks, the best of which for reaching the Plantation is Hollin Bank (aka Plantation car park).

PLACES TO STAY There are multiple fantastic places to stay across the Peak District to suit all budgets. **The Plough** (⌂ ploughhathersage.com), a 16th-century inn, offers nice rooms with views in Hathersage, while **North Lees campsite** (✆ 01433 650838) is scenically situated directly beneath Stanage Edge.

ELSEWHERE Outside the Peak District, excellent bouldering for beginners can be found at Bonehill Rocks on Dartmoor, Devon; the Cuttings Boulderfield on Portland, Dorset; RAC Boulders near Snowdon in Wales; St Bees on the Cumbrian coast; and Dumbarton Rock just west of Glasgow in Scotland.

EXTRA RESOURCES

Peak Bouldering, published by Rockfax, details bouldering problems scattered across the Peak District.

⌂ ukclimbing.com
⌂ thebmc.co.uk

↑ The Plantation is located beneath Stanage Edge, a very popular crag with trad climbers (Valdis Skudre/S)

20 BIKEPACKING

WHERE	Dartmoor, Devon; the Ridgeway, Oxfordshire and Wiltshire; the Peak District; the Yorkshire Dales
SKILL LEVEL	Basic cycling and bike handling skills are required – some off-road trails can be technical and demanding, but there's always the option to dismount and push. Reasonable fitness is required (how much depends on the terrain tackled, distance travelled, weight carried and bike used). You also need to know how to pack light and right, taking only what's necessary and loading your bike properly.
RISK FACTOR	There's always some danger you'll take a tumble when riding off-road, but bikepacking is more about enjoying the journey than chasing thrills and suffering spills on steep, technical trails. Encounters with other vehicles on road sections are more of a risk. Wear a helmet and be alert.

As a lifelong cyclist who loves larking around on trails, exploring new places and sleeping outside, I should have been bikepacking for decades, but the whole concept is a relatively new one. More accurately, it's a fresh take on a long-enjoyed activity. People have been bike touring for donkey's years, using panniers to carry camping gear while cycling around country roads, often venturing far and wide, around regions, countries and even continents. Bikepacking – a term popularised in the 2000s – takes the concept of cycle touring off-road and on to trails, with the steed of choice typically being a mountain bike or, more recently still, a gravel bike. Instead of relying on a couple of large panniers, gear is usually stashed in smaller purpose-made packs

↑ Bikepacking across the heather-covered Peaks (Patrick Kinsella)

attached to various parts of the frame, so you can pedal right out into the wilds, tackling rough, tough and technical trails, and exploring remote corners of the outdoors.

The concept of bikepacking is pretty self explanatory: it's exactly like backpacking, but instead of carting your tent, sleeping bag and other overnight equipment on your back, you attach it to your bike. In practice, there's more to get your head around, because packing a bike properly is nowhere near as simple as stuffing gear into a rucksack. The dynamics are similar – you need to distribute the weight sensibly and evenly, so your centre of gravity remains as low as possible, and you're not lopsided – but with a backpack you can usually achieve this by simply putting the heavy stuff at the bottom, whereas with bikepacking, there's more to think about. But it can't be rocket science, surely? I set out to learn, and my voyage of self-education turned into a four-act play.

DARTMOOR TORING

My first foray into the world of bikepacking was several years ago, when Alpkit began making Sonder bikes and a range of kit specifically designed for the pursuit. I was essentially making it up on the hoof, and didn't have a full set of bags, so I ended up carrying far too much on my back – a terrible idea when cycling, because it makes you top heavy and throws your balance off, which can be particularly calamitous when riding rugged trails.

Nevertheless, I spent a couple of happy days high on Dartmoor, exploring the moor and cycling up and over atmospheric tor tops such as wonderfully spooky Houndtor, riding until darkness descended, then sleeping under a tarp strung up between the wheels of my upturned bike and various boulders and scrappy trees. Criss-crossed by terrific tracks and trails, and (at the time of writing) the only place in England you can legally wild camp, Dartmoor is absolutely perfect for bikepacking. Enthused, I wanted to do more. Lots more.

RIDING THE RIDGEWAY

After several more solo outings, I convinced three of my oldest friends – George, Steve and Dan – that we should do an overnight escapade on our mountain bikes. A route I'd long wanted to ride is the Ridgeway, a national trail that traces an ancient route along a chalk ridge across the centre of England, running 139km (87 miles) between Ivinghoe Beacon and the World Heritage Site of Avebury in Wiltshire. Often referred to as 'Britain's oldest road', the Ridgeway has been used by travellers, traders and soldiers since prehistoric times, and the section between Goring-on-Thames and Avebury can be cycled. Perfect.

Leaving our cars at Pewsey, the closest railway station to Avebury, George and I caught the train with our bikes to Goring, where we met Dan and Steve. By now I'd accumulated much more bikepacking kit, but once it was shared around the group we still had to resort to carrying our bulkiest gear in backpacks. This was our first mistake. The second was hitting The Swan pub on the banks of the Thames in Streatley for lunch, before we'd cycled so much as a kilometre. When we finally saddled up and got going, we immediately had to drag our heavy stomachs straight up a steep climb on to the ridge. Steve, who isn't a regular cyclist, let his feelings be known, and I could hear him twinning my name with some very colourful nouns and adjectives that went well with the old English surroundings.

↑ Rolling along the Ridgeway (Patrick Kinsella)

Once we were rolling along the Ridgeway proper he cheered up slightly, although the trail was a tad more undulating than I'd perhaps described it, so the air went blue a few more times over the next 48 hours. The route proved to be just as spectacular as I'd hoped, though, with the broad chalky track taking us from the downs above the Thames Valley, along the seam between Oxfordshire and Berkshire, into the Vale of the White Horse. Here we paused for the night in a campsite at Fernham, beneath the famous Uffington White Horse – an enormous equine figure carved into the hillside some 3,000 years ago.

Aside from affecting your balance, carrying a bulky backpack while cycling makes you much heavier, leading to saddlesoreness, and we were all walking like cowboys after dismounting from our steeds towards day's end. A couple of late-afternoon pub pit stops once we'd descended from the Ridgeway helped a little, with curative refreshments taken at The White Horse in Woolstone and The Woodman in Fernham, before we set up camp. It was a fine summer's evening, and I was under a tarp again, while the lads were in a mixture of lightweight tents and bivvy bags.

Sadly, the saddlesoreness returned with a vengeance the minute we set off in the morning, and of course we had to climb back up on to the ridge. Steve had stopped swearing by now – in fact he'd stopped talking to me altogether. The trail turned on the charm again though, and riding through the North Wessex Downs Area of Natural Beauty was spectacular. Large birds circled overhead, and despite Steve's fears that they might be vultures waiting for him to drop, they turned out to be red kites.

The track was rutted and technical in places, but good fun to ride, and even Steve's mood lifted on the approach to Avebury. We hollered down the final descent all together, pedalling right into the planet's largest prehistoric stone

↑ Camping beneath tarps and in lightweight shelters is necessary when bikepacking (Patrick Kinsella)

circle. After clanging celebratory ales in The Red Lion, perfectly positioned at the trailhead, George and I left Steve and Dan happily ensconced in the pub, and cycled the extra 10km to Pewsey to retrieve the cars. We discussed plans for future forays as we went, although the chances of convincing Steve to join us on any more jaunts seemed slim.

PEDALLING THE PEAKS

We'd seen plenty of other trail traffic while riding the Ridgeway, with people pedalling past us with 'proper' bikepacking rigs – usually riding gravel bikes, with a small amount of kit arranged perfectly and precisely around the frame, and no stupid pack wobbling around on their backs, giving them sore bums and bad balance. This was the bikepacking I really wanted to do, and when an opportunity arose to join a group of pros in the Peak District, I jumped on it.

Swedish clothing and luggage brand Fjällräven and Specialized bikes had just embarked on a collaborative project, jointly designing a range of bikepacking equipment and apparel, and they wanted some crash-test dummies to trial it. With my outdoor journalist helmet on, I join a small group of fellow pedal-pushing pen pilots in Sheffield, where we're met by Stef and Dave from guiding company Pannier, who specialise in cycle touring and bikepacking expeditions. Our bikes are mostly set up when we arrive, with the new range of bags attached to the handlebars, seat and frame. All we have to do is load our gear into them. Once packed, my bike looks the business – exactly like the rigs ridden by the real-deal bikepackers I'd seen on the Ridgeway. Except… we're cheating a bit (actually, quite a lot) because our tents are already set up at the overnight camp, so we're travelling pretty light. All except Stef, that is, who has a couple of watermelons in his panniers.

Across the group we're riding a mixture of Specialized e-bikes and standard-spec gravel bikes, all with drop handlebars and off-road tyres. I'm on the latter, and soon feel envious of those with battery power, as we pedal out of Sheffield beneath a cloudless sky, riding past the Botanical Gardens, Endcliffe and Bingham parks, and Whiteley Woods, and straight up one of the seven hills that famously circle the old Steel City. Within an hour we're on the edge of the High Peak, surrounded by serenity, with the post-industrial skyline of Sheffield hidden behind hills and already a mere memory. It's shimmering hot and the vibrant blooming heather casts a purple haze across the moor.

Leaving the road we get our first taste of the Peak District's tremendous trails, cycling along stony tracks and sections of slabby rock pavement that demand good concentration and some bike handling skills. The group includes riders with a wide range of experience and ability, including Becky, who's partway through a Land's End to John O'Groats bikepacking odyssey, following an almost entirely

→ Bikepacking over bridges and around berms in the Peak District (both Patrick Kinsella)

TRUE GRIT

While cycle touring has been popular ever since bicycles were invented, the evolution of minimalist bikepacking kit can be traced back to endurance expeditions and events popular in North America, such as the extreme 320km (200-mile) IditaBike race in Alaska (which has evolved into the Iditarod Trail Invitational & itialaska.com) and the epic 4,418km (2,745-mile) Great Divide Mountain Bike Race (now the Tour Divide, & tourdivide.org), which traverses the length of the Rocky Mountains from Canada to the Mexican border. You can take on several iconic bikepacking events and challenges in the UK, too, including the enormous Pan Celtic Race (& pancelticrace.com), a self-supported, ultra-endurance challenge that sends riders through the Celtic nations of Wales, Scotland, Ireland, Cornwall, the Isle of Man and Brittany, which takes a different route each year. There are, of course, many far more accessible gravel-riding and bikepacking events, such as the two-day Dunoon Dirt Dash (& dirtdash.cc/dunoon) in Scotland and the Dorset Dirt Dash in southwest England (& dirtdash.cc).

off-road route. Others, though, have rarely ridden on unsealed surfaces, let alone on a gravel bike, where there's no suspension to absorb the bumps, beyond a bit of dampening that Specialized have built into the steering tube.

After rounding Redmires Reservoir and climbing steadily, we pause for breath atop Hallam Moor before dropping off the High Peak and swooping and whooping along a glorious descent beside stunning Stanage Edge, passing rock climbers clinging to the famous crag on our right. We grab lunch in the Yorkshire Bridge Inn before exploring more magical trails through the Hope Valley. The midsummer sun is relentless, and the heat so mind-meltingly extreme that we witness a startled sheep leap right off a bridge into a stream, narrowly missing a bloke bathing below. We too seek relief with a refreshing dip in the river, where we finally relieve Stef of his watermelon cargo.

Then it's onwards, for a lap of lovely Ladybower Reservoir where, in 1943, RAF 617 Squadron – better known as the Dam Busters – practised low-level flying in total darkness, while testing Barnes Wallis's 'bouncing bomb'. This endless summer and near-drought conditions have left the water level so low we wonder whether the bones of the submerged villages of Derwent and Ashopton, drowned during the construction of the reservoir, might soon start poking above the still surface of the water. The midsummer days are long, but it's getting late by the time we've looped the lake, especially after two people suffer punctures, so once back on track we put the pedal down and gun it for the campsite.

Our overnight camp is scenically situated under Kinder Scout in Edale, one of Britain's most iconic outdoor spots thanks to its natural good looks and exciting history. On the flanks of this hill, the Mass Trespass took place on 24 April 1932, when an unlikely alliance of the Ramblers Society and the Young Communist League staged a large-scale act of civil disobedience in protest about the lack of access to the countryside and set in motion events that eventually led to the creation of national parks and a network of national trails in Britain, as well as the Countryside Rights of Way Act of 2000. The Pennine Way, Britain's first national trail, literally starts (or ends) at the door of the Old Nag's Head in Edale – one of the finest pubs in the country. We don't get as far as the bar, though, because Sheffield chef Gian Bohan is waiting at camp with ice-cold beer, which he follows with a fantastic fire-cooked feast, before finishing us off entirely with negroni nightcaps. Finally falling into the Fjällräven tent, I sleep heavily.

The morning ride back to Sheffield soon blows the cobwebs from my head, though, as we cycle along the bottom of Stanage Edge, through Hope Valley and past Hathersage, a picturesque Peak District village where I got married. The fantastic finale is a spin around Lady Canning's mountain-bike trails before we burst back into the hubbub of the city suburbs.

TRAILS & HIGH ALES IN THE DALES

Pedalling in the Peaks is superb, but I'm anxious to round off my inaugural proper bikepacking season with a self-supported adventure, so soon afterwards I head further north, to the epicentre of England's gravel-riding scene, the Yorkshire Dales. This time I'll be carrying all my own gear, including camping kit, but I do have the advantage of having an e-bike to play around on: the Ribble Gravel

↑ A gravel e-bike designed for bikepacking, fully loaded and ready to roll (Patrick Kinsella)

AL e. The idea with e-bikes is not necessarily to get a helping hand on every hill (although you can do exactly that), but to use the battery power to go further and explore more, and to stay in the saddle on even the most viciously vertical ascents that would otherwise see you pushing the bike along the trail, rather than riding it.

At the excellent Dales Bike Centre in the heart of Swaledale, I carefully load my e-steed, attaching specialist bikepacking bags, stuffed full of camping equipment and supplies for an overnight adventure, to various parts of the Ribble's frame, which is designed specifically to take such cargo. By the time I set off along the sensational Swale Trail, the bike feels very well balanced, but heavy – and I'm immediately grateful for the extra power as I pass through Grinton and begin a staggeringly steep ascent. A map check at the summit informs me I've missed a turn and climbed the hill entirely unnecessarily, but at least I know what the e-bike is capable of.

↑ Bikepacking the Swale Trail in the Yorkshire Dales (Patrick Kinsella)

Back on track, I follow the gravel trail through the valley, tracing the serpentine River Swale's south bank to Gunnerside. Crossing to the north I pedal along the cusp of Melbecks Moor, with the lovely lumps and bumps that characterise the Yorkshire Dales National Park rising to my right and the river rushing along on my left. Near an old lead mine at Crackpot Hall, on Beldi Hill, the track crosses Swinners Gill via a rough ford below a footbridge. Splashing through the water on slippery rocks tests both my bike-handling skills and the grip of the Ribbles' tyres, but we pass without me ending up on my arse. And then, at a fork in the way just before Keld, my mission takes me away from the river and up on to Black Moor, along a rideable section of the Pennine Way, that same long-distance trail that began beside our campsite in the Peak District, over 160km south of here.

I'm aiming for the Tan Hill Inn, England's highest pub and a legendary watering hole for Pennine Way walkers and Dales cyclists. I'm on a bridleway, but the riding gets increasing tough as the track becomes rough and rugged, taking me across multiple ghylls and ditches. By the time I reach the brow of Low Brown Hill the sun is starting to set the horizon ablaze and I fret that I won't reach the pub before dark. After a final push across Stonesdale Moor and over Lad Gill Hill, however, I spy the roof of the famous inn, lying at the end of a sweet single-track descent.

For a nominal fee, camping is allowed on the moorland around the pub, and I find a spot amid the boulders to string up a tarp and lay out my bivvy bag before going in search of sustenance at the inn, where a live band are in full swing. In December 2021, a sudden snowstorm on a Friday evening resulted in 61 people getting trapped for several days in this iconic pub, which sits pretty at 528m above sea level. No such luck for me, though. I'm literally here on the warmest night of the year, which makes for a balmy evening under the stars, but also means I wake up with a cloud of midges enjoying my blood for breakfast.

I get my stove on and cook some porridge, but the incessant attention of these irritating insects encourages me to pack my bike up and get going straight after breakfast. By 9am I'm enjoying a morning swim in the River Swale, wallowing below the waterfalls around Kisdon Force, near Keld.

It's a cruisy cycle back to the Dales Bike Centre on lanes, roads and rubbly trails through Swaledale, rolling along, unencumbered by a backpack, with plenty of juice left in the bike battery for a cheeky cheat on the steepest climbs. Looking down, I feel the bike is pretty much perfectly packed. It's a far cry from my early efforts. I've mastered this and I'm enthused about where I can take it next. A return to Dartmoor is definitely happening. I fancy a multiday mission, cycling coast-to-coast across Devon, along the Two Moors Way that links Exmoor and Dartmoor. My mates have just about started talking to me again – maybe I can convince them to come along for the ride… We can stick sweary Steve on the e-bike.

ESSENTIALS

GETTING STARTED To go on a guided bikepacking trip, contact Stef at Pannier (⌂ pannier.cc). To hire a gravel bike for an exploration of the Yorkshire Dales, visit the excellent Dales Bike Centre near Fremington (⌂ dalesbikecentre.co.uk).

SPECIAL CONSIDERATIONS As with all off-road cycling, it's important to be considerate to other trail users, whether they're on wheels, foot or horseback. Don't descend around blind corners at speed, and greet people on the paths.

KIT BAG You can enjoy bikepacking on a mountain bike or a gravel bike. The latter has drop handlebars (like a racing bike) and a rigid hard-wearing frame, with disc brakes on the wheels and chunky off-road tyres. You will need lightweight minimalist camping kit (a tent or tarp, sleeping bag and mat, stove, etc). There are now myriad bags available specifically designed for bikepacking, from brands like Alpkit, Chrome and Fjällräven.

GETTING THERE **Dartmoor's** gateway towns are Okehampton (north), Ivybridge (south), Bovey Tracey (east) and Tavistock (west). Okehampton and Ivybridge have train stations. The trailheads for the rideable section of the **Ridgeway** are found in Goring-on-Thames, Oxfordshire (closest train station Goring & Streatley) and Avebury (closest railway station Pewsey).

The **Peak District trails** are easily accessed from Sheffield, which is well serviced by trains. To reach **Swaledale and the Dales Bike Centre**, take the M1/A1, turning

↑ Wild camping while bikepacking on Dartmoor (Patrick Kinsella)

west at Catterick. The Leeds-Settle-Carlisle railway line is one of Britain's most scenic, crossing the Yorkshire Dales and stopping at stations including Horton in Ribblesdale, Ribblehead, Dent (England's highest main-line station), Garsdale and Kirkby Stephen.

PLACES TO STAY The rules around wild camping on Dartmoor are in flux, check the current situation with the Dartmoor National Park authority (⊘ dartmoor. gov.uk). There is no accommodation on the **Ridgeway**, but Oxford Oak Camping (⊘ theoxfordoakcamping.co.uk) in Fernham, with views of the Uffington White Horse, is just off the ridge, about halfway along the route. In the **Peaks**, Newfold Farm campsite (⊘ newfoldfarmedale.com) in Edale, beneath Kinder Scout, is superb. In the **Yorkshire Dales**, you can camp at the Tan Hill Inn (⊘ tanhillinn.com) for £5. Useful if you're staying longer, the friendly Dales Bike Centre (⊘ dalesbikecentre.co.uk) offers really good cyclist-friendly accommodation, with bike-washing facilities, a bike shop/hire/repair hub and a café/restaurant on site.

ELSEWHERE With a comprehensive web of bridleways covering the country, there are excellent bikepacking routes to explore all around Britain. Just get a map and start planning.

EXTRA RESOURCES
⊘ bikepacking.com

21 GHYLL SCRAMBLING

WHERE	Eskdale, the Lake District
SKILL LEVEL	Ghyll scrambling is quite accessible to most people of average fitness when enjoyed with a guide. To do it independently, depending on the route taken, you may require rock-climbing skills, need to know how to negotiate fast-moving water and be capable of doing a risk analysis in a dynamic environment, where water depth changes rapidly.
RISK FACTOR	Under the supervision of a good guide, risks are carefully managed, especially in terms of jumps and climbs. Routes vary and leaps are always optional, but potential dangers during any ghyll-scrambling adventure include slips and falls (potentially large ones), hitting submerged rocks during jumps, and being caught by fast-flowing water. Helmets should be worn, along with PFDs (life jackets) on some routes, and sometimes a harness and climbing rope may be required to safely ascend certain sections.

Wherever water meets elevation, creating fast-moving streams and cascades on hillsides and in mountain environments, you will generally find humans in among the elements, doing daft things for kicks. The sport of following tight and twisty waterways, as H_2O hurtles downwards in search of river and sea, is called canyoning, an adventure activity explored in this book in the Wonderful Waterfall country of Wales, amid the Bannau Brycheiniog/Brecon Beacons (page 158). But there is another way to approach this kind of natural playground. To really challenge yourself, you can make like a salmon and try going against both gravity and current, travelling upstream. But who would do that? Ghyll scramblers, that's who.

The people of Cumbria are hardy hill-dwelling folk, who seem to like making things as tough as possible for themselves (see *Fell running*, page 238). But, to be fair, the concept of tracing a waterway upwards towards its source, clambering through rocky clefts and following the steepening folds of a fell, is an alluring one. Here in the Lake District, such gullies are called ghylls, and the practice of scrambling up them began back in the 1800s, with rock climbers such as Keswick's famous Abraham brothers, George and Ashley, using the course of small rivers and streams as a way of approaching the routes they intended to climb, on peaks such as Scafell. Back then, the idea was to stay dry, and the challenge was to clamber along the precipitous banks of the gorge and around the waterfalls without falling in, which helped sharpen their climbing skills. These days, however, plunging into the water – often from quite a height – is central to the enjoyment of ghyll scrambling, and most people are attracted to the activity by the prospect of leaping into pools between the falls.

However, true ghyll scrambling is more about the quality of the ascent rather than the thrill of the jumps. To trace the pursuit back to its source, I joined a father-and-son team who have been deeply involved in guiding people on the activity for decades, on a ghyll-scrambling adventure along the Esk.

← Licence to ghyll – leaping into the Esk (Patrick Kinsella)

ESK-APADE

After waddling through the unusually sun-soaked Cumbrian countryside for a good 40 minutes, incongruously clad in a wetsuit, I'm more than ready to fall into the cool embrace of the Esk by the time we reach our get-in point, just beyond a stunning dry-stone bridge near a fork in the river. And I'm not the only one. For this escapade I have joined Andy Brown and his son Chris – both Lakes locals – and a group of lads celebrating a stag do. They're a friendly bunch, but some are a little jaded from their previous evening's exploits and an uphill hike clad in neoprene hasn't helped. Chris knows how to fix them, though, and he politely orders us all to splash into a pool at the base of the ghyll we're about to explore. There is no hangover cure on earth more effective and instantaneous than sudden full immersion in mountain-fresh water, and within seconds of taking the plunge they are reborn, in full sweary glory.

The footpath from the car park just beneath Hardknott Pass to the starting point has been disarmingly pretty, and en route I've been getting a history lesson about the origins of the adventure pursuit we're about to enjoy from Chris, who divides his time between Cumbria and the Austrian Alps, where he guides people in the mountains. Brought up in the fells, he educates me about the Abraham brothers and the evolution of ghyll scrambling in the 19th century. Chris and Andy used to spend most of their time taking people hill hiking and rock climbing, but the growing demand for ghyll-scrambling sessions from visitors seeking a slightly different Lake District experience means they now do little else. Fortunately, this doesn't seem to have dimmed Chris's enthusiasm for the endeavour, and he's beaming as he leads us upstream into the gob of the ghyll.

Besides the wetsuits, we're all wearing trainers or lightweight boots with good soles, a PFD (life jacket), climbing harness and a helmet. Andy talks about foot placement as we wade upstream through the river. The dry rock is grippy, but the minute your foot enters the water, most surfaces become as slippery as ice, and several of us take unintended swims as we wander.

UP TO THE GHYLLS An initial scramble takes us up a jumble of rocks to an abrupt drop-off, where we form a line on the ledge, like lemmings waiting to leap. This first jump is a gentle introduction to what lies ahead, and it allows Chris to talk us through the basic techniques of how to fall into rockpools without breaking yourself. While airborne, you can do whatever you like with your arms and legs, but by the time you hit the water, body position is important, otherwise you can end up in a world of pain. Arms and elbows need to be tucked in tight, so the impact doesn't cause you to punch yourself comedically in the face – pinching your nose is a definitely no-no, but placing arms across your chest and gripping on to the shoulder straps of your PFD is ideal. Legs need to

↑ Into thin air (and cold water) (Patrick Kinsella)

be shut together, for obvious reasons, and your knees need to be slightly bent, to absorb the impact and slow your rate of descent, just in case the landing zone is shallower than expected or you've strayed too close to a submerged object. The bigger the jump, the more important it is to get these things right.

The first drop is just a couple of metres, from a solid launching place into a nice pool with no nasty obstacles to avoid, but it's high enough for us to put all this sound advice into practice. I hit the water as instructed, descend about a metre below the surface and then pop back up like a cork. Tapping one hand on my helmet to let Chris know I'm fine, I start swimming upstream to the base of a waterfall, clearing the landing zone before the next person takes the plunge. Doing front crawl while wearing a PFD, a climbing harness and running shoes is never going to lend itself to a graceful or efficient stroke, but the current is stronger than I expected, and it takes some effort to reach the other side.

The next section requires some free climbing, as we scale the ghyll's steepening walls next to the cascading water. There are plenty of hand- and footholds, so it's not too tricky, and a fall would only send you backwards into the pool, but the adrenaline starts to kick in nevertheless. In single file, we edge around the crag at the top of the waterfall, skirt along the rocky banks and then watch Chris as he launches himself, Superman style, across water flowing fast through a narrow gap. It looks dicey, but he gets a good handhold on the crag opposite, and then scrambles up the other side of the ghyll. Messing up this dive-swim could result in someone getting flushed over the edge of the waterfall we've just ascended, so Andy positions himself in a place where he can grab anyone that makes a mistake. This is getting exciting.

DROP ZONE By the time we reach the top of the next waterfall, we're already two men down. Fortunately, they haven't been washed away, they've just realised the experience is far more full-on and demanding than they can handle after a heavy night, and have opted to bail early and head back to bottom along the footpath that runs parallel to the gorge. The rest of us push on, wading through waist-deep water, swimming across pools, scrambling over boulders and clambering up a sequence of narrow chasms with the charging water walloping our faces every step of the way. The remaining lads are all fully restored now, and I've rarely felt so alive.

Andy explains that the water levels in the ghyll can rise and fall with surprising speed, and they need to check them carefully before each outing. Some of the sections we're doing today would be far too dangerous to attempt after heavy rain, when the water is in full flow, but at the moment they're perfect.

We pause for while to play around in a pool where a little ledge provides the perfect launch pad for doing dives, bombs and backflips, but then embark on a section where the level of technical difficulty gets dialled right up. The first challenge is a horizontal traverse across a long section of the gorge wall. This is the kind of thing the old-school climbers would have practised as they explored the waterway while attempting to stay dry, and it takes real concentration, effort, tenacity and some skill to keep clinging on.

Andy is impressed by the performance of the lads. 'We've never had so many people on a group successfully get around this bit,' he tells me, just as I'm about to give it go myself. No pressure then... But almost as soon as he finishes speaking, the guy in front of me falls off the crag into the water, and has to claw his way to the other side where his waiting mates laughingly drag him out. Thankfully, I manage to make the whole climb, which ends in a jump and a swim.

The next two waterfalls are steep, and the vertical route to the top of them takes us over jagged rocks, rather than deep water, so Andy free climbs up first and then sets up a rope on an anchor point. It's not really required, but it's nice to know it's there if you're struggling to find a foot- or handhold, or to stop yourself falling backwards on to a nasty landing zone. At the top we reach a large, deep pool. The water is gin clear, and Chris produces a snorkelling mask from his pack and hands it to me. I hold it to my face and duck beneath the water, where I can see every detail of the submerged ghyll – the visibility is extraordinary.

Soon, though, this calm water will be much disturbed, because there are several jumps into this pool, and none of them are small. The first is all-out fun, but the second, which requires an extra scramble up another large crag (where Chris has rigged another rope for those who need it), is definite dare material. The drop is a good 8m, and the jump-off point is more technical too, with a couple of steps required before you propel yourself off a little ledge from one leg. And then there are a couple of submerged boulders to avoid at the bottom. The combination of all this soon sorts the stags from the fawns, and amid lots of banter, several of the group decide not to venture up. The ones that do soon sound a whole lot less cocky when they get to the edge, and before long the erstwhile peaceful ghyll is echoing to the sound of shrieks – as they pluck up the courage and leap – and then big booms as they hit the water, making surprisingly cacophonous explosions that echo through the gorge.

My preferred approach to these kinds of challenges is to just go for it, without hovering around and overthinking things, so when my turn comes I check there's no-one below me and then immediately launch myself into the abyss. There's just enough freefall time to think about various outcomes while I'm airborne, and then SMACK – I hit the water with a big bang and no small amount of splash. Once the adrenaline is already coursing through your veins and you know the experience isn't going to kill you, another jump is always much more exciting than terrifying, and several of us go back for a second and third fling.

↑ Falls gold – climbing the cascade (Patrick Kinsella) → Chris explores beneath the surface in a gin-clear plunge pool (Patrick Kinsella)

LINGO OF THE LAKES

The concept of upstream, anti-gravity canyoning is not exclusively endemic to Cumbria – elsewhere in the UK and Ireland it's known as gorge scrambling, and in Japan the activity is called *sawanobori* – but the landscape and language of the Lake District are certainly both unique, and here these sorts of shenanigans are only called one thing: 'ghyll scrambling'. Dating from Viking times, the Old Norse word ghyll (sometimes spelt 'gill' on maps) describes a deep, water-carved gully or gorge running down a fell (hill).

TOP FUN Once everyone has had enough airtime, Chris informs us that we're about halfway along the ghyll, which provokes some wailing from the lads, who pronounce themselves knackered. Andy and Chris, who have been here many times before, catering for groups of people with mixed fitness levels, are totally prepared for this outcome. A show of hands reveals I'm the only idiot who wants to continue going up instead of obeying the gravitational pull of the pub, so Andy takes the boys back to the start along the footpath, while Chris and I head off to tackle the top half of the Esk Gorge. Briefly I worry that I'm putting him out, but actually Chris now has even more of a spring in his step than before. 'This is my favourite part of the whole thing,' he grins. 'It's stunning up here, and hardly anyone comes this far.'

Now there's just the two of us, we move a lot faster up the ghyll, and the surroundings feel much wilder. Trees increasingly overhang the gorge, which is tight and otherworldly in its depth, with every word, splash and incidental noise bouncing back off the walls. When Chris leads me through a hole in a massive boulder, it's like passing through a hidden portal into a totally different dimension. I wouldn't be all that surprised to see an Ewok emerging from the foliage or peering over the top of a rock, but instead tiny ring ouzels and wheatears swoop around, skimming the water and catching insects.

We concentrate less on the jumps now, and more on the scrambling and clambering. Chris knows this place well, he's been coming here for years, but it's a dynamic environment and he's still discovering new climbing routes to try out and test his mettle on.

After scaling several smaller waterfalls, and wading and swimming through some lovely long stretches of the gorge, occasionally breaking out the snorkelling mask to explore beneath the surface, we eventually reach a large pool, fed by a big waterfall at the far end. Chris explains that the exit from this pool, leading to a climbing route up the waterfall, is the crux move of the whole experience. And then he promptly dives in, swims across the water and, after a few attempts, clambers out and makes the rest of the climb look easy. Following in his wake, I soon discover why the get-out is so deceptively tricky. Finding the first foothold is a nightmare, but once I get a toe into it, I manage to haul myself up, jam a knee into another hold and finally get clear of the water completely. I'm stoked to have made it, doubly so after Chris tells me he recently brought a team of ghyll-scrambling instructors here, and several needed assistance for that move.

But the ghyll won't let me go looking so smug. On the very final section, there's another tricky move, this one several metres up a waterfall, and while Chris free climbs around it with no dramas, I fall straight off into the water. Eventually, with a little help, I get up it and then we're abruptly spat out at the top of the gorge into a wide open area, with views of the Lake District's tallest peaks piercing the blue sky all around us.

It's almost a shock, after being in the intense, tight grip of the ghyll for so long, and I stand wide-eyed for a while, staring up at Scafell Pike (England's highest mountain) and the picturesque pyramid of Bowfell. We're not at the source of the Esk – that's much higher up, and its uppermost branches spread right across the flanks of the fells – but this is the top of the gorge. And now it really is time to shed the wetsuit and go with gravity towards the Woolpack Inn, to sign off the adventure with a celebratory pint of local ale.

↑ Topping out below Scafell (Patrick Kinsella)

ESSENTIALS

GETTING STARTED Chris and Andy (☏ 07974 390 977, **e** andy@ghyllscrambling. co.uk & chris@ghyllscrambling.co.uk, ⦿ ghyllscrambling.co.uk) guide ghyll-scrambling trips up the Esk Gorge and at other lovely Lake District locations (Stoneycroft Ghyll and Canyon, Secret Ghyll, Adventure Ghyll) in spring, summer and autumn. Their family-run business has been providing boutique adventure escapades since 2010.

SPECIAL CONSIDERATIONS Ghyll and gorge scrambling is a potentially dangerous pursuit, where local knowledge is required, along with technical expertise, so it is highly recommended you go with a professional guide who knows the area and the waterway very well. Never jump into water without knowing how deep it is, or what obstacles might lie beneath the surface.

KIT BAG You will need a hard-wearing wetsuit, a helmet and potentially a PFD and climbing harness (all of which should be provided if you're doing a guided experience). Bring your own trainers or boots (good grip is essential, soft rubber is best – Adidas-Terrex Hydrolace Canyoning shoes are literally made for this kind of pursuit, which is good to know if you intend doing lots of it), swimwear, a towel and some food – you'll burn lots of calories. Gloves (preferably neoprene) can be good in colder conditions.

GETTING THERE Ghyll scrambling can be enjoyed at various locations around the Lakes, but the Esk Gorge is considered by many to be the pinnacle, with the best scrambles and biggest jumps. Parking is found just below the infamous Hardknott Pass

↑ Cumbria's Lakes are fed by thousands of ghylls (ss)

(well known to cyclists as one of the steepest hill climbs in the country), which carries the B-road between Eskdale and the Duddon Valley. While the pass provides an exciting (nerve-wracking) drive, it's best to approach the meeting point via Eskdale, leaving the M6 at junction 36 when coming from the south, or junction 40 when approaching from the north. Andy will send you detailed directions.

PLACES TO STAY The National Trust's excellent **Eskdale Campsite** (⌖ nationaltrust.org.uk/holidays/eskdale-campsite-lake-district) near Boot, Holmrook, has tent and van sites and camping pods. It's perfectly positioned for meeting up with your ghyll-scrambling guides at Hardknott Pass, and for exploring many other adventures in the Lakes. There are myriad other accommodation options in the Lakes, ranging from VW Campervan hire places (⌖ vwcamperhire.net) to comfortable B&Bs and hotels. See ⌖ visitcumbria.com for more.

ELSEWHERE 'Ghyll scrambling' is unique to the Lake District (no-one will know what you are talking about if you say those words outside of Cumbria), but similar pursuits can be enjoyed elsewhere in Britain, under the name gorge scrambling (page 158), which differs in that it typically follows the flow of the water, in a downwards direction. Popular places to go gorge scrambling include Dartmoor, the Peak District, the Brecon Beacons and Snowdonia.

EXTRA RESOURCES
⌖ visitcumbria.com/activities/ghyll-scrambling

22 FELL RUNNING

WHERE	Langdale Fells, the Lake District
SKILL LEVEL	Fell running requires the ability to run on technical terrain, often completely off-piste and in challenging conditions, and to navigate to checkpoints along an unmarked and non-signed route using a map and compass.
RISK FACTOR	The terrain can be extreme. Falls, getting lost, exposure and dehydration are the biggest dangers.

O f all the adventure pursuits out there, running is surely the most fundamental, especially when it takes place off-road. Humans have been running ever since they stood on two legs, albeit not purely for fitness and fun – and there are plenty of people who still struggle to see anything remotely pleasurable in the activity. Millions more, though, swear by the transcendent enjoyment and escapism that can be found in wild running, and it has become enormously popular all around the world. In Britain, though, there exists a unique version of the sport, known as fell running.

↑ Fell runners negotiating a pathless peak in Cumbria (Duncan Andison/S)

'Fell' is a word used mainly in the north of England, especially around Cumbria, to describe a hill or peak that protrudes above the treeline. The legacy of the Vikings' visits to these islands runs deep up there, and the noun derives from the Old Norse word for mountain – similar words are used across Scandinavia for such hills (*fjell* in Norwegian, *fjeld* in Danish, *fjäll* in Swedish). Accordingly, fell running is, generally, regarded as a pursuit that happens in the high bits of northern England, particularly the lumpy parts of the Lake District. This is where the first fell running contests took place in the 1800s, with shepherds competing to show off their endurance levels and knowledge of the local hillscape. And consequently, for many people (like me), from the south of England and elsewhere, fell running has always had a bit of mystique swirling around it. What is it, exactly, and can we gain access to the club? (There literally is one, it's called the Fell Runners Association, and there are over 7,000 members.)

Fell running is similar to trail running in that it takes place off-road, on rugged surfaces, amid wild environments. However, often there are no actual trails involved. Which, of course, makes it very different, and a lot harder. With no trails to follow, you must make your own way across open terrain, without getting lost. In proper fell-running races, there are no directional arrows or course markings, either. Competitors carry a map and compass, and navigate their way to compulsory checkpoints in a prescribed order, but the exact route they take is up to them. No digital navigational devices are allowed, and in this way it's more akin to orienteering. Some degree of elevation is always involved (you can't go fell running without the fell). And it's always self-supported. Don't expect aid stations with water, isotonic drinks and cut-up bananas and oranges. You're on your own out there, so taking adequate layers and provisions to stay fuelled, watered and warm is essential. Neither should you expect a T-shirt or a medal just for turning up and getting to the end. If you're lucky, you might get a cup of tea and perhaps a pie. But entry to fell running events is typically very cheap – usually £5 to £10, a fraction of the price you'd pay to do a trail-running race – and it's very community based, often involving the local mountain rescue organisation.

'Fell running is probably closer to running naturally than any other sport,' Cumbrian-based athlete Ricky Lightfoot explains, when I ask him about the appeal of the pursuit. 'It can take you through knee-deep bog, forest plantations or deep gullies where possibly man has never set foot before.'

Besides being a former trail-running World Champion, Ricky recently became only the second human in history to beat all the equines in the legendary Man versus Horse race in Wales, and his words make me even keener to head to those historic hills (sorry, fells) where it all began, and earn my fell-running stripes.

FELLED AT THE FIRST HURDLE

I'm a fairly experienced trail runner, but I've never before attempted an official fell-running event. I did once do an 'intro to fell running' jaunt with a legend of the sport, Steve Birkinshaw, at the Keswick Mountain Festival. Steve had just broken a 27-year-old record (set by fell-running titan Joss Naylor) by running to the top of all 214 of the famous fells collectively known as the Wainwrights in under seven days, covering over 515km (320 miles) of technical terrain and climbing more than 36,000m (the equivalent of going up and down Everest four times, while doing two marathons each day). It's hard to appreciate that level of endurance, but these are the sort of shenanigans top fell runners get up to, with precious little in the way of recognition (outside of the fell-running community) or financial support.

But, while that was undeniably a fell-running experience and I've independently run around other fells since, it's not the same as taking part in an actual fell race. And until you've done that – or ticked off one of the great fell-running round challenges (page 246) – you really can't refer to yourself as a 'fell runner'. Ideally I wanted my first race to be on 'proper' fells too, in the historical home of the activity, but living at the wrong end of the country made that tricky. This year,

↑ The Langdale Fells from afar (Patrick Kinsella) → The starting line of the Langdale Horseshoe (Patrick Kinsella)

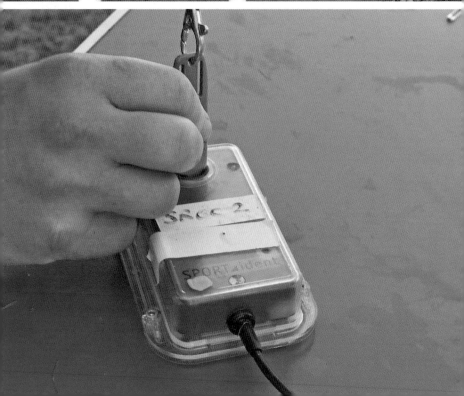

however, with winter approaching and the race calendar winding down, I found myself planning a trip to the Lakes during a weekend when a classic event was taking place. So I attempted to enter. And was immediately rejected.

I've been running on rough stuff for over 20 years, tackling trails and races all over the world, from the tors of Dartmoor to the Australian deserts and New Zealand's Southern Alps, via the mountains of Mauritius and foothills of the Himalaya in northern India. I'm neither fast, graceful or competitive, but I am dogged and have managed to complete ultra-distance events of 80km-plus in one outing, as well as multiday events and challenges that involve running more than a marathon distance for multiple days on the trot. But none of that impressed Dan Duxbury from Ambleside Athletics Club when I tried to enter the annual Langdale Horseshoe race he organises.

Dan's reply to my emailed entry request was friendly, but he politely explained the Langdale Horseshoe is at the extreme end of the fell-racing spectrum, requiring self-navigation skills and covering over 33km (21 miles) of hard, high terrain in October, when the weather could throw anything at participants. For all these reasons, he asks entrants to prove they've taken part in other fell-running races in the Lakes or Scotland in the previous two years. Which I couldn't do. Damn it. Tenacity is a prerequisite of fell-running though, and I replied explaining my running background and pointing to other adventures I'd done on challenging terrain that required self-navigation. I even went and walked some of the route, to do some research. And eventually, after a long, lovely conversation, Dan relented. 'Okay,' he wrote. 'Come and see me on the day… And have a tenner handy if you decide to do it!'

IN AT THE STEEP END Now, standing on the start line of the Langdale Horseshoe race, having talked my way into being allowed here, I'm absolutely terrified. Outside the appropriately scary sounding Old Dungeon Ghyll Hotel, one of Dan's crew checks I'm carrying all the compulsory gear: waterproof jacket and trousers – tick; whistle – tick; map and compass – tick; food and water – tick. Then I swap my tenner for a race number and an electronic dibber, which goes around my neck and is used to prove you have reached all the checkpoints, in the right order. 'Good luck!' Dan grins. I'm going to need it. Despite my claims of competence, I suddenly feel completely out of my depth. It's an amazingly mixed crowd, with people in their late teens to those well north of 60, but they all look frighteningly fit and wiry framed. I've seen more fat on a packet of vegetarian sausages than there is on evidence here.

The atmosphere is super friendly, though. Everyone around me seems to know one another, and they're all laughing and chatting in distinctly local accents, mostly about previous experiences in this race, but there's also lots of speculation

↑ The Old Dungeon Ghyll Hotel is legendary among runners, climbers and hikers (Patrick Kinsella)

← Fell runners follow no specific course, but have to check in with dibbers (Patrick Kinsella)

about the weather, which isn't great. I'm worried about everything now, from my choice of footwear (are these shoes too trail orientated?) to my lack of local knowledge and the fact that a stubborn-looking mist has descended all around us, threatening to make this even harder than I'd expected. During my recce ramble I'd scored a bluebird day, and while the terrain looked breathtakingly steep and technical, at least I could see the peaks I knew we were going to be running to. Now, as I stare at the feet of Raven Crag, the faces of the fells are completely obscured.

Luckily, there's not too much time to ruminate on this. With minimal fuss – as befits the unpretentious culture of fell racing – Dan gets us underway. It's a mass start, and the field self-seeds, with competitive folk eyeing a win tearing off in front and people like me – if indeed there are any other grommies like me in this line-up of 300-odd people – happier to start further back. I have set myself a couple of modest objectives: I want to finish the race (ideally in one piece), and I don't want to come absolutely last. Anything beyond that is a bonus. However, given my lack of local knowhow, I also don't want to lose sight of everyone, so I position myself in the middle.

↑ The unmarked, often trail-free landscape of the Lakes makes fell running uniquely challenging (Patrick Kinsella)

The first kilometre and a half is pretty flat and fast, as we run along the base of the posse of peaks that collectively comprise Langdale Fell. Then, shortly after crossing Dungeon Ghyll (a ravine) and passing the National Trust's Sticklebarn, we hook left and the climbing begins. Puffing like a steam train, I haul my way up the path, which traces a cascading stream to Stickle Tarn, a plateau lake. So far, so good – I'm keeping pace with the people around me and I'm happy to note that, like trail running, the most common approach is to power walk the really steep stuff and save your running legs for the rest of the race. As we run around the water's edge, however, the 700m peak of Pavey Ark rears out of the mist, and suddenly things start to look more serious.

The ascent of Pavey Ark – one of several Wainwrights on the race route – is a proper thigh burner. The only approach is to keep clambering, pushing your hands down on to your knees and trying not to lose ground. Topping out would usually reward with a stunning view, but we've climbed into the clouds and visibility is down to about 50m. From my recce, I know there's a steep drop-off to my left, but I can't see it. I clamber across the fell top as quickly as possible and locate the first checkpoint, where a marshal records my number and holds

DOING THE ROUNDS

Besides races, challenges – usually based on completing a 'round' of summits in 24 hours or less – are a big part of fell running. The big three, all named after the first fell runners to complete them, are the **Bob Graham Round**, a 106km (65-mile) Lake District circuit that starts and finishes at the steps of Keswick's Moot Hall and climbs 42 fells with total ascent of 8,200m (27,000ft); the **Charlie Ramsay Round**, a 93km (58-mile) route taking in 24 peaks in the Scottish Highlands (23 of them Munros – peaks of over 914m/3,000ft); and the **Paddy Buckley Round**, a 100km (61-mile) loop of 47 summits in Snowdonia, Wales.

FURTHER READING *Feet in the Clouds: The Classic Tale of Fell-Running and Obsession* by Richard Askwith is an excellent book about the history, culture and allure of fell running.

out a box that beeps when I dip my dibber into it. One down, six more to go. I set off in the direction of 723m-tall Thunacar Knott, another Wainwright, and locate the second checkpoint. And then we leave the path and go fully off-piste, scarpering across the wide-open terrain of Martcrag Moor.

FEAR & ROAMING There are some strict rules around fell running, such as the ban on using digital devices to navigate, and then there are codes of conduct. For example, it's not the done thing to hang on to the heels of others, leaving them to do all the navigating. However, it's perfectly acceptable (highly sensible even) to follow 'trods' – footprints left on the landscape once those in front have run through. It's also fine to form little groups as you go, and to keep an eye on those well ahead (bearing in mind that they might have erred with their navigation). I'm fretting so much about falling out the back of the race that I'm running much faster than I usually would while doing this sort of distance over the kind of terrain we're tackling. I'm also being chased through the fells by the spectre of cut-offs. Because, if you don't reach some checkpoints by a certain pre-decided time, marshals will pull you from the course and your race is over. This is a sensible safety measure, ensuring the poor marshals don't get stuck up on the top of exposed fells for too long, but the fear of getting cut really snaps at your heels.

Charging across the moor, I'm aware that checkpoint 3 is where the first cut-off will be enforced. A guy ahead of me sinks to his shins in a sudden bog, so I swerve and take a different line. I avoid the bog, but hit a slippery section of mud and instantly go down on my backside and skid for several metres. The runner behind me registers my mishap and takes another route. Covered in gloop, I

↑ Warm and waterproof clothing is usually mandatory equipment for fell runs (Dale Towers/S)

get up and carry on, only to sink right to my thigh in another bog about 100m further on. This kind of stuff is what makes fell running so tough, and if it carries on I'm going to miss that cut-off.

Fortunately I find better ground and even a hint of a path leading to Angle Tarn, and push on to the checkpoint near Esk Hause, arriving with 30 minutes to spare before the cut-off. Is that enough? I'm not sure, there's still a long way to go. By now I'm with a cluster of around 20 runners – all strangers, but we're travelling at roughly the same pace. We pass west of the 885m Est Pike, which is a Wainwright, but it has no checkpoint so there's no point going to the summit. Soon after, there's a disagreement about the direction to take to reach 902m-high Bow Fell, yet another Wainwright, but one with a compulsory checkpoint. We waste valuable minutes dithering and debating, and then the group splinters. The mist is relentless, and it's hard to place exactly where I am on the map. My watch (which I'm wearing purely to record the route for posterity) would give me a grid ref if I asked it, but I resist this illegal move and press on. After initially making a mistake and needlessly ascending a rise, I consult my compass again and desperately re-route. It's micro mistakes like these that lead you to either get lost altogether, or fall sufficiently behind to miss the cut-offs. Eventually the checkpoint looms, and I'm relieved to discover I'm still on track, albeit with less margin of error to play with.

Next, though, is the crux area of Crinkle Crags, where there's a large drop, known ominously as 'Bad Step', and a fifth checkpoint to find among the magical

↑ Runners on the final descent of the Langdale Horseshoe (Patrick Kinsella)

mess of rocky towers and folding felltops that give the feature its name. After successfully locating the checkpoint, and even making up a bit of time, I fall in with a group of three other runners who seem confident about the best way to descend. And yet, we still end up downclimbing a precipitous section of the crag, with my shoes sliding horribly as I hug the rocks for dear life. After this hairy section, the ascent to the Pike of Blisco is almost joyful, not least because when I reach it comfortably within the prescribed time limit, I know it's the last checkpoint with a cut-off.

Safe in the knowledge that nothing can stop me finishing now, the final descent across the flanks of Wrynose Fell is glorious, especially since the mist finally lifts, like a net curtain being drawn up, revealing a stunning view across Langdale to the peaks and pikes I'd been scrambling around a few hours earlier. I even pause to grab some photos, and everyone else seems equally giddy. After running across the finish line I grab a locally made pie – there's one for each participant, and it's far better than any finisher's medal or T-shirt I've picked up at races in the past (I'd have happily paid most of my entry fee just for that pie), and then hunt down Dan, to let him know I'm alive. Runners are still crossing the line, some even more muddied and bloodied than me, having obviously taken tumbles. My entry number is splattered in fell filth, but I'm not going to wash it – that will go straight up on my wall at home, muck and all, as evidence that I'm a fell runner now. Of sorts. I'm back – albeit in 236th position in a field of 256 finishers. But that's mission accomplished for me. Until next year…

↑ Entry is £10 and you get a pie for finishing – tastier than any medal (Patrick Kinsella)

ESSENTIALS

GETTING STARTED Not all fell-running events are brutally hard. To get into the sport, it's a good idea to start with an easier challenge, join a club or go out with a specialist guide such as Dave Taylor (⚲fellrunningguide.co.uk). Fell Runners Association (FRA) races are graded and coded with letters: S is for short (10km or less), M is medium (10–20km) and L is long (20km or more). But be aware that these distances are only part of the story, and the terrain plays a huge part in determining how tough the course is. Accordingly, there's also an A/B/C rating for each race, with A being the hardest and hilliest. If navigation skills are required then you'll see NS next to the race name, and if prior fell-running experience is a prerequisite then ER will also appear.

SPECIAL CONSIDERATIONS Always check local weather forecasts before setting out on a fell run and carry appropriate gear with you. Be aware that even when lowland and lake-level forecasts seem benign, conditions can change very fast in the fells.

KIT BAG Good fell-running shoes with grippy soles are crucial. Some events have compulsory equipment lists, which always include map and compass, whistle, waterproof layers and food, and might even specify an emergency bivvy.

↑ Langdale Fell (Ian Duffield/S)

GETTING THERE To explore the Langdale Horseshoe, arrive via the A591, between Kendal and Keswick, turning off at Ambleside and following signs for Langdale. There's a National Trust car park by the Old Dungeon Ghyll Hotel, and another by Sticklebarn.

PLACES TO STAY There are two hotels at the foot of Langdale Fell: the **Old Dungeon Ghyll Hotel** (where the iconic Hiker's Bar is beloved by fell runners, walkers and rock climbers), which is where the race starts, and the **New Dungeon Ghyll Hotel**. There's a National Trust campsite at Great Langdale.

ELSEWHERE Cumbria is the historical heartland of the sport, but recognised fell-running races and challenges take place in Wales, Scotland, the Peak District, Staffordshire moorlands and the Long Mynd in Shropshire. Dartmoor and Exmoor also offer suitable fell-running terrain. Visit the FRA website and check the event calendar.

EXTRA RESOURCES
⌀ fellrunner.org.uk

23 VIA FERRATA

WHERE	Honister Slate Mine, Keswick, the Lake District
SKILL LEVEL	Low. No technical climbing skills required – you just need a good head for heights and a reasonable level of fitness.
RISK FACTOR	Low. So long as you listen to your instructor, keep your karabiners clipped on to the safety wire and your helmet on, there's little risk.

Seatoller in the English Lake District is a long way from Italy's Dolomite Mountains, but believe it or not, the two places are connected by a series of paths. Iron paths, no less. On the towering walls high above Honister Pass, midway between beautiful Buttermere and Borrowdale, hundreds of metal hand- and footholds protrude from the mine-scarred slate rock. Creating a *via ferrata* – which means 'iron path' in Italian – these permanently fixed features form a vertiginous route around the exposed edges of high Honister Crag, leading up to the summit of Fleetwith Pike. Every day, small groups of climbers scale these ladders into the sky, pitting themselves against gravity and defying the terrifying prospect that a single slip would seemingly send them plummeting hundreds of metres into the jagged jaws of a slate quarry far below.

In fact, travellers on the Honister Slate Mine via ferrata are extremely safe, unlike the men who clambered, crawled and climbed their way through the Dolomites in the era when these paths came into their own. Although fixed pieces of protection had been used to aid the ascent of mountainsides in alpine areas of Europe for decades prior to the outbreak of World War I, it was during the so-called Great War that semi-sophisticated systems of tunnels, ladders and ropes were developed to move troops around in the Italian mountains, where a high-altitude conflict was ranging on a near-vertical battlefield between Italian and Austro-Hungarian soldiers. Less known than the terrible events that unfolded at sea level, on the fields of Flanders, this theatre of war raged for three years between 1915 and 1918, and was critical to the outcome of the global power struggle, with the Italians preventing the Austro-Hungarians from crossing the alpine range and occupying the strategically important Venetian plain. Even viewed amid the shocking carnage of WWI, the conditions on this skyscraping frozen front were appalling, and fighters on both sides died in their thousands, often in deliberately caused avalanches, with broken bodies left where they fell.

Years later, with wartime tales of alpine heroics in the face of horror having become legendary, these rough, tough routes were restored, with much more reliable metal holds and steel cables replacing the weathered ropes and wooden ladders used by the soldiers. In other mountainous parts of Italy, and across alpine areas of Spain, France, Austria, Germany and Switzerland, new iron paths were built amid the peaks, and via ferrata climbing became a popular adventure pursuit. There are now over 1,000 routes to explore in the Dolomites alone, with people often pushing themselves through a ceiling of fear and physical exertion to experience the stunning beauty of the region, and the history that haunts it.

Here in Britain, the Honister Slate Mine was the first location to harness interest in this uniquely accessible form of climbing, with the construction of a via ferrata route in 2007.

← A horizontal traverse high above Honister Pass (Patrick Kinsella)

While it can't claim a battle-hardened history quite as dramatic as the Dolomites, the iron path here does take climbers on a thrilling journey through the stunning landscape of the Western Fells, along an age-old and multi-storied route used by miners for centuries as they chipped away at the slate face of Fleetwith Pike. It traverses terrain immortalised by Britain's premier peak-bagging pioneer and most famous fell-walker, Alfred Wainwright, and ascends through views that steal any remaining breath you might have left in your lungs after clambering up so many rungs. Up against extremely stiff competition, it's been awarded the Lake District's best visitor experience – but this begs a question: is it really a bona fide adventure pursuit, or just another tourist attraction? There's only one way to find out.

FIRST STEPS

At 08.30, on a sunny autumn morning, the keen Cumbrian air whistles through the deep cleavage that is Honister Pass, between Seatoller Fell and Dale Head. Besides the breeze, which is just about chilly enough to hide behind if I start to quiver when things get steep, it's a beautiful day – perfect for a walk along an iron path into the clouds. Three of us are making nervous small talk and mentally preparing to take on the Via Ferrata Xtreme, the longest and most demanding of the climbing experiences offered here at the Honister Slate Mine. If everything goes to plan, the challenge should take us three hours to complete, and we've been told to expect plenty of vertical ascent, punctuated by several overhangs, a ravine traverse across a Burma Bridge and a clamber up a suspended sky ladder.

Rob and Anita, my fellow climbers, are both doctors, which feels reassuring, although there's not much anyone can do to cure the results of a catastrophe on a crag. And Rob is already shivering, something I put down to the fact that he's ill-advisedly wearing shorts (it's only later that he fesses up to being a bit afraid of heights). We meet Gary, our guide, and he gets us geared up in harnesses and helmets, and equips us with specialist gear including a pulley device and a quickdraw (a length of leash with a twist-lock karabiner on either end), before going through the safety brief, which is simultaneously very simple and incredibly serious. It can be summarised thus: be sure to keep at least one karabiner firmly closed on the steel safety line at all times, otherwise you might tumble to your death. And if you hear falling rock, resist the urge to look up or your face may meet the stones first, rather than your helmet, which is far better qualified for the job.

After departing the base, located amid the last working slate mine in England, we wander along some ancient rail tracks, past a disused trolley and into the darkness of an old mine shaft, one of hundreds of tunnels that honeycomb this fell. With his heardtorch pointing the way, Gary explains how skiddaw slate has been mined here since Norman times. For centuries, men would drag sleds of stone

→ Gary goes through the gear, and then leads the way into the mine (Patrick Kinsella)

GETTING YOUR GRADES

None of the standard difficulty-rating scales can be applied to Britain's via ferrata experiences because they don't fall into any of the main climbing camps (rock, ice or aid), but in Italy – where there are many more vie ferrate and people can access them independently – the routes are graded. There are several systems in operation, with one of the most popular being the **Fletcher/Smith Rating System**, which awards a route a number according to how technically difficult it is, and a letter to represent how committing it is (in terms of the surrounding environment and how easy – or not – it might be to abort the adventure and downclimb the route); 1A is the shortest, safest and easiest, 5C the most challenging. Then there's the **Hofler/Werner Rating System**, which simply assigns each route a letter, ranging from A (simple) to G (technical mountain-climbing experience and skills required). All existing via ferrata routes in the UK are either guided or inside, so none of them are really risky or especially committing. The Honister Xtreme route is fairly long, however, with overhangs and big drops that require a good head for heights, so the climb might be rated as a 2A on the Fletcher/Smith Rating System, or a B or C on the Hofler/Werner System. It's the ideal introduction to the activity, and perfect if you want to explore more challenging routes in places like the Dolomites.

across the crag, labouring along perilous paths and tracks. The route of the via ferrata we're about to take follows the incredibly steep route of the Victorian-era narrow-gauge railway system, constructed up the face of Honister Crag between 1880 and 1895. An extraordinary feat of engineering ingenuity, the railway ran from 'the Hause' in Honister Pass, to Ash Gill at the summit, transporting miners and gear up and down the fell. An 'aerial flight', constructed with strong steel cables, carried the chunks of slate they hacked out of the mountainside down to the mine for processing. Battered by the relentless onslaught of Cumbria's oft-angry weather, the railway and aerial flight were abandoned by 1956. The scrap merchants cleaned up most of the remains, like heavy metal vultures, and for decades the upper parts of the mine were visited only by birds and the occasional risk-seeking trespasser. In,1997, however, local businessman Mark Weir bought the mine and realised the tourism potential of this highly featured vertical playground. The via ferrata was built in 2007, with the Xtreme course opening in 2012, and myriad other climbing and adrenaline experiences can now be enjoyed inside the mine and out on the crag.

Eventually we emerge from the ink-dark insides of the mountain to an open area directly beneath the crag. Here, next to signs cheerfully offering more warnings about the potentially terminal consequences of not doing things properly, Gary demonstrates how to clip on to the steel safety wire that will shadow us for the entire route, whether we're edging across the rockface or clambering up the rungs of the via ferrata. Each time you meet a point where the cable is attached to the rock, it's necessary to unclip in order get around and progress along the next section. This is why we have two karabiners, so one remains attached at all times. We spend a little time practising how to twist open the karabiners with one hand, a skill that will make our progress around the route a whole lot smoother if we can master it, and then Gary sends us over the edge.

ABOVE THE ABYSS Like an abseiling experience, this initial step – when you first put all your weight, faith and, indeed, life, in the hands of the equipment – is the most terrifying to take. Beneath us, Honister Crag completely falls away, and suddenly we are dangling over a sheer drop of hundreds of metres, straight down to the serpentine pass way, way below. If I'd been feeling a little bit blasé about how challenging a via ferrata experience might be, this is the point when it dawns on me that, perhaps, it's going to be quite confronting.

The beauty of via ferrata, in its modern incarnation, is that it typically allows people with no technical climbing skills to experience what it feels like to cling on to a fell face or mountainside for dear life. (If that's something they want to do – which the ever-growing popularity of this pursuit suggests it is.) The psychology of adrenaline sports, deliberately terrifying tourism experiences and even fairground rides, is an interesting one. Perhaps we all need to feel the proximity of death every now and then in order to appreciate being alive.

↑ Honister Pass holds the UK record for the most rainfall in 24 hours, but it's beautiful (Patrick Kinsella)

The alpinist Joe Simpson, famous for his very-near fatal fall during an ascent of an Andean peak in Peru, retold in the film *Touching the Void*, has memorably described the deadly but mysteriously alluring emptiness that's ever present on your exposed side when you're climbing, as the 'beckoning silence'. What feels like it can kill you never fails to thrill you.

We're some way along the route, concentrating hard on our changeovers and making sure the karabiners click properly shut after attaching to each new section of wire, before we twig that Gary isn't with us. Thankfully, he hasn't taken the quick way down, he's just observing how we're getting on from a vantage point above – this, it turns out, is just a little practice loop. Soon all four of us embark on the iron path proper, negotiating our way up, down and around a series of gullies, and along a horizontal traverse across an exposed section of the crag. While you don't need any technical climbing skills to scale most via ferrata routes, constantly clinging on to the rungs does demand a decent amount of physical exertion, especially where there are overhangs. As with any kind of climbing, the main trick is to trust your feet – if you constantly attempt to support your body weight with your arms, you will quickly tire and lactic acid builds up in your bloodstream, making your muscles useless.

Soon we reach a deep scar in the crag, spanned by a long Burma Bridge – a wobbly-looking affair comprised of three thick cables strung across the divide to form a rudimentary triangular-shaped bridge over the massive drop. To cross, you must walk along the bottom cable, steadying yourself with hands placed on the two slightly higher parallel cables that run either side. Gary shows us how to use the pulley devices we've been carrying to attach our harnesses to the ever-present safety line, which runs overhead here, ready to catch anyone who takes a tumble. Swallowing his acrophobia, Rob goes first, and soon loudly lets us know exactly how exhilarating the experience is. Or terrifying. With the breeze sending his words howling down into the valley, it's hard to interpret his colourful Geordie-accented adjectives. Anita follows her partner's footsteps, and I join them 50m or so behind. With the three of us on the bridge, all moving at once, it bows and sways excitingly. It's best to push the side cables out as far as you can, and take measured steps forward, but that's easier said than done when you feel like you're tiptoeing through thin air, with mere millimetres of metal between your feet and the beckoning abyss. By the time Gary joins us, the whole thing is writhing around like a flying snake.

On the other side, many more metal rungs take us ever higher on the crag, with views opening up across the Lakes, until we reach the bottom of a sketchy-looking skyladder. By this stage, with lactic acid fizzing in my veins, this final clamber up the rope netting feels – and, I'm sure, looks – pretty graceless and ungainly, but eventually I top out and lie sprawling on the rock. This is the end of the climbing

↑ Anita heads uphill on the iron road (Patrick Kinsella) ← Gary grapples with a Burma bridge (Patrick Kinsella)

part of the adventure, but we still need to hike through the upper intestines of the mine. Entering Ash Crag tunnel, we wander through the scattered debris left by centuries of activity. Medieval monks were once busy up here, breaking rocks and collecting slate for the roofs of monastic buildings around Furness Abbey. Later on, when the slate was being harvested for industry, miners working at this height would stay up here, instead of traipsing up and down, and the remains of their little sky villages built into the rocks can still be seen.

And then we pop out of the gloom, on the top of Fleetwith Pike, and the landscape of the Lakes explodes open all around us. Removing our helmets, we walk across the summit to a trig point, which marks the 648m peak. Below, Buttermere ripples while over to the west stands Haystacks, where Alfred Wainwright's ashes were scattered by the shores of Innominate Tarn after he meandered off this mortal coil in 1991. The downward dawdle, along the public footpath to the base of the crag, is pretty, but pedestrian compared to the way we ascended. The via ferrata experience has left me buzzing – and I'm sure it's not just the lactic acid working its way through my system. For me, it qualifies as a genuine adventure activity beyond doubt, and my appetite has been well and truly whetted. I'm definitely heading to the Dolomites to explore more.

↑ From the top, Gary points across Buttermere to Haystacks, where Wainwright's ashes were spread (Patrick Kinsella)

ESSENTIALS

GETTING STARTED Via Ferrata Xtreme tours run year round and can be booked through the Honister Slate Mine (⊘ honister.com), along with other climbing adventures (inside and outside the mine) and adrenaline experiences such as infinity bridge crossings and freefall jumps.

SPECIAL CONSIDERATIONS Temperatures on the crag can be a lot colder that in the pass, and conditions can always change quickly on the fells.

KIT BAG It's best to layer up (baselayer, fleece, waterproof shell), to keep the elements at bay. Wear comfortable, quick-drying trousers with plenty of dynamic stretch (not jeans or heavy cotton tracksuit bottoms). Gloves can be useful (wear a pair with good grip – soft material palms will not suffice). Sturdy footwear is a must – hiking boots or grippy trainers are fine, but a pair of approach shoes offering a decent degree of rigidity and foot support across the sole are best for edging around rocks and climbing the rungs of the via ferrata. On guided experiences, a harness, helmet and all technical equipment will be supplied.

GETTING THERE The Honister Slate Mine is found near Seatoller on the Honister Pass (Borrowdale, Keswick, Cumbria CA12 5XN). Drive south along the B5289 from either Cockermouth or Keswick. Stagecoach buses 77 and 77A travel from Keswick to the Honister Slate Mine.

PLACES TO STAY Buttermere offers myriad accommodation options, from campsites to lakeside B&Bs and hotels, including the **Bridge Hotel** (⊘ bridge-hotel.com), super scenically situated between Buttermere and Crummock Water, and surrounded by famous fells. There are many more hotels and holiday cottages throughout Borrowdale.

ELSEWHERE **Kendal Climbing Wall**, also in the Lake District, boasts Europe's first indoor via ferrata route (⊘ kendalwall.co.uk/via-ferrata). Elsewhere in the UK, guided via ferrata climbing experiences are offered at **Kinlochleven**, near Fort William in Scotland (⊘ verticaldescents.com); **How Stean Gorge** in the Yorkshire Dales (⊘ howstean.co.uk); on **Dartmoor** in Devon (⊘ devonadventure.co.uk/via-ferrata); and near **Falmouth** in Cornwall (⊘ viaferratacornwall.co.uk). Within **Wookey Hole** in Somerset, you can even take on an underground via ferrata route above a subterranean river (⊘ wildwookey. co.uk). And if you can get to the Dolomites, tackling a via ferrata route there is must.

EXTRA RESOURCES
⊘ via-ferrata-dolomites.com

24 SWIMRUN & SWIMHIKE

WHERE	Buttermere & Crummock Water, the Lake District
SKILL LEVEL	To take part in a swimrun event, or do a swimrun or swimhike challenge, you need to be able to swim (in an outdoor setting, sometimes across fairly large stretches of wild water) and run or hike on potentially technical trails (or even fells with no marked paths), dealing with all the naturally occurring obstacles and challenges traversing such terrain involves. On some routes you will need to be able to navigate using a map and compass.
RISK FACTOR	You can potentially get lost or suffer a fall while tackling trails, but more serious risks need to be factored in during the wet sections of a swimrun or swimhike course. All well-run events will have some on-water safety for the swim legs, but attempting a challenge independently means you are responsible for your own wellbeing. It's highly advisable to have a safety paddler (in a kayak, or on a SUP board) with you while attempting to swim across any large stretch of open water, where cramp or fatigue can set in.

Wild swimming has become a massively popular activity in recent years, with oceans of newspaper and magazine space dedicated to it and endless guidebooks written about the subject. As certain commentators have rather acerbically observed, people have always swum in open water – around the coast and in rivers, lakes and lochs – they just didn't call it 'wild swimming' and bang on about it all the time. There's some truth in this, but there's also no doubt that the mass embrace of outdoor swimming as regular form of exercise, and the large number of well-organised groups of swimmers we see splashing about on Britain's beaches and waterways these days – many of them continuing to swim all year round – is a relatively new phenomenon.

And in my book, that's a good thing. Everyone should enjoy the aquatic element of the landscapes they live in and visit, and the more people taking dips in rivers, lakes and coastal coves, the greater the pressure that will be brought to bear on water companies, environmental agencies and governments to clean up their act and return the nation's waterways (a precious, shared natural resource for the whole population) back to a proper state of health.

This surge in participation in outdoor swimming is comparable to the mass blossoming in popularity of trail running (or 'wild running', if you like) over the last few decades. Indeed, it's often the same people taking the plunge in the wild water as it is running through the wild woods, so the fact that a multisport has evolved, combining these two pursuits, is no surprise. Given there are only two activities involved, and that the focus of many people who take part is on the completion of a route rather than any competitive element, maybe the moniker 'multisport' is misleading, but nevertheless, swimrun – and its slightly slower sibling, swimhike – is most certainly an adventure pursuit.

← Swimrunning events are increasingly popular around the country (bezikus/S)

The concept of swimrun has always really appealed to me. I love the idea of taking on a linear or circular cross-country course where you have to carry all your own gear and tackle sections of trail and traverse open stretches of water - it feels like a proper adventure. The only problem with it is finding a good entry point. Most of the action happens around organised races and challenges, and there are some iconic annual events - none more so than the Scilly Swim, where participants take on a course that features six sea swims (one of them 4.8km in length) between the Isles of Scilly, way off the coast of Cornwall, with land legs to be walked or run in between. I'm determined to have a crack at that one day, but my sea swimming fitness levels aren't quite there yet, so I've been on the lookout for a more manageable challenge to get me started. And it's a search that took me from one end of England to the other.

TESTING THE WATER

After some rudimentary DIY adventures, running along my local clifftops and then swimming back around the coast, my first proper swimrun experiences were with a friend who was scoping out a series of routes for races he was organising in south Devon. Together we swam around the headland of the Kingsbridge Estuary near Salcombe, from South Sands Beach to Starehole Bay, ran sections of the South West Coast Path and then got wet again swimming across Hope Cove. On another occasion, he talked me into doing a 'short' exploratory swim leg along the River Dart, which turned out to be over 3km long, before running a longer route back. Thankfully, the incoming tide was with us during the Dart swim, and it was like travelling horizontally on a magic carpet. A seal even joined us for nearly 1km, lazily keeping pace and every 100m or so popping his head up for a bemused look at the odd creatures who'd so clumsily entered his environment. We swam past ruins and boathouses on the riverbank, beneath the boughs of great overhanging oaks, and were tickled by the dangling limbs of willow trees. It was magical, and I was hooked. My buddy, Ceri, still organises events involving swimming and running, but they're more like aquathlons than swimruns (see opposite).

The Dart swim convinced me that I am capable of doing decent distances in the water - so long as the tide is on my side - but my swimming technique still leaves a lot to be desired, and partly because of this, I've long been looking for a non-competitive swimrun or swimhike challenge to take on, rather than a race. There are several around, the most famous being the fabulous Frog Graham Round in the Lake District. This is loosely based on the renowned Bob Graham Round, a monstrous fell-running challenge that sees people pegging it up 42 fells (peaks), taking on 8,200m (26,900ft) of ascent and running at least 106km (66 miles) in the process, starting from Keswick's Moot Hall and finishing back there within 24 hours. The Frog Graham Round, devised by a devoted swimhiker called Peter Hayes, removes some of the ground distance and elevation, still leaving nearly

SWIMRUNS & AQUATHLON EVENTS

The most tempting way to describe competitive swimruns – sometimes known as aquathlons – is to say they're like triathlons for people who can't afford the bike or simply don't like cycling. That's not quite fair, though, because there are elements of these multisports that, arguably, make them tougher than a tri. For starters, for longer-distance swimruns you usually have to be completely self-reliant, and after transitioning from the swim to the run, or vice versa, participants must carry all their kit with them for subsequent legs. So if you swim in a wetsuit, you either keep it on and run in the soggy neoprene, or you have to carry it. Equally, you can choose to either swim in your running shoes (and then put up with them squelching along the trails), or throw them in a tow bag for the aquatic sections. Also, while some short, sporty aquathlons take place in more controlled situations, most swimrun and swimhike courses cover wild terrain, with rugged trails rather than the generously predictable sealed surfaces most triathlons take place on. And, lastly, while most multisport challenges put you through one discipline at a time and then allow you to move on to the next one, with swimrun you typically have to do multiple land-based legs, punctuated by several swims.

65km of running, but adds in sizeable swims across four of the big beautiful puddles the Lake District is named after: Bassenthwaite Lake, Crummock Water, Buttermere and Derwentwater.

I would dearly love to have a crack at the full Frog Graham Round (and I am determined to one day), but I know I'm not yet swim-fit for such an epic route, so it was with much delight that I discovered there is a smaller version. Aptly named the Tadpole, this much more manageable challenge involves two of the Frog's wet legs, with swims across Crummock Water and Buttermere, plus about 11km (7 miles) of fell running around the banks of both lakes, and around the rearing flanks of Rannerdale Knotts, just below the peak of Whiteless Pike.

SWIMFUN

It's free to download the route of the Tadpole from the Frog Graham website, but because it's a DIY challenge you have to do all the risk assessment and organise safety arrangements yourself. The only part I was a little bit worried about was the first swim leg, which although not enormous, does take you right across Crummock Water from the eastern bank by Rannerdale to the western shore at Low Ling Crag, and if the wind kicks up it can be pretty choppy on this large lake. For these reasons, and the fact that the deep water can be heart-wobblingly chilly all through the year, the guidelines strongly recommend people attempting the swimrun challenges do so in pairs and/or with someone else doing water safety. Fortunately, a good friend

who lives in the Lakes, Tom, volunteers to accompany me across on his paddleboard, keeping an eye on things just in case I run into any trouble.

We meet at the National Trust car park beneath the craggy rise of Rannerdale Knotts on a bluebird morning, with barely a cloud in the Cumbrian sky, a serendipitous result for late September, when conditions can often be much more challenging. As Tom inflates his board and I squeeze into my Alpkit wetsuit, the water across the way looks positively inviting. I opt to keep my shoes and socks dry for the first running leg at least, and stash them in a Lomo dry bag designed specifically for swimrunning, which ingeniously transforms into both a tow float and a backpack.

A little gasp escapes me as I press the start button on my watch and wade barefoot into the lake, where Tom is already up on his board. Once I'm up to my waist I put my goggles on and take the plunge properly, shattering the shimmering reflection of Mellbreak in the still water, and then begin swimming towards the a 512m fell that dominates the view on the far bank. My stroke is frustratingly graceless and inefficient, and I set off far too fast for my swim-fitness level, which despite weekly sea sessions throughout the summer still isn't where I would like it to be. I'm soon out of breath and forced into making several pauses, treading water and pretending to Tom that I'm checking that I'm still going in the right direction, while really gulping great mouthfuls of air and telling myself to relax.

As it happens, although the day is fine, Tom is having to deal with a lively breeze that's whipping along the lake and blowing him around all over the place, so he has opted to kneel rather than stand up on his SUP. On the upside, I'm comfortably warm in my wetsuit, and by the time I'm about a third of the way across, I manage to settle into a more measured stroke. Once I calm down and get my breathing sorted, I'm able to punch out the rest of the swim without any dramas.

Low Ling Crag soon looms to my right, but I keep going to the main shoreline, just left of this little arm of land that reaches out into the lake, and run on to the stony beach by the rocky ankles of Mellbreak. As I bid goodbye to Tom, and he paddles back across the water to our start point, a family arrive on kayaks and shout a cheerful hello. The sight of people doing these things is not the least unusual here, in this adventure paradise, and as I lace my shoes up and prepare to set off running, the father tells me that he did the Frog Graham Round not long back, and shares some detailed horror stories about chafing that I could have happily not heard.

RUNFUN Setting off around the scenic trail that hugs the west bank of Crummock Water, I'm soon cooking in my wetsuit. I'd been deliberating overnight about wearing a shorty, but the autumnal chill of the September dawn convinced me a full wetsuit was the better option, and now I'm regretting it. The sensible solution would be to roll the top down, but for some reason

↑ Setting off on Crummock Water (Patrick Kinsella) ← Exiting Crummock Water with Whiteless Peak behind (Patrick Kinsella)

(probably a nagging doubt that I'd be unable to get the thing done back up again, since Tom had to help me into it earlier) I just plough on, with steam rising off me and a dry sensation growing in my mouth. It feels spectacularly stupid to get dehydrated here, amid all this lovely liquid, but like the luckless Ancient Mariner in the famous poem by one-time Lake District local Samuel Taylor Coleridge, I find that out on the trail there's simultaneously water, water everywhere, nor any drop to drink. Ruminating on this rhyme while running over the bridge across Scale Beck, I'm tempted to stick my head in the rushing water that has just plummeted off the sheer edge of Gale Fell, via Scale Force waterfall – the highest cascade in Cumbria – but a gang of sheep loitering around the water's edge persuade me otherwise.

Well away from the roads and cafés, this side of the lake is much quieter than the eastern bank, but I still run past several gaggles of walkers, chatting and ambling along the shoreline path. I must look bit weird, wobbling along in my wetsuit with sweat flowing off my brow, but most meanderers offer friendly 'hullo's instead of quizzical stares, and I guess the sight of swimrunners amid this aquascape just can't be that unusual. However, the trails get busier and the groups more curious as I reach the southern end of Crummock Water and approach the tourist honeypot of Buttermere. Weaving through hand-holding couples and clusters of Sunday walkers, like a lost frogman completely out of his element, I cross a busy bridge by a lively waterfall at the bottom of Far Ruddy Beck, and keep scampering across Buttermere Dubs. Bimbling through Burtness Wood, which hugs the western bank of Buttermere, I pass dog walkers every few metres, and by the time I reach Horse Close – a knuckle of tree-covered land that punches out into the famous

↑ Steaming along a run section, beside Crummock Water (Patrick Kinsella)

lake, and the starting point for the second swim – I have quite an audience. And they're all clearly wondering what the hell I'm playing at.

Having splashed through multiple puddles along the trail, my shoes and socks are now soaked, so I simply leave them on, fish my goggles out of the bag and start wading in, grateful for the cool embrace of the water. With the dark dagger-like backdrop of 648m Fleetwith Pike puncturing the azure sky to my right, I dive in and strike out for the opposite bank, where – all going to plan – Tom will be waiting. After leaving me at the end of the first swim, the idea was for him to paddle back across Crummock Water and then run along the eastern banks of the lakes to meet me at the get-out point from Buttermere. When we'd discussed logistics, I'd figured that if I survived the first swim, this second, shorter one shouldn't cause me too many problems, and decided it would be sufficient for Tom to safety spot me from the far shore. What I hadn't realised, however, was that I was going to feel quite so dehydrated by this stage. To ward off the threat of cramp, I gulp down an energy gel before getting in and swallow several mouthfuls of the lake water while swimming across. It tastes brackish, but beautiful to my parched mouth.

LAST LEG Right enough, Tom is exactly where he promised to be, on the beach in front of Crag Wood, kitted out in his running gear and raring to go. In fact I hear him before I see him, whooping out encouragement from the bank. This time, when I get out of the water I can pull my wetsuit off altogether, and although the swim has cooled me down considerably, this is a big relief. I grab a dry T-shirt out of my float-bag-come-backpack and stuff the dripping neoprene suit in its place, and then we're ready to roll. Tom, who organises running events

↑ Entering Buttermere, with Fleetwith Pike behind (Patrick Kinsella)

such as the sensational Serpent Trail Race in the South Downs, is a highly experienced runner who has twice done the Bob Graham Round, so this is an easy afternoon out for him. He knows the fells well, too, having lived in the Lakes for several years, and it's great to have him for company on this last leg.

We trot along the east bank of Buttermere, tracing the Pike Rigg path into the bustling village itself, before crossing Mill Beck and then turning right to begin the long ascent up the rise of Whiteless Breast, a foothill of the main fell, 660m Whiteless Pike. It's a steep, hands-on-thighs kind of climb, during which our previously lively conversation gives way to heavy breathing. Fortunately, the fairly forgiving route of the Tadpole takes us left just before the point where the peak really rears up, and instead of scrambling skywards we get to run down a gently descending path along Squat Beck, passing just to the right of Rannerdale Knotts.

ESSENTIALS

GETTING STARTED Your local open-water swimming and running groups are good places to find out about swimrun activity around you – peruse Facebook to find these. Also check the websites of event and race organisers such as Love Swimrun (⌀ loveswimrun. co.uk), Ötillö (⌀ otilloswimrun.com) and Mad Hatter (⌀ madhattersportsevents.co.uk) which all have information about the sport and useful links.

SPECIAL CONSIDERATIONS On-water safety is a big deal for swimrun – whether you're in a river, lake or the sea, there are multiple potential hazards in any wild aquascape, and even if you know the waterway well, conditions can change quickly. Many races and events stipulate that entrants must compete in pairs, and responsible organisers will have boats and boards on the water with dedicated observers watching out for swimmers in distress. However, water safety needs to be taken into serious consideration when you're training or doing independent swimrun challenges, too.

KIT BAG You don't necessarily need a wetsuit to do a swimrun (in fact, over a certain temperature, some events ban them), but most of the time they are recommended, and they help with buoyancy as well as keeping you warm. The design and fit is very important, though – remember you will need to run in it. Triathlon wetsuits (designed to be quick in the water and speedy to transition out of) tend to be a bit too tight for running. Swimrun is now so popular that many wetsuit brands have designed dedicated suits for the sport, using different thicknesses of neoprene in various areas to supply buoyancy without overheating the wearer, and with little pockets for gels and attachment points for tow bags. Swim hats are popular for events and good for making you visible in the water, and you will also need goggles and a pair of quick-draining running shoes. A tow bag is required if you want to keep kit dry, and can really add to on-water safety,

The very last section is a lovely pacy descent through a fantastic fold in the fell known as the Valley of the Bluebells because of the high tide of wildflowers that floods through the area each spring. An old folk tale claims these blue flowers bloom in such vibrant abundance here because of blood spilt on the ground during a big battle between valorous locals and invading Vikings, but there's little evidence to support this. We're here at the wrong time of year for bluebells anyway, but it's gorgeous nonetheless, and with the end of the challenge literally in sight I get a bit carried away and start making promises I may live to regret.

'Next year, Tom…' I blurt, between breaths. '…I'm absolutely, definitely coming back to do the Frog Graham Round. Don't let me wriggle out of it. This is officially the start of my training for the big one.'

some aquathlons don't allow them. Some people use hand fins/paddles, but they're not always allowed in races either. It's good to have a warm dryrobe (or similar) and a flask of something hot and restorative at the end.

GETTING THERE When driving towards Buttermere and Crummock Water, take the B5292 west from Keswick or south from Cockermouth, then turn south along the B5289 at Low Lorton. There's a free car park by the beginning of the Tadpole route, but you need to get in early. Paid parking can be found in Buttermere.

PLACES TO STAY There are lots of places to stay in and around Buttermere, ranging from a YHA hostel to homely B&Bs and posh hotels. Book early to secure accommodation in summer and around bank holidays. **Syke Farm** (⌀ sykefarmcampsite.com) offers camping, glamping (in yurts) and shepherd's huts right by the lake, but it can get busy and noisy at times.

ELSEWHERE The Lakes obviously lend themselves perfectly to swimrun, but the sport is very popular elsewhere too, from Wales to Sweden and plenty more places besides. In the UK, the premium destination for the sport is the Isles of Scilly, but there are no easy courses or events there.

EXTRA RESOURCES
⌀ froggrahamround.co.uk/tadpole
⌀ swimrun.com
⌀ scillyswimchallenge.co.uk
⌀ nationaltrust.org.uk/buttermere-valley

25 WINGSURFING, WINGFOILING & KITESURFING

WHERE	Beadnell Bay, Northumberland; Troon, south Ayrshire, Scotland
SKILL LEVEL	Wingsurfing is far more accessible than kitesurfing, and complete beginners can usually get to grips with the basics after a lesson or two (although transitioning to a wingfoiling board is a significant step up). However, both winging and kitesurfing can be enjoyed by anyone with a basic level of fitness, if given the right guidance and correct equipment. To become a proficient independent wingfoiler and/or kitesurfer takes years of practice and dedication.
RISK FACTOR	High winds can create problems for people doing any of these sports. The size of the wing/kite can be adjusted, to lower the risks and make the activity more manageable, but there is an upper threshold above which all individual water-based, wind-powered pursuits become dangerous, and even experts put their boards away if the Beaufort scale begins edging towards Force 8, when the winds are pushing 34 knots (62km/hr). Kitesurfing is by far the more risky of the two sports when conditions get feisty, with the possibility of being dragged high into the air or along the ground a very real and potentially extremely serious possibility, leading to broken bones or worse. However, reputable wingfoiling and kitesurfing instructors will not operate in winds above a certain speed and will keep a close eye on conditions to manage the risks carefully. When wingfoiling or kitesurfing independently, getting caught in rip tides or colliding with other water users or rocks and other submerged features are risks that need to be considered, especially if you're not familiar with the area.

People have been making pilgrimages to the shores of Northumberland for well over a thousand years. The 'Holy Island' of Lindesfarne has long exerted a pull on the pious (not to mention attracting the violent attention of Vikings), while wildlife lovers flock to the Farne Islands, a sanctuary for sea animals including grey seals and puffins, and hikers and history buffs love to explore paths and places ranging from the remains of Hadrian's Wall to the ruins of Dunstanburgh Castle. But these days, a whole different group of people is drawn here by features altogether more elemental: the wind and the water. This stretch of craggy coast, where northern England meets southern Scotland and the North Sea waves roll in from the direction of Scandinavia, is a breeze basket, which makes it ideal for water-based, wind-propelled adventure sports such as kitesurfing and, more recently, the newly popular pursuits of wingsurfing and wingfoiling.

The concept of **wingsurfing** – where the surfer clings on to a handheld 'wing' instead of using a sail or kite attached to a harness or board – has been around for over four decades. It only picked up proper momentum in the last few years, however, when innovators started constructing lightweight wings with polymer kite material stretched out by inflatable

← Wingfoiling is soaring in popularity around the coast of Britain (VillegasPhoto/S)

airbeams, and began using smaller boards with hydrofoils attached to them. This set-up quickly evolved and spawned the sport of **wingfoiling**, which sees surfers use a super-light and easily manoeuvrable handheld wing while riding a foilboard that lifts out of the water once it's in motion, and they can then travel at exhilaratingly high speeds, thanks to the lack of drag.

Conceptually, wingfoiling sits somewhere in-between windsurfing and kitesurfing, except it's much more versatile than either of its siblings, and the kit is far simpler, quicker to set up, easier to carry and cheaper to buy. As a result, from a virtual standing start just a few years ago, wingfoiling has exploded in popularity and is now the fastest-growing wind-powered watersport in the world. Look out from almost any British beach on a breezy day and you will spot someone in a wetsuit, racing along on what appears to be a hover board, below what looks like a giant paper aeroplane. Interest and participation in wingfoiling is soaring, the sport is destined to grow much bigger in coming years and I've been desperate to give it a go ever since I first clapped eyes on someone sailing past me clutching a wing and wearing a grin. And what better place than Beadnell Bay, where one local waterman has been pioneering the pursuit since it arrived on these shores?

TAKING TO THE WING

On the Northumberland Heritage Coast, the northerly winds blow straight down from the not-particularly-distant Arctic, and both water and air temperatures

↑ James demonstrating wing power on the beach (Patrick Kinsella)

can be confronting, making a good wetsuit de rigueur even in the summer. And yet, late in October, I seem to have scored a bluebird day that belongs to a much earlier month. There's a lively breeze, but it's coming from the south, and as I drive towards Seahouses and turn right along the coast to Beadnell Bay, the sun is beaming and everyone is in T-shirts – although Geordies will, of course, wear short sleeves in a snowstorm, so this is not the world's most reliable barometer.

At the very moment I pull into the public car park in Beadnell Bay, Kevin Anderson is just returning to the container where he keeps all his gear, to grab his own board and wing. A well-accomplished watersport athlete, who still competes at a high level in various events, Kev runs KA Adventure Sports, which offers kitesurfing, stand-up paddleboarding and, in more recent years, wingsurfing and foiling sessions here on the bay, as well as coasteering and other adventures further afield. I've had a lot of phone conversations with Kev in recent months, as we have been attempting to tee up this meeting, and he comes across as a very down-to-earth, unflappable character. But today he's proper excited. The conditions are perfect for wingfoiling, the wind is improving even as we make our introductions, and he clearly doesn't want to waste a second of this late-season gift from the gods – Njörd obviously isn't always this generous.

I can tell he is itching to get out on the water, but first Kev takes me along the beautiful breeze-stroked beach to where one of his instructors, James, is

↑ Lessons in winging it (Patrick Kinsella)

teaching a couple of noobs the fundamentals of wingsurfing. Before you can get anywhere near a foilboard, Kev explains, you need to get your head around the basics on a more stable board. These guys are doing what KA describes as a 'Wingtro' session, learning how to wingsurf while standing atop a standard SUP, with an extra couple of fins strapped to the bottom midway along the board for improved stability and tracking. The transition to a smaller, more nimble board with a hydrofoil will come later, if they stick at it.

The students have been out on the sea for a couple of hours, and they're already shooting the breeze, holding their wings aloft and angling them to harness enough wind to be pulled along across the crest of the waves. They take regular tumbles, but they are also upright for impressively long periods of time, considering this is their first time on the water with a wing. The wind keeps getting stronger, and at Kev's suggestion, James summons the two learners in to swap over to a slightly smaller wing, which will keep them safer on the water and reduces the danger of a shoulder injury in the event of the wing getting caught by a large gust and them forgetting to let go. It's far easier to avert disaster with a wing (which you can simply drop) than it is with a kite, which is more firmly attached to you, but still, good instructors read and respect the wind at all times.

As we walk back across the broad blonde beach, James demonstrates just how well these wings can catch a whiff of wind; taking a small skip and deftly angling the wing in the right way, he rises a metre or more into the air and just hangs there on the uplift, laughing, for several seconds. I suspect, quite rightly, that there's far more to this malarkey than this little demonstration suggests, but nevertheless, I'm excited by the simplicity of the set-up.

↑ Kev wingfoiling on Beadnell Bay (Patrick Kinsella)

WING MAN While the two fledgling wingsurfers pump up their new, smaller wings, Kev can resist the Siren call of the sea and the wind no longer, and he hightails it through the dunes to grab his board. Keen to see how the pros do it, I follow him down to the shore, and watch as he speeds out towards the horizon. Within a few minutes, he's a dot below a colourful triangle that stands out like a butterfly wing in front of the dramatic dark backdrop of Dunstanburgh Castle, the ruin of a 14th-century fortification silhouetted against the sky on the far side of Beadnell and Embleton bays.

Watching through my telescopic lens, I see Kev hurtling towards the shore, with his board gradually levitating until he appears to be hovering about a metre above the water. As he gets closer I can make out the stem of the hydrofoil beneath the board, which provides the lift, vastly reducing the drag and making him go even faster. Experienced wingfoilers can reach speeds of 27 knots (over 48km/ hr). Inevitably, Kev makes the whole thing look easy, and when he gets within about 100m of the beach he just dips a shoulder, flips the wing around to execute an effortless turn, and heads back out across the bay.

WINGING IT After looking at a couple of Kev's runs, I'm pumped up and keen to have a crack myself. I climb into my wetsuit and track down James. He has just finished with his lesson, and takes me under his wing to show me the basics. We start on the beach, and I learn how to hold the wing above my head in order to harness the wind. Although it all looks very simple, and clearly comes as second nature to Kev and James, the precise positioning of your hands and arms is crucially important to avoid the tip of the wing coming into contact with the ground or the water. For a good half an hour or so, I practise on the sand, zig-zagging up and down the beach, feeling the pull of the wind for 50m or so, and then swapping hands and changing direction. The wing is attached to my wrist with a leash, and when I get it wrong and the wind threatens to take me over (which is often, to begin with) James just tells me to drop the whole thing, and it flaps harmlessly to the ground.

All the while the wind has continued to increase, the gusts have gathered momentum and the sky has become more bruised than blue. For a while I'm not sure that they're going to let me out on the water at all, but when Kev finally finishes his session, he gives me the green light, under the strict instruction of James. We're running out of time, though, as the day is definitely changing humour. I know I'm not going to master the art of wingsurfing in a single session, let alone get up on a board with a foil, but I am determined to stand up and surf a few waves with a wing in my hand. And that's exactly what I end up doing. It's a pedestrian performance compared to what I've just seen Kev doing, riding high on his board like the Silver Surfer, but I realise he has invested years of practice to get to this point. My journey has only just begun, and I have an awful long way to go.

KITE GUNNER

On the opposite side of the country to Beadnell Bay, north of the border in south Ayrshire, Scotland, the west coast town of Troon looks out over the Firth of Clyde. Protected from the wickeder waves of the wild Atlantic by the Isle of Arran, and blessed with perfect prevailing winds, Troon's South Beach offers some of the best conditions in Britain for wingfoiling and kitesurfing, and board riders come here from all over Europe to enjoy the seascape. This is the operating base of Kitesurf Scotland, run by Grant Clayton, who returned to Troon after spending years competing on the professional international kitesurfing circuit and managing kitesurfing schools in places as far flung as Australia, to set the school up in his home town, the place where he learned his craft over 18 years ago.

Kitesurf Scotland offers lessons and courses all year round, and I had been hoping to further my embryonic education on how to become a wingsurfer here, maybe even move on up to have a flirt with a foilboard, and to try my hand at kitesurfing too. The morning I arrive to meet Grant is blue and crisp, but the wind is whipping along the seafront of South Bay and I know long before I meet the master that conditions are not right for beginners to be out on the water. It is, however, a glorious day for experienced kiters to show off their aerial skills.

Walking towards the beach from my parking spot, I spy kites flying high in the sky before I can even see the sea, and soon enough I can make out the wetsuited figures dangling below them. They're soaring a good 10m or more into the air, and pulling off all sorts of tricks before landing gracefully (most of the time) and

↑ Grant Clayton carving beneath his kite in Troon, Scotland (Patrick Kinsella) ➔ Aldo assists with a kite on South Beach, Troon (Patrick Kinsella)

continuing to carve across the waves. I wander up the sand to where a couple of kitesurfing flags indicate the location of the school. Lessons are clearly cancelled today, though – the alfresco classroom is deserted and all the teachers are out playing in the wind, which is whipping and gusting across the beach at a very lively 25 to 30 knots. These are the kind of conditions where the experts have a whale of a time, and everyone else contents themselves with watching.

A guy approaches me, incongruously attired in a wetsuit and a top hat, fresh from the waves and grinning like a Cheshire cat. He nods a friendly greeting, and I ask whether Grant is around. 'There he is,' says top hat man, who proceeds to introduce himself as Aldo. 'That's Grant.' He points to a person performing a pirouette high above the waves. 'He'll be in shortly, I reckon.' I'm not so sure. It looks very much like Grant is in his element to me, but I don't mind – I'm enjoying the display and it's making me reconsider my preconceptions about kitesurfing.

If I am completely honest, while I've always fancied having a go, it does look like one of those sports where there is an awful lot of faffing about with gear to be done before you can get out and experience the fun stuff, and that has always put me off a little bit. The comparative simplicity of wingsurfing and foiling is what drew me in the direction of those activities, but until today I had not fully appreciated the potential of a kite to take you to the heights these guys are exploring. It's absolutely sensational to watch, so I can only imagine what it must feel like to experience first-hand. Although, of course, I'm looking at people who are right at the pointy end of the sport here. While I watch and take photos, another bloke arrives and Aldo – who, it transpires, is Grant's right-hand man and a kitesurfer with 20 years' experience under his hat – helps him get set up. 'I've been kitesurfing for decades,' the newcomer tells me. 'Since the beginning of the sport really. But I still can't get close to what these guys are capable of.'

I wade into the waves and get some close-ups of Grant as he races past, in between pulling off enormous jumps with epic amounts of airtime. He spots me and gives me a good-humoured gurn and a shaka hand sign, before getting his game face back on and going for another couple of runs. When he comes in, not long afterwards, Grant is absolutely buzzing – every bit as excited as Kev had been back in Beadnell Bay. 'What a morning!' he enthuses as we walk back up the beach. 'I've been out for hours.'

Grant explains that he had to cancel a whole day of lessons because the conditions were way too feisty for beginners, or intermediates for that matter, but it doesn't sound like he begrudges the lost income – far from it. I get the distinct feeling that he'd happily have every day like this. The biggest thing on his mind is the data downloading from a nifty little device on his board, which will reveal exactly how high he has flown during the morning's biggest jumps.

SPROUTING WINGS

Although it seems like the newest wind-powered pursuit to hit the water, wingsurfing has actually been around since 1981, and the sport was conceived by Jim Drake, an American aeronautical engineer who invented windsurfing in the late 1960s. Whereas windsurfing immediately gained popularity after Drake launched and patented his pioneering rig in 1967, and remained massively popular until being eclipsed by kitesurfing in the 21st century, wingsurfing struggled to take off for over three decades, until much lighter materials were used in the construction of the wing, and it was combined with a foilboard. Once all that happened, and affordable wings were made available to the public – which wasn't until around 2019 – wingfoiling suddenly soared. Foilboards can also be used by kitesurfers, and other variations on the theme include wing skating, where the foilboard is swapped for a skateboard.

There's a fierce but friendly rivalry going on between the gang clustered around his campervan HQ, with everyone vying for maximum elevation bragging rights for the biggest 'boost' (wind-assisted jump). Grant's personal record for a boost on South Troon Beach is a monstrous 20.7m.

Of course, the conditions today (and for the foreseeable, according to the forecast) mean I'm all out of luck in terms of progressing with my wingsurfing and foiling journey for the moment, let alone getting a taste of kitesurfing. But I'll be back on a board soon enough – I have the salty taste of it in my mouth now, and I am determined to earn my wings properly.

↑ The foil reduces water resistance and allows wingers to travel extra fast (VillegasPhoto/S)

ESSENTIALS

GETTING STARTED   To do a course and learn how to wingsurf, wingfoil or kitesurf, contact **KA Adventure Sports** in Beadnell Bay, Northumberland (⌖ kaadventuresports.co.uk) or **Kitesurf Scotland** in Troon, south Ayrshire (⌖ kitesurfscotland.co.uk).

SPECIAL CONSIDERATIONS All wind-powered watersports are technical. There is a lot to learn, especially if you're completely new to such activities, so don't expect to become an expert after a one-day course. Learning to read forecasts and watch the wind is imperative – some wind is crucial, of course, with 11–16 knots (21–27km/hr; Force 4) being ideal for learning. Anything above 22 knots (41km/hr; Force 6) is too much for noobs.

KIT BAG Wingsurfing, wingfoiling and kitesurfing are sports that require specialist and quite expensive equipment, all of which will be provided by the company you are learning with. I don't recommend going out and buying your own wing, kite or board before taking a few lessons, earning some solid knowledge and making sure you enjoy the pursuit enough to continue with it. Even choosing the right wetsuit is a multilayered consideration, with shorties and thinner suits allowing more flexibility, but thicker full-body suits supplying better thermal protection, allowing you to go out for longer and in all seasons. If you want to enjoy year-round surfing of any sort in Northumberland or Scotland, a good a 5/4 full-length wetsuit is well worth considering.

GETTING THERE To drive to **Beadnell Bay**, take the A1 north from Newcastle or south from Edinburgh. Buses run from Berwick-upon-Tweed, where there's a mainline train station.

↑ The beach at Troon (Rodney Hutchinson/S)

To drive to **Troon**, take the M77 from Glasgow to Kilmarnock and then the A77 to the coast, before following signs. Trains from Glasgow Central Station to Troon take 40 minutes, and the town is around 8km from Glasgow Prestwick Airport.

PLACES TO STAY There are lots of B&Bs, holiday lets, hotels and inns around the **Northumberland Coast Area of Outstanding Natural Beauty**, close to Beadnell Bay, including the excellent-value Dunstanburgh Castle Hotel (⌖ dunstanburghcastlehotel.co.uk). The Camping and Caravanning Club (⌖ campingandcaravanningclub.co.uk) has a good site right on the bay, with a full range of facilities, which is open to non-members.

There are lots of hotels around **Troon**, including the Old Loans Inn (⌖ oldloansinn. co.uk) and the Salt Lodge (⌖ saltlodgehotel.com), as well as more budget-orientated options including a Premier Inn close to Glasgow Prestwick Airport. Campers and vanners can try the Camping and Caravanning Club-affiliated Glenburn Dairy site in Troon (⌖ campingandcaravanningclub.co.uk).

ELSEWHERE Besides Beadnell Bay in Northumberland and Troon in Scotland, top spots for wingfoiling and kitesurfing in Britain include **Poole Harbour** (⌖ poseidonkiteschool.com) and **Portland** (⌖ otc-watersports.com) in Dorset, **Southend-on-Sea** in Essex (⌖ southendkitesurfing.co.uk), Brighton and Shoreham in Sussex (⌖ brightonkitesurfandsupacademy.com), **Rhosneigr** in Anglesea (⌖ funsportonline.co.uk), and **Porthcrawl** in south Wales (⌖ blastkiteboarding.co.uk).

EXTRA RESOURCES
⌖ kitesurf.co.uk
⌖ rya.org.uk

26 FASTPACKING

WHERE	The West Highland Way, Scotland
SKILL LEVEL	Fastpackers use skills commonly learned while hiking and trail running: you need to be competent at navigation and know how to negotiate sometimes-technical trails while moving at pace. The ability to interpret weather forecasts is handy, and you soon learn to pack very light, with gear evenly distributed and weight arranged so your centre of gravity is low.
RISK FACTOR	The biggest dangers are getting lost and encountering severe weather. Take quality gear and use a layering system, including waterproof shells. Depending on where you're fastpacking, local threats could include the risk of exposure and natural hazards. In the UK, the risk of injury from wildlife is low (adders can be present on some trails in summer), but when fastpacking in North America or even parts of Europe, you need to be bear aware. Wherever you are, trail injuries such as twisted ankles and falls resulting in scrapes and grazes are fairly common, however, so take a first-aid kit. Avoid pitching your tent under trees in windy weather, always check the local forecast and let someone know your plans and expected finish time/date. Take a phone, in case of an emergency.

Fastpacking is, in essence, speed hiking. Army folk call it 'yomping', and squaddies are often sent on long marches across moors and other challenging terrain with full packs. In civilian life, however, it's a more pleasurable pursuit (in theory), usually undertaken by those who want to walk long-distance footpaths – such as the Pennine Way, or Offa's Dyke – but lack either the inclination or the luxury of being able to spend weeks doing so. Some people naturally move quickly while trekking, and would rather keep going each day than stop at a campsite, hut or B&B halfway through the afternoon. Others simply enjoy the challenge of doing a trail in double-quick time.

Often, fastpackers, like many ultrarunners, will walk the uphills and run or trot the descents and the flat parts of a path, but there are no set rules. The pursuit is popular in North America, where it's often combined with 'thru-hiking', which simply means completing a long-distance route from trailhead to trailhead in one continuous linear trip, instead of doing separate sections. Most fastpackers carry all their own gear and wild camp, because being self-sufficient and not prebooking campsites, huts, hostels, pubs or B&Bs means you can keep going for as long as you like each day, with no fixed stops.

Britain boasts many long-distance paths (LDPs), from the 321km (200-mile) Cape Wrath Trail at the top of Scotland to the longest of the lot, the 1,014km (630-mile) South West Coast Path, which traces the sole of England's boot-shaped bottom. I've walked several in their entirety, run a few and dawdled along sections of others, and many more are on my ever-expanding to-do list. But it's challenging to find the time and get a ticket of leave to hike a

← Fastpacking towards Kinlochleven and the Mamores on the West Highland Way (Patrick Kinsella)

full LDP alone – let alone with friends or family, who all have equally commitment-cluttered calendars – so increasingly I found myself experimenting with an approach that I only recently learned had a name. Fastpacking was a revelation for me. It opened up opportunities to explore corners of the country and entire trails I didn't think I was going to see for years.

One LDP I've been eyeing for decades, but never found the time to do, is the West Highland Way. This is hardly a hidden hiking trail, I realise. As Scotland's original long-distance route, leading from the outskirts of the country's biggest city right into the heart of the Highlands, it sees a phenomenal amount of foot traffic, with over 100,000 people plodding along part of the path annually, and an estimated 36,000 completing the whole thing. I've read about how hectic it can get, and for that reason (and to avoid the monstrous midges) I waited until well into autumn before setting off to try and fastpack the 154km (96-mile) route from Milngavie to Fort William. Which seemed like a genius idea when I planned it.

↑ Damp on day 1 – the official start of the West Highland Way (Patrick Kinsella)

HEADING UPHILL

Walkers and runners often joke about routes being 'uphill' when tackled south to north, but when you do the West Highland Way (WHW) in that direction, the path literally does ascend, from the lowlands of suburban Glasgow into the Scottish Highlands (which have that name for good reason). Still, south to north is the most popular direction to do this path – partly because of prevailing winds, but mainly because people like to end on a high, and Fort William is the more dramatic trail terminus of the two.

Having decided to do the route uphill, my fastpacking adventure gets off to a slapstick start. It's raining (of course) as I set off from the station at Milngavie (which is inexplicably pronounced Mull-guy), and upon reaching the 'official' start of the WHW in the town centre, a stranger kindly agrees to leave the shelter of a café to take a picture of me by the obelisk. I then promptly pull up my hood and stride off, in completely the wrong direction. Eventually I clock my mistake and return to the big sign pointing along the proper route, passing my volunteer photographer, who grins and asks if I want another shot. Smart arse.

The trail escapes the city pretty quickly, and I practise picking up my pace while padding along the tree-lined path through verdant Mugdock Country Park. Trail running only partly prepares you for fastpacking, because trotting a track in shorts, T-shirt and lightweight shoes is altogether different to cantering while carting several days' camping provisions. Happily, I've managed to get all my gear – tent, sleeping bag, mat, stove, food and clothes – into a large (35l) daypack.

↑ The West Highland Way crosses several waterfalls as it traces the shore of Loch Lomond (Patrick Kinsella)

It's compact, but heavy, and there's no room for my camera, which is strapped tightly to my chest so it won't (I hope) knock my teeth out when I break into a jog. I'm wearing light Keen hiking boots, which offer ankle support without adding weight, and using Salewa trekking poles to take some stress and strain away from my knees. It might not look graceful, but I'm able to travel at a reasonable clip, alternating my cadence between normal walking (for the ascents), marching (on the level bits) and running (during the downhill sections).

The sun even appears as I get into the Campsie Fells, a series of volcanic hills north of Glasgow, and soon I have to shed a few layers. Rounding Dumgoyach and Dumgoyne, I go past Drymen, the first overnight stop for most WHW walkers, and continue towards the shores of Loch Lomond. After a later-than-planned start, the day is already waning by the time I reach the top of Conic Hill, where a bemused bovine keeps me company as I gaze down at the immense loch below. Descending as fast as I dare along the deeply scarred rough-and-tumble track, I start making my way around the eastern shore of the loch, which lies in the fault between the Lowlands and the Highlands, and make it as far as Rowardennan Forest before darkness really has me in its grasp. Wild camping is widely allowed in Scotland, but it's not permitted for several months along parts of the WHW, including this section, which gets unbelievably busy during the season. Luckily,

↑ Loch Lomond from Conic Hill (Patrick Kinsella)

I'm well outside the no-camping window, so I set up my Alpkit Soloist tent right next to the lapping water, light my stove and boil some loch water for a much-anticipated brew.

ALONG THE LOCH Loch Lomond is Britain's largest lake by some measure (surface area) and the WHW traces most of its massive length. The guidebooks describe this section as the hardest, but I love scampering along the tortured trail, clambering and scrambling over rocks, ascending tree-root ladders and crossing stone-strewn streams and waterfalls, with Ben Lomond – the most southerly of the Munros (Scottish mountains over 914m/3,000ft; page 328) towering to my right. Atop a crag above Rob Roy's prison (where the outlaw-come-folkhero supposedly kept captives during his decade-long dust-up with the Duke of Montrose in the 18th century) I surprise a gang of goats, two of which greet my sudden arrival by smashing their heads violently together, before nonchalantly resuming their nibbling.

The route rambles on, past Rob Roy's Cave (where both the eponymous outlaw and fellow Scottish hero Robert the Bruce are believed to have taken shelter at different times). The wonderful woodlands of oak and beech are ablaze with autumnal colour, and the constant cascades tumbling off the flanks of Ben Lomond are supercharged by the recent rain. Arklet Falls, beside Inversnaid Hotel, is absolutely thunderous. A small castle-topped island, Eilean a' Bhò, appears to float towards the northern end of the loch, never getting any closer.

↑ Wild camping at the foot of the Devil's Staircase, with Buachaille Etive Mòr for a backdrop (Patrick Kinsella)

↑ Mountain bikers share the trail with hikers and runners on the West Highland Way (Jon Sparks/A)

WHAT THE FKT?

If fastpacking isn't extreme enough, you can try running entire long-distance paths. Most well-known LDPs have a recognised 'Fastest Known Time' (FKT), details of which are registered and recorded on the website *ᕯ* fastestknowntime.com. At the time of writing, the current FKT for running the West Highland Way unsupported is an extraordinary 17 hours 57 minutes and 35 seconds, set by Paweł Cymbalista. No less amazing (when you've seen the section along Loch Lomond) is the fact that some people mountain bike the West Highland Way – the current FKT for doing it on a bike was set by Rab Wardell, who rode the route in 9 hours 14 minutes and 32 seconds.

Eventually, though, the route leaves the lairy lochside trails to gambol through Glen Falloch along an ancient military road – still an unsealed track, but one that's tame enough for me to trot into the Trossachs. But by the time I reach the turning for Crianlarich, a deep darkness has descended, infused with stinging rain. I find shelter, and a couple of other campers, in pine woods just off the track, and pitch my tent for a second night out.

Laying in my sleeping bag, listening to the rain and looking at the map, I calculate I'm halfway along the WHW, and concede that I won't be completing the whole thing in three days, as originally hoped. Oh well. When you're fastpacking, it's best to keep plans bendable. Sometimes you just can't pack as fast as expected, because of adverse conditions, tricky terrain, unforseen factors and entirely predictable ones – like the clocks going back in the middle of your trip, stealing away a precious daylit hour, as happens to me this very eve. Reading about the trail ahead, I realise that, even allowing an extra day, I'm going to need to get a wriggle on.

UP FOR MOOR
Mercifully, the rain has stopped when I awake, and I'm packed and on the path by the time the first blush of dawn colours the clouds. The way takes me along the River Fillan past hunting herons, ancient graves, a monastic site where St Fillan did his finest work in the 8th century, and the Lochan of the Lost Sword, a lake into which Robert the Bruce is rumoured to have lobbed his blade after losing a battle in 1306. After Tyndrum the track runs parallel to the railway line, and a steam train atmospherically puffs past as I march along the military road, passing between Beinn Bhreac-liath and Beinn Odhar, a couple of Corbetts (Scottish mountains between 2,500 and 3,000ft/762m and 914m; page 328). Ahead lies beautiful Beinn Dòrain, unmistakably a Munro, but before I reach its rise the WHW veers left, crosses the railway and road, and arrives at Bridge of Orchy.

The stiletto-sharp Highland peaks appear to poke holes in the bulging clouds that have hung ominously over me all morning, and it starts to pour, so after quickly admiring the wonderful whitewater of the rushing River Orchy I don't dillydally. Climbing out of town, the route leads to a cairn atop Màm Carraigh, where the views across Loch Tulla and around the crown of surrounding peaks, including Stob Gabhar and Stob Choire, are stunning. Apparently. Sadly, all I can see is a wall of water, so I descend to Forest Lodge. I soon forget the missing vista, however, when I'm welcomed on to Rannoch Moor by a family of red deer, including a young stag. I tip my dripping hood to the aspiring monarch of the glen, and keep moving, lest I drown in the deluge.

As I tramp across the evocative wild emptiness of Rannoch Moor, an immense heather-bearded Highland plateau, the clouds occasionally relent, rising to reveal views of Black Mount, topped by the magnificent Munros of Meall a'Bhuiridh and

↑ Marching along the old military road (Patrick Kinsella)   → Red deer on Rannoch Moor (Alex Nicol/S)

Buachaille Etive Mòr, which guard the gateway to Glen Coe. The light is fading by the time I reach rowdy River Bà and pass the ski tows of Glencoe Mountain Resort, and in the gathering gloom I almost trip over a tent set up by the side of the track – the inhabitants are probably terrified, since I've started talking loudly to myself, like a lunatic, explaining that I want to get as far as possible before making camp, to have a fighting chance of finishing the WHW in daylight tomorrow. The rain is tumbling in torrents, and even another meeting with a seemingly tame stag in the grounds of the swanky hotel here can't persuade me to pause. I press on, past Altnafeadh to the bottom of the Devil's Staircase.

I don't fancy climbing these satanic steps in the dark, especially after snapping one of my trekking poles during a stumble, but there's little in the way of unswamped level ground to sleep on. Eventually, by a footbridge, I find a spot that's just about big enough to pitch my tent on. My Haglöfs Gore-Tex jacket and overtrousers have done extraordinarily well, and I'm amazed to find my thermals dry when I climb out of them, but everything else is soaked – except my sleeping bag, which I've double wrapped in a dry bag. As I climb into this comfortable cocoon, the cacophonous cascade a few metres from my head sends thoughts of flash floods rushing through my brain. But only for a few seconds. After that I'm unconscious.

INTO THE GREAT GLEN Daybreak reveals the true charms of the most scenic camping spot I've ever occupied. My tent is nestled beside a stunning stream, next to a waterfall, with Buachaille Etive Mòr forming a dramatic backdrop. It's the kind of serendipitous scenario that can only arise when you're fastpacking – no commercial campsite boasts a setting this good. Lovely as it is, I've a train to catch and there's little time to linger. After breaking camp I tackle the Devil's Staircase, which ascends to a scenic saddle between Beinn Bheag and Stob Mhic Mhartuin, where I'm treated to a voluptuous view of the Mamores, with Ben Nevis and Aonach Mòr lurking behind. With the weather revealing the landscape to me in occasional snippets, the clouds parting like curtains opening to a spectacular theatre set for each new act of the adventure, it makes each vista I do see extra special. The relief is brief, and I'm assailed by rain again as I jog into Kinlochleven, where a welcoming café is serving restorative homemade soup. And this is so nearly my downfall.

My phone and watch both die just after I climb out of Kinlochleven on to the lower flanks of Am Bodach and Sgurr an lubhair, Munros in the Mamores. The straight stretch through Lairig Mor feels long and lonesome, not least because rain relentlessly pelts my face as I run, and the only sign of life I pass for several hours is Tigh-na-sleubhaicg, the evocative ruin of an old crofter's cottage in the middle of nowhere. The military road eventually rounds a corner at Blar a'

↑ Climbing the Devil's Staircase (Patrick Kinsella) ← West Highland Way waymarker (Patrick Kinsella)

Chaorainn and passes the ominous-looking water of Lochan Lùnn Dà-Bhrà, home to a monster, apparently, and an island that was the one-time abode of Macbeth, the King of Scotland so maligned by Shakespeare's propagandist play.

An information sign finally confirms the remaining distance to Fort William, but then cruelly gives me two options: the proper route of the WHW, which is longer and more undulating, or a shortcut. After fastpacking for 3½ days, I'm not going to start cutting corners now, so, swearing loudly, I set off along the official path, moving as fast as my now-swollen knees will allow. The trail takes a rollercoaster route through the hills and trees on the fringe of Nevis Forest before finally emerging on to a wide track, high above Glen Nevis, with the big Ben over to my right, its lofty head firmly in the clouds.

Without any means of telling the time, and increasingly concerned that I'm going to miss my train, I leg it along the winding forestry road that descends into the bend of the glen before spitting me out on to the road by the banks of River Nevis. Here I collar a passing cyclist and breathlessly ask the time. 'Half-past three,' he says. Unbelievably I have over two hours to do the last few clicks into Fort William.

But the trail has one last trick up its sleeve. Bizarrely, at some point, the official ending of the WHW was moved from its original, logical location, at the entrance to the town, to a seemingly random spot at the far end of the high street, well past the train station. On the upside, walking to this marker does take me pass a pub, where I confirm the right time, take shelter from the rain and raise a pint to celebrate the completion of my first fastpacking foray since I learned the term. It won't be my last, either – but I think I'll do the next one in the dry season.

↑ Finishing the West Highland Way in the rain (Patrick Kinsella)

ESSENTIALS

GETTING STARTED Fastpacking is an independent adventure pursuit – just get yourself to one of the trailheads and start trotting.

SPECIAL CONSIDERATIONS Wild camping, instead of advance-booking sites or other accommodation, means fastpackers can be completely flexible with their daily distances. However, wild camping is not strictly legal in most parts of Wales and England. It's permissible in most parts of Scotland, with the exception of certain parts of the WHW in high season. Wherever you wild camp, it's very important to be discreet and considerate and to use Leave No Trace principles.

KIT BAG The secret to a successful fastpacking trip relies on the selection of equipment that is both very lightweight and fit for purpose. You will need a large daypack, tent (or tarp/hammock in summer), sleeping bag, inflatable mat, headtorch, stove and food (prepacked dehydrated meals are best), plus enough layers – including waterproofs – to stay warm and dry. Take a map and compass. Running or speed-walking with a pack affects your balance and increases stress on joints, especially knees, so many fastpackers use trekking poles. Lightweight boots are good for stability and ankle support. Between May and October, hikers, campers and fastpackers in the Scottish Highlands can be horribly harassed by plagues of midges, tiny biting flies that descend upon you in clouds; take insect repellent, lightweight long-sleeved tops and a hat with face netting.

GETTING THERE Trains run between Fort William and Glasgow Queen Street several times daily, and you can catch connecting trains to Milngavie station (pronounced Mull-guy). There are also buses.

PLACES TO STAY There are multiple campsites, inns, hotels and B&Bs along the route and in Fort William. In Milngavie, there's a conveniently located Premier Inn about 15 minutes' walk from the station and the start of the West Highland Way (⌀ premierinn. com > Glasgow (Milngavie)).

ELSEWHERE Fastpacking adventures can be enjoyed on any long-distance path or multiday hiking route. The world is your oyster.

EXTRA RESOURCES Cicerone's *The West Highland Way* by Terry Marsh is a good guidebook. Harvey produces a waterproof map of the West Highland Way – this is a wise investment.

⌀westhighlandway.org
Long Distance Walkers Association ⌀ ldwa.org.uk

27 SNORKELLING

WHERE	Oban, Scotland
SKILL LEVEL	There is more to snorkelling than most people might think, but it can be an easy and accessible activity for beginners to dive into. You need to be a reasonably competent and confident swimmer, happy to have your face in the water. Having the ability to interpret tide tables and weather forecasts is also very beneficial, for safety reasons and to ensure you time your snorkel to enjoy optimal conditions – in some places, these skills are crucial. Night snorkelling demands a bit more, in terms of navigation. More advanced skills – such as how to swim efficiently with fins, safely use a weight belt and make the most of your underwater time – can be learned on snorkelling courses.
RISK FACTOR	Caution needs to be exercised during any water-based activity, and snorkelling is no exception. Designated snorkel trails are located in places where swimming conditions are usually safe, but always check weather forecasts and tide charts carefully – look out for strong offshore winds and be aware that conditions can change quickly on the water. Wherever you're snorkelling, do your research and make sure there are no rips or surprise currents that might catch you out. Also, be very aware of motorised traffic such as boats and jetskis – sometimes it's wise to use a swim buoy and/or a dive flag to alert others to your presence. It's best to use a buddy system when snorkelling, and never practise apnea techniques (sustained breath holding) when snorkelling alone – see the *Freediving* chapter for more about this, page 14. Other risks include sunburn (when snorkelling in warm water without a wetsuit make sure your back and neck are protected) and injury from marine flora and fauna; the latter is rare, but don't chase or provoke animals such as seals, or touch anything with bare hands unless you know exactly what it is. When night snorkelling, it's surprising easy to get disorientated – plan carefully and take a torch.

A diving mask is a window to a whole new world, a subaquatic universe that usually remains unseen, hidden beneath the waves. Once you start exploring under the surface of the sea, it quickly becomes apparent that this different dimension is a deeply intriguing place, full of fantastic flora and fauna, and you just never know what you're going to find down there, or which animals you might meet. One entry route is by taking up scuba diving (page 86), but the trouble with using compressed air is that your visiting time in this awesome alternative world is severely limited. If you get an hour out of your tanks, then you're doing well. But it doesn't have to be like that.

← Subaquatic sightseeing in Scotland (Shane Wasik/Basking Shark Scotland)

While descending to 30 or 40m to check out a reef wall or a wreck is always an amazing experience, often when you're simply doing a shore dive the vast majority of the sealife and things of interest are encountered around the rocks just a couple of metres below the surface. And to explore this shallower aquascape, it's far better to substitute heavy tanks for a simple snorkel, through which you can keep breathing for hours on end if you want to, while keeping your face in the water to observe all the marine action and drama unfolding.

Snorkelling is one of those activities that many of us dabble with on holiday, and often really enjoy, but people often don't fully appreciate just how far it can take them. If you kit yourself out properly, with a wetsuit thick enough to keep you comfortable for long periods of time (even in quite chilly water) and decent fins to provide some propulsion when it's required (to duck dive down, or keep pace with a new-found fishy friend) you can do some serious exploring with a snorkel and mask, and enjoy encounters with impressive denizens of the deep – and the not-so-deep – including marine mammals, incredibly intricate sea creatures and some of the largest fish on this big blue planet.

What's more, compared to many outdoor activities it's really cheap and accessible. And in some parts of Britain, especially around Scotland's stunning and curvy coastline, snorkelling trails have even been designed to help point people towards some of the very best areas of our wonderful wet wilderness. Having just learned that one such snorkel trail had recently been established near Oban, I packed my aquatic adventure kit for a trip north, to experience a couple of sea snorkels in very different conditions.

TRAIL BLAZING

'Turn your torch off for a minute,' Shane says. I do as instructed and the intensity of the Scottish night instantly envelops us. We're swimming in 2 or 3m of water, just off the coast of Oban, beneath Dunollie Castle, but the darkness of the late October evening is so complete that the location is kind of irrelevant. The only way to distinguish between the inky sea and the black air is by touch. But suddenly that changes. 'Watch,' Shane whispers. And then he starts rapidly moving his arms back and forth just below the surface, and something magical happens. A thousand pinpricks of bright greenish-blue light explode into existence around his limbs, like a nebula of stars emerging from a dark sky. I copy his lead, flapping my wetsuited wings around and instantly I'm surrounded by subaquatic sparks too. It's bioluminescence, and it is beautiful. And weird. In fact the whole scenario is a little surreal, considering I was sitting in a warm, brightly lit café enjoying a coffee just half an hour earlier.

Shane and I explored this same stretch of coastline earlier in the day, when the sun wasn't exactly 'out', but it was high in the sky somewhere above the cloud cover that habitually hangs above the Scottish Highlands and Hebridean islands at this time of year. Suffice to say, it was light and everything looked very different, both above and below the water. Many of the creatures we met were different

too, and even the ones that were here earlier are now behaving differently under the cover of darkness – especially the crabs. The moonlight must do something to these guys, because there seems to be a lot of late-night hunting, munching, mating and fighting going on.

In recent years, the Scottish Wildlife Trust has set up a series of award-winning snorkel trails around the sensational shoreline they oversee, with multiple sites scattered widely across the country, from the Isle of Harris off the northwest coast to Berwickshire in the Borders, on the southeast coast, just above Northumberland. This year, trails in three new areas were established, including seven in north Argyll, such as the one Shane and I are scoping out, a little over 3km north of Oban, just off a satisfyingly Scottish-sounding beach called Wee Ganavan, or Camas Bàn.

The trails are all light-touch. No physical infrastructure has been put in place to interfere with the natural seascape, but each site has been identified as a safe place for people to snorkel, where an abundance of marine wildlife can be observed and enjoyed. Access to the water is generally very easy, there are typically parking and toilet facilities nearby, and downloadable PDFs providing details of practical information such as put-in points, plus a visual guide to the flora and fauna you can expect to see, are available from the Scottish Wildlife Trust's website.

DAY FLIPPING Shane Wasik is a local, a marine biologist, an underwater photographer and a qualified snorkelling instructor, so I really couldn't ask for a better buddy to be in the water with. His company, Basking Shark Scotland,

↑ Pat night snorkelling off the coast of Oban (Shane Wasik/Basking Shark Scotland)

takes people on snorkel safaris all around the Hebridean islands, where they often bump into the very big – but entirely non-threatening – basking sharks that patrol these seas with their great mouths agape. We're extremely unlikely to encounter any such behemoths here, but there is plenty of other wonderful wildlife to meet, and often it's the smaller species that prove the most interesting.

Besides operating basking shark trips and numerous other aquatic adventure activities, Shane teaches snorkelling courses, ranging from introductory level to advanced (and extending into freediving for those who really want to extend their single-breath underwater time). Having assessed my level of experience and ability in the water, and looked at the tidal and weather conditions on the day we meet, he decides to take me on a drift swim around Dunollie Point for our first snorkel experience. This means we get in the water just south of the official snorkel trail, to explore the rocks and walls around the point, but then swim around to Wee Ganavan itself, which is a more sheltered spot, deemed much safer for people to explore independently, when they're not lucky enough to have a marine biologist and pro snorkelling instructor with them.

We meet in a lay-by below the ancient ruins of historic Dunollie Castle, where a fortification of one sort or another has looked out over the waves for at least 1,400 years. After Shane has stopped laughing at my hopelessly inadequate 3mm wetsuit (perfect for warm Devon days, but not made for autumnal snorkelling in Scotland) he furnishes me with a 10mm steamer, a hood, gloves and weight belt. We discuss the plan for the day, and once we're sufficiently suited and booted, walk along the road – looking like two lost frogmen to passing cars – and around the corner to the entry point.

A handy slipway leads down into the saltwater, which takes several minutes to seep into my thick suit. Almost the instant I put my face in the cold water, before I've really had a chance to recover from the shock of the temperature, I spy a magnificent sea urchin, the size of a large grapefruit. Before long I realise there are dozens of similar animals all around me – rival gangs of colourful sea urchins and anemones clustered on the rocks. Occasionally, Caledonian MacBrayne (CalMac) ferries chug through the channel between the Isle of Kerrera and the mainland, going in and out of Oban Bay en route to and from Mull, Lismore and various other islands of the Hebrides. But we stick close to the shore, well out of their way, and explore mostly in the tidal zone where the most interesting wildlife can be seen – such as a conical shellfish that Shane swears is known as a 'mermaid's nipple'. I daresay Attenborough has a different name for the creature, but I probably wouldn't remember it, whereas this one does stick in my mind.

The current is quite fast, and we have to kick our fins fairly hard against it in order to stay in the one place for any length of time. Hanging on to fronds of fluttering seaweed, Shane and I spend a few minutes watching marauding crabs

↑ Suited and booted for a winter snorkel at Dunollie Point (Patrick Kinsella) → Discovering urchins in front of Dunollie Castle (Shane Wasik/Basking Shark Scotland)

↓ The harmless, but behemoth basking shark is Britain's biggest fish (Shane Wasik/Basking Shark Scotland)

SNORKELLING WITH SHARKS

Basking sharks are the second-biggest fish on the planet; growing up to 10m/33ft in length, they are slightly smaller than the world's biggest, the whopping whale shark. Along with seals, dolphins and the occasional orca (killer whale), basking sharks are often seen off the coast of Scotland. For more about the chance to snorkel with these gentle giants, see the Basking Shark Scotland website (baskingsharkscotland.co.uk).

make their way around the rocks and wave their pincers at us in warning if we peer too closely at them. There are multiple species here, including green, brown, velvet and spider crabs. More sedate are the starfish, which lie in occasional constellations on the sea floor. The tide is low, and when we're joined by inquisitive wrasse, we're able to duck dive down into the forest of seaweed and get right into the cracks and crevices of the sunken boulders to play hopelessly one-sided games of chase with the fish. The visibility is good, and gliding over the top of this marine wilderness, I'm struck – as I often am when snorkelling – how close this sensation feels to flying.

At one point, once we've reached Wee Ganavan and are within the terrain of the new snorkel trail, Shane beckons me over and indicates something nestling in the palm of his glove. It's a twig, I think, somewhat unimpressed, but then I look closer and see what he is getting excited about. He's nursing a baby pipefish, a perfect, almost impossibly miniature version of the long, thin adult fish that I've seen many times before. How Shane spotted it I'll never know, but it transpires he has an excellent eye, and is constantly pointing out imp-sized animals such as shrimp that most people would miss. A few minutes later he locates a nudibranch – a group of extraordinary marine animals sometimes referred to as sea slugs, a description that does absolutely no justice to the stunning colours and body shapes they display. Divers and other regular aquanauts prize their encounters with these delicate dandies of the deep, and I'm delighted to see one.

After about an hour exploring the snorkel trail at Camas Bàn, we head towards the beach and swim right through a massive shoal of fish that put on a flashy kaleidoscopic show in the shallows. When they stay still long enough for us to get a good look, it turns out they are see-through sand smelt, a completely

↑ Nudibranchs are super colourful sea slugs (Unlisted Images, Inc/A)

translucent fish with all its organs on display. We get out on to the sand at Wee Ganavan, and then waddle the short distance back to the van to get out of the wetsuits. It's a Thursday afternoon in term time and the fish aren't the only wee ones in schools, so while Shane goes off to collect his kids I head into Oban to replace some of the surprising number of calories I seem to have burned through, judging by the size of my appetite.

LUNAR KICKS While wandering through the bustling Highland town, I look up at the iconic folly of McCaig's Tower and see a host of heavily pregnant clouds furiously frowning over Battery Hill. Taking shelter in a café, cuddling a cup of steaming coffee while rain strafes the pavement outside and the evening starts to descend, I do question why I'm about to voluntarily get back into the increasingly ominous-looking ocean. Making like a local, I order a pint of Irn Bru to gird my loins, and hope it won't sink me.

We have arranged a rendezvous for 19.00, and by that time the clouds have miraculously marched on and stars are even twinkling in the Scottish sky. Climbing back into a damp wetsuit is never nice, and doing it in the darkness of an October evening doesn't improve the experience much, but it's such a vigorous exercise pulling on a 10mm-thick neoprene suit that at least I feel warmed up by the time I'm done. Shane has some extra toys for us this time around, in the shape of mega-bright diving lights, which we strap to our gloved hands.

And, once I'm actually in the water, I remember how much I love night swimming, snorkelling and diving. There is something really exhilarating about

↑ Aerial view of Wee Ganavan, one of several snorkelling trails close to Oban (Shane Wasik/Basking Shark Scotland)

being in the sea during the hours of darkness, especially when you're armed with a good torch. Fish are attracted to the light, so they come and find you, and with your attention being so intently focused on the small circle of rock or sea floor illuminated by your beam, you explore the terrain in intricate detail. And, of course, there's the slightly chilling, buzz-inducing thrill of never knowing what lies lurking in the raven-dark abyss beyond that beam. Or behind you.

After playing around in the bioluminescence for a bit, we swim towards the northern part of the Wee Ganavan site, opposite Maiden Island. Shane is hoping we'll encounter some cuttlefish, which can bedazzle divers with their flamboyant displays, but the colourful cephalopods remain elusive this evening. Nautical nightlife is often very eccentric. Halfway across the bay, Shane pauses at a fishing buoy. On the underside of the float he finds a delicate decorator crab, flamboyantly dressing itself up in bits of seaweed. On a roll, he also spots a cling fish moonbathing on top of the buoy. This is a rare species in these waters and can survive out of water for some time, although it wouldn't last long in daylight, with greedy gulls always on the lookout for an easy lunch.

ESSENTIALS

GETTING STARTED To join a snorkelling trip or do a snorkelling course, contact Shane via his website (⚓ baskingsharksscotland.co.uk).

SPECIAL CONSIDERATIONS Snorkel trails are often located in marine conservation areas. Please leave everything as you find it, and don't assume you can go collecting crabs, lobsters or shellfish.

KIT BAG Use a good snorkel (with purge valves) and a mask with tempered glass – this is your window to the underwater world. Quality fins (don't call them flippers) are also an excellent investment; if you're likely to be snorkelling in cooler water where booties are required, diving fins with adjustable heel straps are best. Unless you're snorkelling in really warm water it's best to wear a wetsuit, which will significantly lengthen the time you can comfortably spend in the water and improve your enjoyment of the experience. The thickness of the best wetsuit will depend on when and where you are snorkelling – on an autumn night in Scotland I was in a 10mm suit, with a full hood, gloves and booties, but when snorkelling in Cornwall in midsummer, a much thinner suit with short arms and legs will suffice. A wetsuit will make you much more buoyant, so a weight belt might be required to enable you to duck dive and explore underwater – make sure you get the weighting right in shallow water before swimming out of your depth, and practise how to take the belt off in case you need to do so in an emergency (better still, do a course). When night snorkelling you will need a diving torch.

I find a lonely hermit crab scuttling along the sandy bottom, but when we reach the rocks on the far shore it's crazy busy, with hundreds of crabs swarming all over the place. It's like a bustling town centre on a Saturday night, all feeding frenzy, flirting and fighting. Absolute scenes. From the relative serenity of the surface you would never guess how much drama is happening down there – it would make an excellent reality TV show. The tide is fully in now, and we have to duck dive a lot deeper to get down among the action, but most are so preoccupied they barely bother raising a pincer towards us even when we get really close.

Eventually the power packs on the torches indicate they're going to start fading soon, and before the chills start to overpower the thrills we decide it's time to call it a night. Shane leads the way and I follow his fins and the beam of his light into the shallows. As we loosen our fins and stagger up the beach, I notice a small group of people on the sand. They must think we're lunatics, I think to myself, snorkelling in the moonlight like this. But no, as we pass and say hello, it becomes clear they're hopping in for a swim themselves – without wetsuits too. People are made of hardy stuff up here. There really must be something in that Irn Bru.

GETTING THERE Oban, regarded as the 'gateway to the isles', is on the west coast of Scotland, 145km north of Glasgow via the A82 and A85. There is a train station, and the railway journey between Glasgow and Oban is considered one of the best in Britain.

PLACES TO STAY There is a wide range of accommodation in Oban, including hotels, hostels and guesthouses. Housed in a classic Scottish greystone Victorian building, Oban's **SYHA hostel** – which has sea views out over the harbour and the Firth of Lorne – is a great choice if you're on a budget (⊘ hostellingscotland.org.uk/hostels/oban). To experience some true Scottish hospitality, a B&B is a really good choice.

ELSEWHERE The Scottish Wildlife Trust has set up **snorkel trails** all around the country's stunning shoreline, from the Isle of Harris (six sites) to Berwickshire (five sites). More snorkel trails are scattered across the northwest Highlands (nine sites), the Isle of Arran (six sites) and Lochaber (six sites), and in 2022, trails in three new areas were established; Torridon (five sites), East Lothian (five sites) and north Argyll (seven sites). Top snorkelling spots elsewhere around Britain include the **Farne Islands** in Northumberland, **Stackpole Quay** in Pembrokeshire (famous for spider crab swarms), **Studland Bay** in Dorset (where you might spy a spiny seahorse) and **Lundy Island** off Devon.

EXTRA RESOURCES
⊘ scottishwildlifetrust.org.uk/things-to-do/snorkel-trails
⊘ www.bsac.com/uk-diving/top-uk-snorkelling

28 BOATPACKING – CANOE & KAYAK CAMPING

WHERE	River Dart, Devon; the Great Glen, Scotland
SKILL LEVEL	The multiple variables involved in any boatpacking trip determine what skills are required to safely complete the adventure. Most importantly, ask yourself what's the nature of the waterway you're paddling, and does it have any significant rapids? Secondly, what craft are you using: a single or two-person canoe or kayak? Here we explore two inland, ostensibly non-technical waterways, but both have characteristics that demand some water knowledge and a few paddling skills. To do this independently, you need to know basic canoe/kayak paddling strokes and be aware of what to do in the event of a capsize.
RISK FACTOR	No matter how benign conditions might seem, whenever you're on the water there are always risks involved, including potentially serious – even life-threatening – ones. However, these can be mitigated with good safety precautions (always wear a PFD and appropriate clothing) and sensible decision making – make a plan, paddle within your limits, check forecasts and if the weather turns against you, be prepared to get off the water.

Paddling a canoe or kayak along a waterway is always exciting – it's a unique way of exploring a new place, or seeing somewhere you know well from a completely new perspective. But adding overnight stops takes the experience to a whole new level.

↑ Canoeing across monstrous Loch Ness can be challenging (www.dvlcom.co.uk/S)

There's something magical about a campsite only accessible from the water. It bestows a feeling of exclusivity that has nothing to do with snobbiness or wealth. To arrive at such places, you first have to embark on an adventure.

Canoe camping expeditions, paddle safaris or boatpacking missions – whatever you call these aquatic escapades, they involve an edifying amount of planning and some careful packing, and often result in long-lasting memories, especially when enjoyed with close friends and family. So long as you're still talking to one another at the end of the outing, that is. Because there's nothing quite like a paddling and camping mission for discovering how well you really get along with someone – especially if you're sharing a two-person boat.

DAD & DAUGHTER ADRIFT ON THE DART

Boatpacking is one of my favourite ways to explore, whether it's around a coastline, along a canal or down a river, and I'm always keen to share the excitement I feel whenever I set out on a paddling adventure with my nearest and dearest. Even if they are recalcitrant teenagers. This was the backdrop to one of my most treasured trips: a kayak-camping escapade along the lower reaches of the River Dart with my daughter Ivy.

Upstream, the Dart is a feisty whitewater river that races across the moor it lends its name to, rushing through rock-strewn rapids and generally behaving in a riotously rowdy manner. By the time it reaches Totnes, however, it has calmed down completely, and between here and the estuary at Dartmouth, the river is a ribbon of comparative tranquility, stretching for about 20km, and perfect for a two-day paddling escapade.

While there are no rapids to contend with on the lower section of the Dart, it is a tidal waterway from Totnes, and getting the timing right is crucial. For it to be a pleasurable paddle, rather than an uphill struggle, you need to start on a falling tide. I know this, and I can read a tide chart, yet I still manage to make a mess of it – mostly because I'm too scared to get Ivy up in the dangerous hours of pre-dawn on the day of our departure, lest she actually bite my head off. Or, worse, refuse to come along at all. Pathetic, I know, but I've been looking forward to this for months.

Inevitably, my timidity backfires. We put in around low tide, and within an hour find ourselves fighting the incoming flow. We're in separate sea kayaks, and although I try to paddle at Ivy's pace to keep her enthusiasm levels up, increasingly I look over my shoulder to see her with both blades out of water, drifting backwards up the river, glaring back at me with adolescent anger boiling in her eyes. 'Told you I wouldn't enjoy this, Dad!' she shouts.

A little tow does the trick, though. She soon cheers up, and we start making good progress. Rounding Sharpham Point, a thunderous noise erupts above us and, startled, we simultaneously stare skywards as a gaggle of low-flying Canada geese skim over our heads and land noisily in front of our boats. We laugh at each other's alarmed expressions, and the mood is buoyant.

On the right bank, a vineyard envelops Sharpham House, an 18th-century Palladian villa. The beautiful bathing house here is available for overnight stays – our accommodation plans are more rudimentary, but we will enjoy the same view, because just around the tree-covered corner is Ashprington Point and Point Field Campsite. Operated by the Sharpham Trust, this basic campsite has everything you need, and not a single thing more. There are long-drop eco toilets, freshwater taps, flat space for putting up tents, and a fire pit. It's perfect, and we have the place to ourselves.

UPRISING I pitch the tent as Ivy collects driftwood, and soon we have a fire roaring, with foil-wrapped potatoes baking beneath the embers. Beside us, the river rises. And then rises some more. When it starts seeping over the top of the bank, I get slightly alarmed and consult my tide chart again. It transpires that we're camping out on a night with one of the highest tides of the year, and a thought occurs to me: perhaps this is why no-one else is here… 'Yeah, nice one Dad!' Ivy comments, as we look around to discover that we're perched on a rapidly shrinking island of dry land.

The chart promises me that the tide is about to turn, though, and fortunately the tent is on the highest part of the field, and we've pulled the kayaks well back

from the river and secured them (if they float off, we're really in trouble). Sure enough, just before the water threatens to put the fire out and flood our tent, the level starts to drop. We rescue our spuds from the glow and enjoy dinner, while the sun sets and oystercatchers, shelducks, redshanks and dunlins dig for muddy treasure in the soggy soil around us.

Dawn doesn't allow tent dwellers to lie in – not even teenagers – but Ivy awakes in a good mood. It's hard to be grumpy in such surrounds. I first found this place years ago, during a wild swim upriver from Blackwater Point to Sharpham, when an inquisitive seal kept me company all the way to Point Field, where it played in the shallows, delighting campers. I'd been planning to return with Ivy ever since. And now we're here. There's no sign of my seal, sadly, but the setting is just as special as I remember.

We break camp quickly to ride the outgoing tide, which totally transforms the experience. It feels as though we're kayaking on a conveyor belt, speeding along, compared to the dawdling pace of the previous day. The clouds part too, and the river changes character from this point on. The Harbourne River joins us at Bow Creek, and as we paddle past pretty Stoke Gabriel, the Dart broadens massively to embrace the estuary. This stretch of river is fringed with verdant woods, colourfully crowding the bank all the way to Sandridge Point. At Dittisham we dodge dinky boats ferrying people to Greenway House, Agatha Christie's much-loved holiday home. Walter Raleigh was once a local too, and the nearby Raleigh Estate around Old Mill Creek is still owned by his descendants.

A steam train puffing along the east bank towards Kingswear overtakes us as we enter historic Dartmouth Harbour, a pretty place protected by twin castles. The river yawns wide and boats bob all around us; yachts, pleasure cruisers, car ferries and England's last coal-powered paddlesteamer. Our take-out point is the jetty just past the main marina, right by the bus stop. We've timed it perfectly, and once the kayaks are safely on the pontoon, I catch the bus back to Totnes to collect the car, while Ivy scoffs a massive ice cream and minds the boats.

She might not admit it, but I reckon she has enjoyed herself, and subsequent Instagram posts confirm my suspicions. I hope Ivy will look back on the experience with fondness. I know that such adventures with my old man made a lasting impression on me, even if I didn't fully appreciate it until many years later. I've often wondered how the dynamic might change during a similar outdoor escapade now I'm an adult. And it was about time I found out.

OLD MEN ON THE GREAT GLEN

There are no tides to worry about while canoeing the Caledonian Canal, which stretches for 95km (60 miles) through the Great Glen, running coast-to-coast across Scotland from Fort William to Inverness. Here you have other concerns:

CANOE OR KAYAK

Like all navigable waterways, the Lower Dart and the Great Glen can be paddled in either a kayak or an open canoe (sometimes called a Canadian canoe). For those planning to camp, an open canoe offers by far the most storage space (although you will need dry bags or barrels), but many touring kayaks have waterproof storage compartments where it's possible to stash everything you need for overnight and multiday adventures. Sit-inside kayaks offer more protection from the wind and rain. Double boats (kayaks or canoes) are perfect for trips when one person is less experienced on the water than their paddling partner. Whichever boat you use, be sure to pull it well away from the water and secure it when you stop for the evening (especially on tidal rivers like the Dart).

three large lochs to cross, two of which are so huge they're classified as open water. On these inland seas, waves can whip up to 2m when the wind gets caught in the glen and becomes furious. As it often does.

In the early 19th century, engineering genius Thomas Telford designed a canal that traces a geological faultline which has been ripping the Highlands in half for millennia, and joined up the deep, dark dots of Loch Lochy, Loch Oich and monstrous Loch Ness. The resulting navigation allowed ships to travel from the Atlantic Ocean to the North Sea without sailing around the treacherous northern extremities of Scotland. It took almost 20 years for the navvies to dig out the route, but within decades the railway had rendered commercial canal traffic obsolete, and the waterway fell silent until recreational boats started using it. In 2012, nearly two centuries after it opened, the Great Glen Canoe Trail along the Caledonian Canal became Scotland's first official wild paddling path.

I've long wanted to do a canoe-camping expedition along this wonderful waterway. And, as it transpired during a random conversation, my Dad – who grew up on a river in Ireland and first got me into paddling – had been harbouring a similar ambition. So one October, after almost letting another season go past, we finally got our acts together, organised a boat and made a plan.

FLYING CANOES 'Paddling the Great Glen is an expedition, not a pleasure cruise,' John Cuthbertson from the Snowgoose Mountain Centre in Corpach cautions us on the day of our departure. 'You'd best get a move on if you want to make camp on the loch shore before nightfall. There's a storm coming.'

Like most Great Glen Canoe Trail paddlers, we're going west to east, so the prevailing wind can give us a helping hand. At its western extremity, the Great Glen begins below Ben Nevis, in the saltwater of Loch Linnhe, but the first proper put-in for paddlers is at the top of Neptune's Staircase in Banavie – where a set

of eight locks forms Britain's biggest liquid staircase, and the Caledonian Canal and Great Glen Canoe Trail start. Leaving the locks behind, we paddle through a rural landscape, cutting across reflections of a sky as blue as the Scottish flag. A brown trout jumps and tranquility surrounds us – at least until a fighter jet roars overhead. By 5pm we reach Gairlochy and start to edge around the banks of 15km-long Loch Lochy, looking for a camping spot as the sun sinks behind the mountains. A flat bit of land by a pebble beach catches our eye, and soon we have a fire roaring and water boiling for a brew. The storm feels a long way off, and after a couple of drams of the local firewater, we settle down for the night.

The gale arrives with a big bad wolf-like vengeance in the wee hours, huffing and puffing and almost blowing our little house in. The poles of our tent creak and groan under the onslaught for hours before a loud bang and a big shudder shock us completely out of whatever shallow sleep state we're in. Dad scrambles for his glasses while I grab my headtorch and try to locate the zip in the place where the door used to be. Once outside, one thing is immediately clear: the bottle of single malt we toasted the first night of our aquatic adventure with is safe and sound. Phew. Sadly, the rest of the scene is more sobering. Incredibly, the wicked wind had picked up our 16ft canoe from where we'd turned it on its side, thrown it right over our tent and ripped the tent flysheet off in the process. The boat had come to rest right beside our feet, miraculously missing us by mere centimetres.

↑ Loche Linhe and the Great Glen, part of an incredible canoe trail (Andy Morehouse/S)

On the upside, the storm seems to have blown itself out with that last giant gust, neither the tent nor the canoe appear broken, we're unsquashed by the aerial antics of our boat, and we haven't lost anything into the loch. After a wake-up call like that, however, further sleep is impossible, so as the first feeble fingers of light claw at the horizon, we pack up and get going. The water is agitated, so we make a break for the far side of the loch, which looks more sheltered. About halfway across, however, the mischievous maelstrom discovers its second wind, whipping up waves which splash over the gunwale of the canoe. Surface water is picked up and lashed into our faces, along with relentless rain, and all we can do is keep our heads down, point the bow into the crests and paddle hard towards the far bank. We battle the elements for an hour before finally docking at a jetty. Dad's hair seems extra white, and it's all blown up on end, giving him a mad – or terrified – professor look. 'We were in real danger of capsizing out there son,' he declares, as I get the stove on and make a brew to calm our nerves. 'Is this some sort of elaborate form of euthanasia?'

PADDLING LOCHS & PORTAGING LOCKS Porridge cures everything, and fuelled by a fill of hot oats and restorative mugs of tea, we set off again, on a loch that, thankfully, has calmed down considerably. The east bank has the A82 road running alongside it, which impairs the wilderness feel of the experience somewhat, so as conditions increasingly clear we hug the forested flanks opposite. While the wind has moved on, the rain returns by the time we reach the end of Lochy and people in a pleasure boat passing through Laggan Locks look at us with pity as we portage our canoe and gear. To fight off the freezing cold feeling, we get going at a quick pace, grateful for the peacefulness of the navigation after the tempestuous conditions on the loch.

It's only a short section of canal, however, and soon we find ourselves afloat on littler Loch Oich. What this loch lacks in size it more than makes up for with bloody history. On our left we paddle past 17th-century Invergarry Castle, once the stronghold of the MacDonnells (a branch of the Clan Donald) until government troops blew it up after the Battle of Culloden in 1746, to punish the inhabitants for their support of Bonnie Prince Charlie. Nearby is the Well of the Seven Heads monument, named after a gory story that began in 1663, when Alexander MacDonald and his brother Ranald were killed by rivals within their clan. Two years later the brothers were avenged by Iain Lom (Bald John), who found, killed and decapitated the seven murderers. En route to Invergarry Castle to present the heads to the clan chief, Lom stopped to wash his trophies at this spring, which was thereafter known as Tobar-nan-Ceann – the Well of the Heads.

At the far end of Loch Oich, our canoe becomes the scene of a slightly tamer family feud. There are two spots along the Great Glen Canoe Trail where paddlers have a choice: continue along the calm canal, portaging around lochs, or veer off on to nature's whitewater highway, and risk riding the river rapids. We have reached the first of these junctions. I'm keen to explore the wild route; Dad is

↑ Two men in a boat – father and son loaded up for a canoe camping adventure (Charlie Horan)

dead against it. We've been squabbling about paddling technique for a few hours, and our team spirit isn't at its best, but just as we begin to bicker we get battered from behind by a vicious squall of hail and wind that blows us into the arms of the lock and settles the argument in Dad's favour.

I soon realise this intervention by the weather is a blessing, because, by the time we've portaged around the lock, Dad is beginning to look a bit blue and I'm starting to worry about him. The rain eases slightly as we continue along the canal, but as the bucolic farmland gives way to buildings on the outskirts of Fort Augustus, two things become clear: we need to get some warm, dry clothes on very quickly, and we're not going to find a picturesque camping spot this evening. 'B&B and pub?' I shout over my shoulder. The wind blows Dad's reply away, but I know what his answer is, and within a couple of hours we're tucking into hot haggis washed down with pints of ale.

SOME KIND OF MONSTER Loch Ness is the biggest of the Great Glen's four freshwater lochs, and it's the scariest, even if you don't believe the stories about what occupies its depths. But, although the third morning of our adventure dawns grey, with unpredictable clouds lurking, the loch looks calm enough as we collect our canoe from where I stashed it overnight. A big guy in a kilt is playing bagpipes for the benefit of a boatload of holidaymakers going through the six gates of Fort Augustus Lock, and for all its touristy overtones, the lilting music drifting across the water and through the glen is undeniably atmospheric. Billy, the pipe player and also the lockmaster, takes a break from strangling the tartan octopus for long enough to point us in the direction of the portaging trolley, and we're soon on our way.

Over 37km long and up to 230m deep, Loch Ness is an intimidating body of water to contemplate from a small boat. The safest approach in dodgy weather is to hug the shores, but that does make for a much longer paddle. The weather seems to be in a benign mood, and the forecast I checked earlier suggested a more settled day, so we strike out across the middle of this inland sea. Strange sets of waves pop up from nowhere on this loch, though, and it's easy to see how these can play tricks with people's minds. Random bits of wood float past too, and we speculate about how these things may have combined to create the monster myth that endures here. Written accounts of a strange beast on Loch Ness go all the way back to AD565, although reports went through the roof in the 1930s. Some Loch Ness maps even helpfully highlight the 'monster zone', where most sightings have happened, so you can paddle over these if you're cynical – or brave – enough.

After yesterday's excitement, we're more concerned with staying dry and in the boat than we are about meeting a monster. Some large waves do rock us at the outset, but the water is soon smoothened out as we paddle. It's astonishing how big the wash from passing boats can get, though, and we regularly have to point the bow into the waves to avert tipping, especially around the popular spot of Urquhart Castle, which dates to 1296. We're paddling in sync now, and manage to knock off at least three-quarters of the loch's length before calling it a day and setting up camp beside a musical stream. It's our final night on the water, so we polish off the single malt and settle down for what we hope will be a monster- and flying-canoe-free night.

On our last day we've arranged to meet Donald Macpherson, who was the project officer responsible for setting up the Great Glen Canoe Trail ahead of its 2012 launch, and now runs a company offering guided paddling trips along the lochs and elsewhere. We rendezvous just after Dochgarroch Lock, at the end of Loch Ness and just past the turn-off for whitewater paddlers intending to play on the wild River Ness. I don't even try to convince Dad to take the river route

ESSENTIALS

GETTING STARTED The Dart: you don't need to have your own craft – **Totnes Kayaks** (⊘ totneskayaks.co.uk) hires single and double sit-on-top kayaks to groups and individuals, and offers guided tours in open canoes and SUP lessons. Trips leave from Stoke Gabriel, close to the most scenic section of the lower reaches of the River Dart below Totnes.

The Great Glen: providers including **Explore Highland** (⊘ explorehighland.com) and **Snowgoose** (⊘ highland-mountain-guides.co.uk) offer boat hire, shuttle services and fully guided experiences along the canoe trail.

SPECIAL CONSIDERATIONS Sadly, while in Scotland you can paddle virtually anywhere, in England and Wales there are currently restrictions on kayaking and canoeing almost all free-flowing rivers, especially in summer, and paddlers can only legally access around 2% of rivers in these countries. However, you can paddle most tidal waterways and estuaries, plus canals and lakes (licences are sometimes required).

KIT BAG To go boatpacking you will need a kayak or canoe, a paddle, life jacket (PFD), dry bags, paddling apparel (or wetsuit), neoprene booties, warm clothes, tent, sleeping bag, stove, headtorch and other camping kit.

GETTING THERE The Dart: Totnes is reached via the A38/A384 from Exeter and the north, and the A38/A385 if you're coming from the south. The railway station is served by trains from London Paddington. Buses run regularly from Dartmouth back to Totnes.

The Great Glen: Fort William is reached via the A82 from Glasgow, or the A84/A82 from Edinburgh. The railway station is served by trains from Glasgow and the Caledonian

this time, because we're meeting Donald, who soon sides with my old man and confirms that running the rapids with a fully loaded canoe would be a ridiculous idea. (He does then agree to take me down them the following day, in an empty canoe, but that's another story.)

The sun breaks through as we negotiate the final stretch of the route, along the canal to Muirtown Locks, while Donald tells us about the history of the canoe trail he helped create, which has become one of the most popular paddling experiences in Britain over the last decade, setting the standard for other routes around the country. Quite a fanfare greets us as we enter the urban surrounds of Inverness, which is unexpected. It turns out the crowd are there to clap competitors in the Inverness Marathon, not to cheer us home, but nevertheless, we're proud of ourselves for completing this coast-to-coast challenge in one piece. And we're still on talking terms.

Sleeper train from London (⌾ sleeper.scot). Buses run regularly from Inverness back to Fort William.

PLACES TO STAY The fantastic riverside **Dart**: **Point Field Campsite** at Ashprington Point is owned and operated by the Sharpham Trust (⌾ sharphamtrust. org); book well in advance, as spots are limited.

The Great Glen: there are commercial campsites along the route of the canoe trail, and you can wild camp on the loch shores (be sure to follow Leave No Trace ethics and observe Scotland's Outdoor Access Code). Note: wild camping beside the canal sections in between the lochs is not permitted. There are B&Bs along the trail at places such as Gairlochy, South Laggan, Invergarry, Fort Augustus and Drumnadrochit.

ELSEWHERE Other great overnight paddling trips include the River Wye (Hoarwithy to Symonds Yat), a 42km, two-day adventure along the Wales-England border with an overnight stop at Ross-on-Wye (camping and B&B options); the River Yare and River Chet (17km from Rockland St Mary to Loddon in the Norfolk Broads); the Oxford Canal (62km from Fenny Marina to Hythe Bridge, Oxford); the Monmouthshire and Brecon Canal (50km from Brecon to Pontypool in south Wales) and Ullswater in Cumbria (12km from Pooley Bridge to Glenridding Pier).

EXTRA RESOURCES
⌾ britishcanoeing.org.uk
⌾ greatglencanoetrail.info
⌾ scottishcanals.co.uk
⌾ canalrivertrust.org.uk

29 SNOWHOLING & WINTER MUNRO BAGGING

WHERE	Cairngorms National Park, the Scottish Highlands
SKILL LEVEL	To go snowholing and winter hill hiking in the Highlands independently, you require advanced skills, including the ability to navigate in whiteout conditions and knowledge of how to assess avalanche danger and build a structurally sound, well-ventilated snow shelter. Unless you're very experienced in severe conditions, you should go with a guide – a winter skills course with an appropriately qualified mountain leader is the ideal way to learn how to keep yourself safe in the hills during the cold months, and to experience a night out in a snowhole.
RISK FACTOR	Constructing and sleeping in a snow shelter carries with it risks of collapse, entombment and suffocation, and when cooking and using candles inside the cave, carbon monoxide and carbon dioxide poisoning can occur if the hole is not made and ventilated well. It's extremely easy to get lost while walking in Cairngorms National Park (or elsewhere in the Scottish Highlands) in winter whiteout conditions, which can result in unexpected (and potentially fatal) falls from cornices and hidden drop-offs, and the risk of exposure and hypothermia if you get lost. Throughout winter, avalanches are a real and present danger.

↑ Winter hiking on the windswept Cairngorm Plateau (Patrick Kinsella)

When imagining a shelter made from ice and snow, many people – myself very much included – will immediately call to mind an igloo. But, when you're actually out there, surrounded by snow, which typically gets blown around and banked up in deep drifts, it makes an awful lot more sense to dig out a den, burrowing into the building material, rather than spending time making bricks and embarking on a complicated construction project. Snowholing, as this activity is called, enables outdoor adventurers to spend relatively comfortable midwinter nights, sleeping among the elements in super-remote places, without having to cart heavy four-season tents around.

Snowholes vary enormously in size and sophistication, from crude caves quickly carved by climbers and mountaineers benighted on slopes, to relatively luxurious temporary abodes built by hill hikers, snowshoers and ski tourers out exploring the wild white expanse, who have come equipped with all the right gear and spent several hours constructing their ice house. In midwinter, when sunlight only graces the Scottish Highlands for eight hours a day (if you're lucky), having the ability stay out overnight enables you to take on longer escapades without resorting to night walking. And who isn't excited at spending the night in a snow cave?

But this is not something to be taken lightly. A poorly built snowhole can, quite literally, be a deathtrap. The location chosen is crucial, and while you don't have to be an architect to construct such a shelter, you need sufficient knowledge of how ventilation works to avoid suffering from suffocation or carbon monoxide poisoning once you fire your stove up or have a candle on the go. Plus, no-one wants to wake up mid avalanche, or to discover the entrance to their cave has become badly blocked by fresh snowfall, or the roof has collapsed. Well I certainly don't, which is why I booked myself on a winter skills course being run by Ian Stewart, a fully qualified mountain leader and expert guide based in the Cairngorms, where he spends almost every day of winter out among the white stuff.

COOL SCHOOL

I swear the ceiling wasn't as close to my face when I drifted off as it appears to be when I awake. Either my nose has grown overnight, or the roof of the burrow I seem to be sleeping in has come down to meet it. Both possibilities are slightly alarming – my prominent proboscis definitely does not need to be any bigger than it already is, and generally I prefer bedrooms to keep to their rough dimensions and not creep up on me under cover of darkness, like some wall-shaped Weeping Angel.

Even putting aside the surprise ceiling drop, coming round in a snowhole is a massively discombobulating experience. It's cold and dark, of course, but as soon as a headtorch is switched on, your entire surroundings are revealed as being brilliantly, blindingly, bright white, from floor to ceiling. It feels exactly as though you have fallen asleep and woken up inside a fridge. For a full minute or two I lie there, staring at the clouds of condensation I'm exhaling, with my sleep-addled brain desperately trying to figure out where on earth I am. And then I remember.

I am two-thirds of the way through a three-day winter skills course, during which Ian is teaching me how to stay alive while hiking in the hills of the Highlands during the coldest, snowiest and most challenging months of the year. We're in the Cairngorms, which is one of the wildest parts of the country at any time, let alone now, in the icy grip of a freezing week in January. It is reasonable to ask why would anyone would want to be out here during this period, but once you've set eyes on the terrific terrain of this high plateau covered in a wonderful white veil, that question answers itself. It's absolutely stunning. The rugged rocks and crags of the Cairngorms are made more gentle by the blanket of snow that lies across them, but this is, of course, dangerously deceptive. Soft snow conceals hard holes, icy slopes form slippery slides that can lead to terrible drops, and fragile frozen cornices (corners of ice overhanging a precipice) can give way, sending explorers of this domain to their doom. You really need to know what you're doing before you set out on a winter adventure here, and Ian is doing his best to equip me with the right knowledge to do just that.

The first day was spent schooling me in essential skills required before setting foot in the icy alpine arena we were about to explore. Around Coire Laogh Mòr I learned to climb and descend frozen slopes with boots and crampons, and practised how to self-arrest with and without an ice axe in the event of a fall. Ian

↑ Ian demonstrating how to ascend ice in boots (Patrick Kinsella) → Pat digging the snowhole (Ian Stewart)

sent me toppling from a variety of starting points – face first, backwards and completely head over heels – and I had to try and stop myself sliding as quickly as possible. It was fantastic fun, but the realisation of how much acceleration the human body picks up in just a few metres, even on a modest slope, is – once you finally shudder to a halt and think about it – terrifying. Unless you have lightning-fast reactions, you need to rehearse these moves repeatedly to be sure of stopping safely if you do take a tumble.

'Get your weight over the head of the ice axe!' Ian yells at me, as I slide much further than I'd like, for the umpteenth time. 'Like this…' He demonstrates each technique with the precision of a bloke who has done all this countless times before. In all the years he's been working and playing in the mountains, however, Ian has used his self-arrest skills just once in a real-life scenario. Reaction is important, he stresses, but prevention is much better. 'I compare it to driving,' he says. 'If you have a fall, you've already had an accident – it's about limiting the damage.'

I do it all over again, with more success. 'We're getting there,' Ian admits. 'Let's try that another ten times. We'll make a mountain man of you yet.'

SNOW DEN On the morning of the second day, we embark on our mission proper: a two-day midwinter ascent of Ben Macdui, Britain's second-highest summit. Ian, his wife Laura (also a mountain leader), photographer Ed Smith and I meet in the ski-centre car park, before hiking through Coire an t-Sneachda, watched by little white snow buntings and ptarmigans. Branching left just before the ice-climbing crag, we ascend Windy Col, which is gentle enough to be climbed without ropes. It's still steep though, and I'm soon sweating. And slipping.

'Listen to what your feet are telling you,' Ian reminds me. 'Is the gradient getting steeper? Is the snow getting icier? Is it time to put on crampons?' Yep, yes and yeah. Of course it is.

On the plateau we traverse a wind-swept ice field to Coire Domhain, where Ian is confident there will be a drift deep enough for us to build a snow cave. A few prods with his avalanche probe confirms the conditions are good, and we begin construction of our overnight shelter. It's 2pm – we have just over two hours of daylight digging time to excavate ourselves a snow home. Everyone starts burrowing, taking turns using lightweight shovels we've brought along specifically for digging. Ed and I work on one entrance, while Laura and Ian start on a second. Several metres in, we turn in right angles and dig towards each other, and when we meet in the middle, all four of us get to work enlarging the central part of the den. The snowhole is structurally finished by nightfall, but we continue to work, making the inside positively palatial. The ceilings are rounded to prevent drips forming and dropping on us during the night, and we use a saw to cut snow bricks to turn one of the entrances into a vent, rather than a gaping

ICE CLIMBING

To take the adventure level up a notch, consider having a crack at ice climbing. There is an indoor ice wall in Kinlochleven, Scotland, which is the UK's National Ice Climbing Centre, but the most exciting way to learn is out among the terrain itself. The perfect introductory route is very close to the spot where our snowhole adventure came to a conclusion, on the frozen flanks of Coire an t'Sneachda in the Cairngorms. Here, you can tackle the Goat Track, as I did with mountain instructor Ian and photographer Ed on the day after our winter ascent of Ben Macdui. The three-pitch, 120m, Grade 1 winter route requires crampons, rope and two ice axes, and must be done with a guide unless you are an experienced ice climber. It's a challenging climb in anyone's book, but the feeling when you top out beneath Stob Coire an t-Sneachda makes it all worthwhile.

Routes in places such as Coire an t' Sneachda and Coire Lochan can be explored as part of a winter climbing course with **Scotch on the Rocks** (⊘ sotrg.co.uk/winter-skills/winter-climbing). Sandy Paterson from Scotch on the Rocks does, however, caution that the terrain encountered very much depends on conditions when you're there. 'I try not to call it ice climbing,' he says. 'During a course we might climb ice, snow, snowed-up rock and frozen turf!'

↑ Ed and Ian ice climbing in Coire an t' Sneachda (Patrick Kinsella)

MARILYNS & MUNROS

Cairngorms National Park is Britain's largest elevated expanse of wilderness, and it boasts five of the UK's six highest peaks, the tallest being Ben Macdui, which is both a Munro and a Marilyn. Munro is the name given to Scottish mountains that stand 3,000ft (914m) or more above sea level, whereas a Marilyn is a mountain anywhere in Britain with a prominence (where the peak stands proud of other surrounding summits) of at least 150m (492ft). Named after Hugh T Munro, who surveyed and catalogued them in 1891, there are 282 Munros scattered across Scotland. Systematically summiting and ticking off these peaks is a popular pursuit known as 'Munro bagging'. In 2020 Donnie Campbell ran to the top of all the Munros in 31 days, climbing a total of 126,143m and running 1,340km. Scottish mountains that miss out on Munro status, but stand over 2,500ft (762m) tall, are known as Corbetts.

opening. Importantly, we ensure the main door is angled slightly downhill to help gasses such as carbon monoxide escape. Finally, we add a bag storage room at one end and a kitchen area at the other, complete with a cooking bench and recessed light alcoves. It's genuinely cosy.

Ian chips part of the wall into a pan and boils a brew. Brilliant. The more we consume, the bigger our house gets. Taking this to heart, we cook up a storm, before chasing the food down with a dram of single malt and settling in for a kip. It's only about 9pm, but bedtime comes early in a snowhole. Inside our cave, the temperature hovers around zero, but clad in thermals and buried deep in a down

↑ Ben Macdui is a Munro and a Marilyn (MountainGlory/S)

sleeping bag and Gore-Tex bivvy, I'm very snug. Until the tea and whisky takes effect at least, when, with bursting bladder, I stagger into a star-splattered night to sign my name in the snow. It's important to periodically check the entrance of your snow cave several times overnight, to ensure you're not getting snowed in, so I'm taking one for the team here.

Outside it's −15°C, the sky is cloudless and the pale landscape glows with eerie moonlit luminosity. Away from the safety of the snowhole, wild thoughts of Am Fear Liath Mòr (the big grey man of Ben Macdui – a legendary Yeti-like monster rumoured to haunt the Cairngorms) invade my head, and I scurry back into the warmth of our den. Quickly I fall back into a deep slumber, before waking up to find the ceiling apparently closing in on me.

This is exactly what happens in snowholes, Ian calmly explains when he wakes. Our combined body warmth, plus the heat generated by last night's cooking, has caused the snow to compact and the roof to literally drop a bit. This is why these holes are very much temporary abodes, usually fit for a one-night occupancy only, even if you spend ages making them large and luxurious. And we definitely did that. Our snowhole is proper fancy, but within a few days it will most likely be gone altogether – unless someone else comes along and refurbs it, which does happen.

The temperature inside is still hovering around 0°C, which is fine while you're in a goosedown and Gore-Tex nest, but becomes a little more confronting when it's time to get up. Ian makes the first move. Still in his bag, he sits up, breaks off a bit of the wall, pops it into a pot and starts to boil snow water for tea. The many

↑ Settling down for the night in a snowhole (Ed Smith)

metres of ice and snow that surround our cave completely cushion us from the Cairngorms, and I haven't a clue what the weather is doing out there. Curious, I venture out the door, and walk straight into the buffeting blows of a boisterous blizzard. The calm conditions of the wee hours have long gone, and fresh snow is swirling around on rowdy gusts of wind. Visibility is virtually non-existent and I'd put the temperature at around −10°C, probably much lower with wind chill factored in. Shivering, I scuttle back inside the snowhole, where Ian hands me a steaming cup of tea.

The temptation to stay put within our little wintry womb is very high, even if the walls are contracting. But we have a mountain to climb today. And not just any old mountain. We have set our sights on Ben Macdui – a magnificent Munro that stands 1,309m above sea level, forming the very crown of the Cairngorms National Park. Although how we're going to find our way up there in this great white mess, god only knows. And Ian. I hope.

MASSIF ATTACK Eventually we emerge from our snug snowhole into the howling, wind-whipped day. Leaving our overnight gear in the cave, marked with a long avalanche pole to help us relocate it later, we set off across the plateau towards the peak, skirting east of Hell's Lum Crag. Spindrift blankets everything – paths, streams, gullies and rocks are all hidden, and even before the whiteout gets really serious, it's hard to locate the seam between ground and sky. And then our surroundings seem to disappear altogether.

'It's like walking around inside a ping-pong ball isn't it?' Ian's muffled voice comes from deep inside a hood, somewhere to my immediate right – in that mysterious wispy white place where my guide used to be, before the Cairngorms conditions closed in and abruptly mugged me of company and most of my sensory indicators. He's right – that's exactly what it's like. And I'm hoping Ian knows how to navigate around the interior of a table-tennis ball, because I haven't a clue which way is up or down anymore, let alone what direction we should be going in, or whether we've just turned towards the peak we're seeking, or the cornice that could send us down from the plateau the regrettably rapid way. This is no place to pick a fight with gravity.

Minutes earlier we'd been admiring the brutal beauty of the landscape, but once the white veil falls across its visage, as it does with rapacious regularity in winter, this scene transforms into a world devoid of, well, almost everything. On the way up here, aboard the overnight sleeper train from London to Aviemore, I'd read about a walker who – just a few days ago, in a similarly dramatic whiteout – disappeared through a cornice on nearby Coire Sputan Dearg. Miraculously he survived a 250m fall, albeit with a wince-inducing horror show of injuries, but it wasn't comforting bedtime reading. And now I'm here in exactly the same

↑ Reaching the summit of Ben Macdui (Patrick Kinsella) ← Ian above Loch Avon (Patrick Kinsella)

conditions. In this mood, the Cairngorms doesn't even suffer experienced Scottish hillwalkers gladly, let alone numpty noobs like me.

Fortunately I'm in good company. Ian has been working in these Highland hills for over six years. He knows the contours like the back of his glove, and uses every wrinkle in the terrain and nuance of the landscape to navigate. Studying his map and compass continuously, Ian identifies features from flimsy shadows: tiny inclines and baby hillocks, slight depressions that hint at frozen streams below the snow. Directing me to stand a few metres ahead, he calculates a bearing based on my comparative elevation. It's bare-bones orienteering, but it works and suddenly the summit cairn looms. Covered as the Munro is in rime ice and shrouded in ethereal mist, I almost mistake its wraith-like silhouette as that of the Big Grey Man himself.

Just 35m lower than Ben Nevis, which is around 100km away to the southeast, 1,309m Macdui was once thought to be the higher peak of the two. Now relegated to second, it sees a fraction of the visitors the bigger ben suffers, and the experience of exploring Macdui is all the better for it. Aside from the spectre of Fear Liath Mòr – the apparent appearance of which has spooked several climbers around

ESSENTIALS

GETTING STARTED To learn a multitude of winter skills in the Scottish hills, contact MIC-qualified mountaineering instructor Ian Stewart (**e** ian@sotrg.co.uk), or check out the full range of guiding services offered at Scotch on the Rocks (⊘ sotrg.co.uk). To do a winter skills course you can also contact Mountain Magic (⊘ mountainmagic.org.uk).

SPECIAL CONSIDERATIONS Rugged though it might be, the Cairngorms and surrounding environment is a very fragile and precious place. Please practise Leave No Trace principles whether you're visiting for the day or spending a night out – that means packing everything (and we mean everything, including used toilet roll) out with you to be disposed of in bins.

KIT BAG To go hiking in the Highlands in winter you need lots of layers, starting with good baselayers (merino wool garments are ideal), fleeces/puffer jacket midlayers and high-performing, waterproof shell trousers and jacket made with a breathable membrane such as Gore-Tex. (A good tip is to remove your midlayer when digging the snowhole, to stop it getting damp with sweat, and carry a spare baselayer. Another great idea is to bring rubber gardening gloves to wear over your main gloves, to keep the better ones protected and dry.) A guide will usually provide an ice axe, crampons and helmet as required, but bring crampon-compatible ('B2' or 'B1') winter hiking boots. An

the summit, including an army climber who fired several shots at it, and Professor Norman Collie, a highly respected mountaineer – we're certainly alone up here. This is unsurprising, given the time of year and the conditions. The summit views are astounding – apparently. All I can see are grinning faces framed by big hoods, but our Munro mission is a success nonetheless.

The veil lifts a little during our walk-off, prompting a revised return route via iconic Shelter Stone rock, with Loch Avon as a beautiful backdrop. Collecting our gear from the snowhole, we hike out via point 1141, a special spot with a prosaic name at the head of Fiacaill a' Choire Cas, which marks the beginning of the descent proper. As we drop, Glenmore Forest comes into view and colour rushes back into our world, finally popping the ping-pong ball properly.

Gravity isn't always the enemy in the mountains, and Ian has one last skill to impart before we leave the plateau: the seated glacade – which is essentially tobogganing without the toboggan. Whooping, we slide on our bums from the Cairngorms back into civilisation, rolling over into the self-arrest position to stop. 'Not bad,' says Ian, observing my technique. 'Another ten times and you'll have that down, Pat.'

avalanche probe, snow shovels and ice saws are also required (a guide should supply). A properly built snowhole will warm up when you're inside, but you still need a good four-season sleeping bag, a good Gore-Tex bivvy bag and quality winter apparel.

GETTING THERE Aviemore is the gateway to the Cairngorms. To drive, head north from Glasgow or Edinburgh and follow the A9. Scotrail's Caledonian Sleeper Train, which runs overnight from London Euston to stations in Scotland six nights a week (Sunday to Friday), stops at Aviemore; cabins are available (⌀ sleeper.scot).

PLACES TO STAY For those nights when you don't have a snowhole to sleep in, Aviemore offers several good B&Bs. An excellent choice is the **Ravenscraig guesthouse** (⌀ aviemoreonline.com).

ELSEWHERE Fantastic hiking can be enjoyed right across the Highlands all year round, but if you are not an experienced winter hillwalker I can't stress strongly enough just how dangerous conditions can be, especially if you attempt to stay out in a snowhole. Go adventuring within your capabilities, and seek professional guidance to expand your skill set.

EXTRA RESOURCES
⌀ cairngorms.co.uk

30 WHITEWATER RAFTING & PACKRAFTING

WHERE	River Findhorn, Moray, northeast Scotland
SKILL LEVEL	Whitewater rafting is accessible to pretty much everyone – you simply need to follow the instructions barked at you by your guide, paddle hard forwards or backwards when they tell you to do so, and hang on tight at other times. There is more individual skill involved in packrafting, where you're solely responsible for getting yourself along a stretch of river, potentially running a sequence of rapids. How difficult this is will depend entirely on the river and the conditions at the time. Packrafts are much less tippy and far more forgiving than technical whitewater kayaks, so you don't need to be an experienced paddler if you're going with a guide. To read and run rapids independently you require knowledge of water dynamics and plenty of paddling experience.
RISK FACTOR	Whitewater is a very dynamic environment where conditions can change daily (hourly, sometimes), presenting new dangers as the water level drops or rises, revealing rocks and other obstacles such as logs and fallen trees. If you fall out of the boat – a common occurrence when rafting – risks include concussion from a head injury and getting caught in a 'strainer', when you're pinned against an obstacle by the force of the flowing water; both can result in drowning. When you're rafting with a river guide they should have good knowledge of the waterway and will have studied the conditions immediately prior to setting out. Safety equipment such as helmets and PFDs (personal flotation devices) should always be worn, and equipment including throw ropes should be taken. If you enter the water, float on your back, feet first. Never attempt to negotiate a stretch of whitewater independently in any craft if you are not an experienced paddler.

When conjuring up mental images of whitewater paddling, most people will think about scenes they may have seen, either first-hand or on the screen, of the world's epic rafting rivers – places like the mighty Zambezi below Victoria Falls on the border between Zimbabwe and Zambia, or the Colorado River charging through the Grand Canyon in Arizona, or any one of a long list of lovely liquid locations in New Zealand, Canada, Chile, Costa Rica and Nepal. Less, I'd wager, would call to mind any of the river systems in the UK, and yet – especially in the wilder parts of Wales and Scotland – Britain boasts some of the best boating waterways in Europe.

One especially exciting place to paddle is the rowdy River Findhorn, where the water that tumbles from the famously well-hydrated Highlands hurtles towards the Moray Firth on Scotland's northeast coast. Rising in the valley between the Cairngorms and the Monadhliath Mountains, the Findhorn is fed by myriad tributary streams, burns and rivers,

← Calm before the storm: rafting on the River Findhorn in late autumn (Callum Lewis/Ace Adventures)

and it arguably offers the very best and most consistent wild whitewater rafting conditions in the whole country. This is precisely what has drawn me here, specifically to the most local of all the operators who run this river, Ace Adventures, because they uniquely take rafts down the extremely thrilling lower section of the Findhorn. This is the only rafting trip in the UK to deliver Grade 3 conditions all year round on a course created by nature (as opposed to a purpose-built water centre). And when I visit, in the middle of November, the flow rate is far feistier than that, with several rapids pushing Grade 4+.

Better still, not only do Ace Adventures offer the country's finest whitewater rafting, they also take people on packrafting trips. Packrafts are ingenious craft designed for solo paddlers, which look a little bit like a miniature version of the larger rafts, because that's essentially what they are. But don't be fooled into thinking that they are just rubber dinghies, of the sort you see families messing around in at the beach. These are very robust, well-thought-through and capable craft that allow plucky paddlers who don't possess all the technical skills to take a kayak along a whitewater river to experience exactly what that feels like. They bounce off rocks, and don't tip over anywhere nearly as easily as a hard-shell kayak, but they enable paddlers to pilot themselves through the jaws of the river rocks, choosing their own lines, running the rapids and going over the drops, taking responsibility for their own destiny. And I can't wait to see if this is even half as exciting (and terrifying) as it sounds.

RAFT CRAFT

'If I shout at you, I'm not angry,' Callum bellows, over the loud rumbling of the river, rushing past some 100m below where we're standing. 'I'm just Scottish, and it sounds that way.' Helmeted and kitted out in thick wetsuits and PFDs, we're gathered in a group around a raft, and the noisy but non-angry Scot is one of our river guides for the afternoon. And it's a good thing he explains his demeanour to us at the put-in point, because there will be a whole lot of yelling over the next few hours. And whooping. And maybe even the odd yelp. Not least when Callum goes for a surprise swim and we're left in control of the boat for a bit. But more of that later.

Today, from a put-in spot that's only a short drive from the Ace Base, we're running the lower section of the River Findhorn. There are ten of us punters in total, and we're split into two rafts, one steered by Callum and the other by Harris. Both are highly experienced raft guides and whitewater paddlers with excellent knowledge of the river, so we basically just need to do what we're told, when we're told. However, no-one in a whitewater raft gets to come along purely as a passenger. We're the engine of the craft and when power is required, we have to dig in hard. At the put-in, Callum goes through the paddle strokes we will need for the day – these are essentially forward stroke and back stroke. It's also very important to keep your top hand on the T-section of the paddle, not just

PACKING A PUNCH

Although running short sections of rapid-strewn rivers in a packraft is enormous fun, these brilliant boats were originally designed more for multiday escapades. They can be packed away into relatively small bags and carried on expeditions, so intrepid explorers can traverse gorges, hike over hills or travel through mountain passes and then, when they reach a river, inflate their mini-rafts and float along with the current, or propel their boats with purpose-built paddles that break down into four or more small sections. The best ones even have heavy-duty water- and airproof zips on the hull, so you can stash your trail gear (backpack, hiking boots, tent, sleeping bag, cooking equipment, food supplies and spare clothes) inside the packraft, which not only keeps the stuff dry, but also acts as ballast for the boat, making it more stable and less likely to capsize. Absolute genius.

for efficiency, but because otherwise someone is likely to get bashed in the face by it when things get hectic, and then the shouting might get a little more angry.

What you do with your body weight is also crucial in a raft, partly to keep the craft the right way up during the most boisterous rapids, but also to ensure that you stay in it. Unsurprisingly, the sides of a big inflatable boat are extremely bouncy, and when the boat hits rocks and standing waves at speed, it's quite common for people to be propelled into the water. If that happens, and you're unable to swim easily to the raft, you need to float with your feet facing downstream, because it's better for your shoes, rather than your head, to hit hard rocks. The raft will then rescue you. No-one gets left behind.

↑ Packraft camping – an aquatic escape (Smit/S)

Callum needs to explain all this prior to the actual put-in, because as soon as we cart the raft down the steep bank and launch at a spot just by Daltullich Bridge – by a twist in the river that's also known by the comforting name of Carnage Corner – the action starts unfolding immediately. Well, almost.

RAPID LEARNING CURVE

Rafting fast past Randolph's Leap we're immediately on the lower section of the River Findhorn, where the rapids soon live up to their name and start looming with relentless regularity around every corner. Briefly, though, we get to appreciate the flaming beauty of the Darnaway Forest in all its autumnal splendour. Today the forest is a riot of fiery colour, from rusty red to glowing gold, and leaves fall like sparks into water stained with the peat that makes it the perfect ingredient for the whisky this region is so famous for (the Single Malt Trail runs nearby – but that's a different kind of adventure altogether).

These wonderful woods are home to some epic trees – including Scots pines, birches, rowan, alder, willow and Douglas fir. One especially splendid sitka spruce reaches so far skyward from the riverbank that it's reckoned to be Britain's second-tallest tree. And the tales are almost as tall as the trees around here too. According to local folklore (but contrary to botanical history books), this is where the last wolf in Scotland was slain by MacQueen of Pall a' Chrocain, a legendary Highland deerstalker, in 1743. Scientific records claim the animals were hunted to extinction in Scotland 60 years earlier, but it's not hard to imagine wolves stalking these woods even now, especially when the howling starts.

Because once Dorback Burn comes racing in from our right, the river becomes restless and rafters get cacophonously excited. The Lobie is our introduction to the rock-and-roll world of rapids on the lower Findhorn, and while its name might be prosaic, running it quickens our pulses. Here the dark water fizzes with bubbles like shaken Coca-Cola as the river rams into rocks, and bashes up against boulders. Both rafts negotiate the obstacles without mishap, and we whoop as Callum hollers out instructions. Soon, though, the challenges become significantly more serious, and the severity of the rapids is signalled by their mischievous monikers, which Callum calls out as we approach. 'This one is Sidewinder! Forward paddle, forward paddle. Stop! Get down and hold on. Up up up… Back paddle hard on the right, forward paddle left side!' And so on.

We get through Triple Step alright – although someone in the other raft gets catapulted in for an unintended swim, and has to be hauled out of the water. But Corkscrew adds a twist to our tale. Here, amid all the anarchy and near-catastrophe that always seems to be unfolding when you find yourself mid-churn in a rapid, I suddenly feel a significant whack in my back, followed by a conspicuous cessation in shouting from Callum. I'm too busy hanging on to

↑ Hitting the rapids in a raft (Harris/Ace Adventures) ← Whitewater packrafting (Callum Lewis/Ace Adventures)

pay too much attention, until we get spat out the end of the rapid. After a few seconds of cheering and congratulatory paddle slaps, someone looks over their shoulder and says, 'Where's Callum?' Hastily we put in a whole load of fairly uncoordinated back strokes to slow the raft down, and within a few seconds our guide's head has appeared by the boat and he deftly clambers back in. 'I was a wee bit hot there,' he grins. 'Just fancied a dip.'

We pause for food while drifting through the woods, as Harris shows Callum photos of his ejector-seat-style exit from the boat, taken as he stood on the rocks with a safety rope and a camera at the ready, perfectly poised to capture chaos and prevent calamity. Not wanting Callum to feel too conspicuous, we join him in getting consensually drenched by doing a bit of cliff jumping, leaping from rock shelves up to 10m high.

There are more rapids to be run yet, though, and we soon set off again to get bounced and buffeted around by Pin Ball, and emit some squeals on Deliverance. And then, after drifting around a sensationally scenic section of the waterway, which slinks around a huge hook-shaped curve, we reach the take-out point on the river right at a beautiful beach by Gorachs Pool. From here we need to carry the rafts across a couple of fields to where the truck is waiting to pick us up and transport us back to base, where I bid my boat buddies farewell. And, as they depart, I start to get my head around the very different challenge that lies in wait tomorrow, when I'll get my first taste of packrafting on technical rapids.

SENT PACKING Against all odds, for the second November day in a row we are treated to clear, crisp conditions, with only a smattering of wispy white clouds and a couple of aircraft contrails crossing the bright blue Scottish sky like a smudged saltire. It's chilly though, and that's why I'm shaking. Honest.

On this particular packrafting escapade, I'm the only punter. But I'm being very well looked after. Callum, Harris and a trainee river guide called Douglas accompany me, also paddling packrafts, and a fourth Ace guide – Heath – comes along in a plastic Pyranha playboat as a safety kayaker. We put in at Logie Bridge, a kilometre north of Ferness, to run the middle section of the River Findhorn. The boys are in their element, nimbly playing around in the eddies, surfing the standing waves and alternately dunking the bow or stern of their boats into the myriad whirlpools that swirl and curl across the surface of the river as it rampages along its route, bashing into boulders, cascading over drops and careering around corners. Harris even manages to roll his raft. The show-off.

Between the sections of whitewater, they recall anecdotes about previous paddling adventures they have enjoyed, without clients, full of drama and – occasionally – danger. As guides and kayakers, they have been out on the Findhorn hundreds of times over the past year, but Callum explains just how much the river can change across the space of a week, let alone over the full course of a season. Water levels can rise and drop in a matter of hours, dislodging debris and washing all kinds of things along the river, so new elements and features appear almost every time they run a section. It's often more risky for them to run commercial trips when water levels are low and various vicious rocks are exposed, at which point they have to portage rafts around certain obstacles. But there's certainly no danger of that at the moment – being late autumn, the volume is high, which means the river is running fast and the paddling is at its most exciting.

The rapids are pretty much all Grade 3 on this stretch, so they're not quite as epic as the ones we ran in the rafts yesterday – thankfully, because they would have chewed me up for breakfast and spat my remains out into the Moray Firth. But I will need to negotiate all the whitewater sections on my own today. With some guidance and advice from the lads of course, who suggest the best lines to take, and offer some hard-earned knowledge about which rocks to definitely steer clear of. The trouble with that type of tip is that, once someone has identified a bad-arse boulder which is best avoided, you tend to end up staring at it, and that will inevitable take you directly towards it. The same thing happens when you're mountain biking: you have to focus hard on the line you want to take,

↑ In a packraft you have to pick the best line (Callum Lewis/ACE Adventures)

not the pitfalls on either side, and your body and boat/bike will then follow. But sometimes this is easier said than done.

Just like the previous day, the rapids are punctuated by fairly long and languorous sections where the river calms right down, and we have a chance to chat and look in the woods for wildlife like red squirrel, deer and raptors. Each time we approach a new bit of troubled water, however, we move into action formation. Callum and Harris act as the advance party, shooting the rapid first to check there are no nasty surprises lying in wait, and then Douglas and I run it in quick succession, with him leading the way and me largely following his line. In the meantime Heath skilfully manoeuvres his tiny kayak around, keeping an eye on everything. Fortunately, though, there's no need for the safety boat to get involved, and while I get buffeted by my fair share of rocks, and occasionally feel like I'm being virtually submerged beneath the hectic flow of brackish H_2O, we successfully paddle our way though rapids ranging from Magnetic and the misleadingly somnolent-sounding Sleeping Whale Rock to the more aptly named Dragon's Tooth.

Yesterday's put-in point is today's take-out place, so when Daltullich Bridge comes into view, I know I'm near the end of my packrafting adventure and start to feel pretty proud that I haven't capsized or fallen out of my cool little craft. But then I recall the name of the bend in the Findhorn that comes just before the raft launching spot, and realise the river has one last test for me: I must get around Carnage Corner in one piece before I can get back on terra firma. As invisible boulders beneath the surface begin to make the water bulge and bubble, as though it's boiling, Callum calls out some final instructions, in his broadest Scottish-but-not-angry brogue, complete with a little warning at the end: 'Go river left, keep your raft pointing downstream, aim for the V, and once you're down the drop, break left in to the eddy and paddle hard upstream, to the pebble beach. Whatever you do, don't continue down the river!'

I've seen what the rapids are like beyond this point, so this seems like excellent advice. Although I don't have too much time to think about it. Callum and Harris are quickly through the rapid and on the beach, and Douglas follows quickly behind them. Then it's my turn. As the pace of the flow beneath my boat accelerates dramatically, I put in a couple of big paddle strokes to keep the pointy end of the packraft facing forwards, hug the left side of the river, and aim for the middle of the drop – the apex of the V – just as Callum advised. I shoot through the gap, put in a paddle stroke to punch over the drop and then find myself in the eddy, doing a textbook turn (which owes more to good fortune than fine paddling skills) to face the beach.

'Nice one!' shouts Callum. 'No bother. Grand job!' I think he's happy. Pretty sure he's not angry, anyway. I could get used to being shouted at like this.

ESSENTIALS

GETTING STARTED Arrange a whitewater rafting or packrafting experience with Ace Adventures (⌀ aceadventures.co.uk).

SPECIAL CONSIDERATIONS The International Scale of River Diffculty, created by the American Whitewater Association, rates the technicality of a stretch of river or a single rapid, from Class 1 (fast-moving water travelling over small rocks with a few ripples and minor waves) to Class 5 (long rapids, which need to be scouted from the shore prior to running them, significant obstacles, water is violent and rescues tricky). There is a Class 6, but recreational rafters don't run these. The rapids on the Middle Findhorn are mostly Grade 3, with tricky irregular waves, some drops and narrow passages. Lower Findhorn rapids can reach Grade 4+ because they're longer, with much bigger waves and drops, and far feistier flow. During Ace Adventures trips, punters can always walk around rapids they don't fancy rafting.

KIT BAG Rafting companies supply everything except swim and footwear. Bring old trainers or neoprene booties. To go packrafting independently, you need a raft (Alpacka make brilliant boats: ⌀ alpackaraft.com, as do British-brand Neris: ⌀ neris.co.uk), a paddle, wetsuit (or drysuit), booties, kayaking helmet, PFD (life jacket), a throw rope, and ideally some experience and a paddling partner.

GETTING THERE All rafting and packrafting adventures start from the Ace Adventures base (Achnagairn, Forres IV36 2QL) very close to the banks of the River Findhorn. To get there, drive along the A9 from Perth, take the A95 to Speybridge, and then follow the B9007 until you see signs.

PLACES TO STAY Ace Adventures offers camping and campervan pitches, plus they have excellent accommodation in bell tents and shepherd's huts.

ELSEWHERE You can experience excellent whitewater rafting, with rapids up to Grade 4, on the **River Teifi** in **southwest Wales** with Cardigan Bay Active (⌀ cardiganbayactive.co.uk). The **National White Water Centre** (⌀ nationalwhitewatercentre.co.uk) in Bala, Wales, offers exciting whitewater adventures on the natural rapids of the River Tryweryn, and **Lee Valley White Water Centre** (⌀ visitleevalley.org.uk) near London offers rafting on the course used for whitewater sports in the 2012 Olympics.

EXTRA RESOURCES

⌀ britishcanoeing.org.uk/competition/white-water-rafting
⌀ internationalrafting.com

EPILOGUE

If I thought I'd seriously scratch the adventure itch or sate my curiosity by researching and writing this book, I was very much mistaken. In my experience, with every extra outdoor encounter you have and activity you learn about, the more ideas, challenges and escapades occur to you, and the bigger your wish list grows. Effectively, all that I've ended up doing here is increasing the number of hobbies I have by tenfold, and filling my garage with even more outdoor toys (much to the annoyance of my wife).

And there are multiple activities that I wanted to include in this book that, for one reason or another, I couldn't – from fatbiking and parahawking to coracle paddling in Wales and cross-country skiing in the frozen backcountry of Scotland. It might sound like I'm trying to set up a sequel here, but actually I'm simply emphasising the fact that there's at least a lifetime's worth of adventures and activities you could chase around the shores of Britain, so start planning and get among it.

I very much hope you do genuinely dive into some of the experiences suggested here, and continue to find exhilarating escapades of your own as you hike, bike, climb, swim and paddle around Britain. Because the more people explore, the greater connection they feel to the trails, forests, shores, moors and mountains around them. As I said in the introduction, we're blessed with an extraordinarily diverse and endlessly exciting landscape here, but the inescapably sad fact is that

↑ Approaching the Campsie Fells at the start of the West Highland Way (Patrick Kinsella)

– especially in England and Wales – we are also excluded from an awful lot of it. The situation is much better in Scotland, where the outdoor code is far more reasonable and locals and visitors have the right to roam (and camp, ride and forage) across the majority of the country, but in England and Wales it's very different. Only a tiny percentage of rivers can be legally paddled all year round, and even during the time it took me to research and write this book, our legal right to overnight on the Dartmoor commons was removed – effectively making wild camping illegal across all of England and Wales.

It's impossible to sit on the fence when fences are the very problem we're discussing, so we may as well just say that it's an awful and unhealthy state of affairs when the vast majority of a country's population finds itself excluded from the natural environment that surrounds them, especially in the wake of a pandemic that saw us temporarily entombed in our flats and houses. There have been mutterings recently about extensively revising the right to roam legislation in England and Wales, significantly improving access to wild and green areas of the countryside and the coast, not to mention cleaning up the water quality of our streams, rivers and sea. The sooner that happens, the better. In the meantime, please keep exploring what we have available to us, and take your family and friends out with you – the more they see and experience, the greater their investment in the environment will become, and collectively we can be a powerful force for positive change.

I'll just get my coat. See you out there…

The award-winning Slow Travel series from Bradt Guides

Over 20 regional guides across Britain.
See the full list at bradtguides.com/slowtravel.

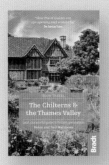

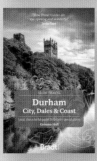

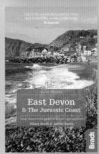

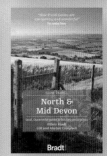

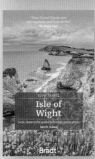

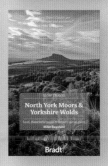

INDEX

Bold indicates a major entry

INDEX OF ADVERTISERS